"A much-needed fresh approach to the environmental concerns of the average person."

—*Ladelle McWhorter, University of Richmond, USA*

"Environmental ethics often seeks to develop a suitably modern solution to the problems imposed by modernity—solutions rooted in enlightenment thinking and romanticism. Mark Coeckelbergh's *Environmental Skill* takes an entirely different approach, demonstrating that it is modernity that is the problem and developing an innovative form of environmental ethics that relies not on better knowledge about the world but more attentive and skillful ways of being-in-the-world."

—*David J. Gunkel, Northern Illinois University, USA*

"This new book by Mark Coeckelbergh is an insightful argument for an environmental philosophy that draws on the resources of and at the same time extends work in philosophy of technology. The notion of skilled engagement with the world as this has emerged from pragmatism and phenomenology is here deepened and re-thought in an effort to understand and respond to the challenges of living in a techno-transformed nature."

—*Carl Mitcham, Colorado School of Mines, USA*

Environmental Skill

Today it is widely recognized that we face urgent and serious environmental problems and we know much about them, yet we do very little. What explains this lack of motivation and change? Why is it so hard to change our lives? This book addresses this question by means of a philosophical inquiry into the conditions of possibility for environmental change. It discusses how we can become more motivated to do environmental good and what kind of knowledge we need for this, and explores the relations between motivation, knowledge, and modernity. After reviewing a broad range of possible philosophical and psychological responses to environmental apathy and inertia, the author argues for moving away from a modern focus on either detached reason and control (Stoicism and Enlightenment reason) or the natural, the sentiments, and the authentic (Romanticism), both of which make possible disengaging and alienating modes of relating to our environment. Instead, he develops the notion of environmental skill: a concept that bridges the gap between knowledge and action, re-interprets environmental virtue, and suggests an environmental ethics centered on experience, know-how, and skillful engagement with our environment. The author then explores the implications of this ethics for our lives: it changes the way we think about and deal with health, food, animals, energy, climate change, politics, and technology.

Engaging with phenomenological and pragmatist ideas and with literature on romanticism and contemporary environmental virtue ethics, this book shows how existing thinking about nature is often still highly romantic, and how the concept of environmental skill provides a more adequate description of our basic existential relation to our environment. By revealing different ways of actively relating to our environment and by encouraging us to develop environmental skill, Coeckelbergh proposes an environmental ethics that imaginatively and practically explores new possibilities.

Mark Coeckelbergh is Professor of Technology and Social Responsibility at De Montfort University, UK. Previously he was Managing Director of the 3TU Centre for Ethics and Technology and affiliated to the Philosophy Department of the University of Twente. His publications include *Growing Moral Relations* (2012), *Human Being @ Risk* (2013), and numerous publications in the area of ethics and technology—in particular, ethics of robotics and ICTS. His research interests include philosophy of technology, environmental philosophy, and moral philosophy.

Routledge Studies in Ethics and Moral Theory

1 **The Contradictions of Modern Moral Philosophy**
Ethics after Wittgenstein
Paul Johnston

2 **Kant, Duty and Moral Worth**
Philip Stratton-Lake

3 **Justifying Emotions**
Pride and Jealousy
Kristján Kristjánsson

4 **Classical Utilitarianism from Hume to Mill**
Frederick Rosen

5 **The Self, the Soul and the Psychology of Good and Evil**
Ilham Dilman

6 **Moral Responsibility**
The Ways of Scepticism
Carlos J. Moya

7 **The Ethics of Confucius and Aristotle**
Mirrors of Virtue
Jiyuan Yu

8 **Caste Wars**
A Philosophy of Discrimination
David Edmonds

9 **Deprivation and Freedom**
A Philosophical Enquiry
Richard J. Hull

10 **Needs and Moral Necessity**
Soran Reader

11 **Reasons, Patterns, and Cooperation**
Christopher Woodard

12 **Challenging Moral Particularism**
Edited by Mark Norris Lance, Matjaž Potrč, and Vojko Strahovnik

13 **Rationality and Moral Theory**
How Intimacy Generates Reasons
Diane Jeske

14 **The Ethics of Forgiveness**
A Collection of Essays
Christel Fricke

15 **Moral Exemplars in the *Analects***
The Good Person is *That*
Amy Olberding

16 **The Phenomenology of Moral Normativity**
William H. Smith

17 **The Second-Person Perspective in Aquinas's Ethics**
Virtues and Gifts
Andrew Pinsent

18 **Social Humanism**
A New Metaphysics
Brian Ellis

19 **Ethics Without Morals**
In Defence of Amorality
Joel Marks

20 **Evil and Moral Psychology**
Peter Brian Barry

21 **Aristotelian Ethics in Contemporary Perspective**
Edited by Julia Peters

22 **Modern Honor**
A Philosophical Defense
Anthony Cunningham

23 **Art and Ethics in a Material World**
Kant's Pragmatist Legacy
Jennifer A. McMahon

24 **Defending Associative Duties**
Jonathan Seglow

25 **Consequentialism and Environmental Ethics**
Edited by Avram Hiller, Ramona Ilea, and Leonard Kahn

26 **The Ethics of Vulnerability**
A Feminist Analysis of Social Life and Practice
Erinn C. Gilson

27 **Eudaimonic Ethics**
The Philosophy and Psychology of Living Well
Lorraine Besser-Jones

28 **The Philosophy and Psychology of Character and Happiness**
Edited by Nancy E. Snow and Franco V. Trivigno

29 **Moral Responsibility and the Problem of Many Hands**
Ibo van de Poel, Lambèr Royakkers, and Sjoerd D. Zwart

30 **Environmental Skill**
Motivation, Knowledge, and the Possibility of a Non-Romantic Environmental Ethics
Mark Coeckelbergh

'That is well said, answered Candide, but we must cultivate our garden.'

Illustration by Fernand Siméon, printed in Voltaire's 'Candide ou L'optimisme', Paris: Jules Meynial, 1922. Reproduction courtesy of the New York Public Library.

Environmental Skill

Motivation, Knowledge, and the Possibility of a Non-Romantic Environmental Ethics

Mark Coeckelbergh

LONDON AND NEW YORK

First published 2015 by Routledge

2 Park Square, Milton Park, Abingdon, Oxfordshire OX14 4RN
711 Third Avenue, New York, NY 10017

Routledge is an imprint of the Taylor & Francis Group, an informa business

First issued in paperback 2018

Copyright © 2015 Taylor & Francis

The right of Mark Coeckelbergh to be identified as author of this work
has been asserted by him in accordance with sections 77 and 78 of the
Copyright, Designs and Patents Act 1988.

All rights reserved. No part of this book may be reprinted or reproduced
or utilised in any form or by any electronic, mechanical, or other
means, now known or hereafter invented, including photocopying and
recording, or in any information storage or retrieval system, without
permission in writing from the publishers.

Notice:
Product or corporate names may be trademarks or registered trademarks,
and are used only for identification and explanation without intent to
infringe.

Library of Congress Cataloging-in-Publication Data

Coeckelbergh, Mark.
Environmental skill : motivation, knowledge, and the possibility of a
    non-romantic environmental ethics / by Mark Coeckelbergh. — 1 [edition].
        pages cm. — (Routledge studies in ethics and moral theory ; 30)
    Includes bibliographical references and index.
    1. Environmental ethics.   2. Environmentalism—Moral and
ethical aspects.   3. Environmentalism—Philosophy.   4. Human
ecology—Philosophy.   I. Title.
    GE42.C64   2015
    179'.1—dc23
    2014041809

ISBN: 978-1-138-88557-8 (hbk)
ISBN: 978-1-138-34675-8 (pbk)

Typeset in Sabon
by Apex CoVantage, LLC

For Roxy

Contents

Preface	xiii
Acknowledgments	xv

1 Introduction	1

PART I
Environmental Motivation and Knowledge: Ancient and Modern Lessons from Philosophy and Psychology

2 The Moral Psychology of Environmental "Sin"	13
3 Lessons from Contemporary Psychology	29

PART II
The Janus Face of Modern Environmentalism: Enlightenment and Romanticism

4 Enlightenment Reason and Liberation Politics	43
5 Romantic Feeling for Nature	63

PART III
Beyond Nature, Beyond Modernity, Beyond Thinking: A Non-Romantic, Non-Modern Approach

6 Beyond "Nature" and Modernity: Towards Non-Dualistic Thinking	83

xii *Contents*

7 Beyond Environmental *Thinking* (1): Skilled Engagement 96

8 Beyond Environmental *Thinking* (2): Exercising Virtue
and Moral Sentiment 119

PART IV
Implications for Environmental Ethics and
Philosophy of Technology

9 Implications for Environmental Ethics (1):
Beyond Walking in "Nature" 137

10 Implications for Environmental Ethics (2):
Exploring the Possibility of Non-Modern and
Non-Romantic Environmental Living 157

11 The Art of Environmental Practice as an Ethics of Skill:
Revisiting the Problem of Technology and Its Relation
to Alienation 181

12 Conclusion: The Possibility of a New Environmental Ethics 200

Bibliography 211
Index 219

Preface

For years I have known about environmental problems. For years I have been reading reports, policy documents, and theories in environmental ethics. I know about climate change, species extinction, usage of non-renewable energy, habitat destruction, bad air quality, soil erosion and contamination, overpopulation, nuclear risk, water pollution, resource depletion, toxins, electronic waste, hormones and antibiotics in food, etc. I know that humans are doing this. I also know that there is a causal connection between what *I* do (e.g. eat meat, drive a car, etc.) and environmental problems. I know about the so-called footprint: my footprint, your footprint. I know about overconsumption and its effects on the planet. I know that our lifestyle—including *my* lifestyle—is not sustainable, or at least not sustainable enough. I even know about solutions. I know that we should work towards a clean and renewable energy future, end overfishing and industrial farming, protect wildlife, eat better food, and so on. I also know that this requires from me that *I* change my life.

But do I change my life? I have been trying to live in a more "green", "environmentally friendly" way—for example, by not using my car as often as I used to do, by biking to work, by eating less meat and by regularly buying some biological products, by sorting my waste, and by limiting my buying of consumption goods (e.g. buying less clothing and electronic equipment, buying second-hand things, etc.). However, I must admit that the degree of change I have made to my life is disappointingly small in comparison to what I believe I ought to do.

I think my "case" is not exceptional. There are many people who, like me, received a good education and are well-informed about environmental issues. There are many people who, like me, know the "facts". But most of us have not made very impressive changes. We are concerned about the environment, but we do not radically change our lives.

This book is motivated by the desire to understand why making this change is so difficult and to explore what we can do about it. How can we understand and deal with this problem, and what can philosophy contribute?

Acknowledgments

I wish to thank the anonymous reviewers of my manuscript for their helpful comments, and I am grateful to all people who, directly or indirectly, contributed to my thinking on environmental ethics and to the publication of this book. I also thank the New York Public Library for the permission to use the illustration included in this book. Let me give special thanks to Joke Noppers for assistance with research on empirical psychology and to my colleague Brent Mittelstadt for correcting the final version of my manuscript. I also would like to express my respect and admiration for people who are exemplary when it comes to having a more practical and engaged relation to the environment.

1 Introduction

1.1. THE PROBLEM: WHY IS IT NOT EASY TO BECOME GREEN?

Today it is widely recognized that we face environmental problems and that we should do something about them. Even if there is considerable disagreement about what the underlying or central problem is, how urgent the problem is (Does this amount to a "crisis"? Should we act now?), and what exactly should be done, since the 1970s many people—especially but certainly not exclusively in the West—recognize that "nature" is in trouble and believe that action is required to protect and preserve "nature". For example, they agree that we should promote "sustainability" and that we should prevent cruelty to animals.

A significant proportion of these people also believe that environmental action should involve changes to the way they live their lives. Today we know so much more about this: We know the "facts" and we know that there is a connection between how we live and what happens to "nature". The sciences show what happens (e.g. what happens to ecosystems or to the climate), alarming reports have been produced from the 1970s up to now, and during the past 50 years "green" ethicists, activists, and politicians have constantly reminded us about the need for change[1]. We realize that we should live in a more "green" way. To care about "nature" has become mainstream, and many of us try to live in a more "environmentally friendly" way.

However, in spite of this growing awareness, we have failed to make substantial and fundamental alterations to our societies and to our way of living. Political change in this area is so slow that even those who care and want change tend to become frustrated, cynical, or apathetic about "the environment" and its problems. And when it really comes to doing things differently and to *living* differently, even those who are sympathetic to green thinking fail to make changes to their lives or limit their efforts to cosmetic "lifestyle" changes, while knowing that these are not enough. Thus, it seems that the main problem of environmental ethics is not that we do not know what to do, but that we are not *motivated* to make the required changes.

2 Introduction

What explains this lack of motivation? Why does this gap between knowledge and action persist? What makes it so hard to change? Why is it not easy to become green, or at least *greener*? If we could find a good answer to these questions, perhaps we could make some real progress in this area: It would help to clarify the underlying problem(s) and suggest a way to address it.

1.2. AIM OF THE BOOK

This book intends to contribute to a better understanding of the problem and an answer by means of a philosophical inquiry into the conditions of possibility of environmental change, involving a discussion of the moral-psychological, moral-epistemological, and cultural-philosophical barriers to change. Rather than directly focusing on the usual normative-ethical questions *what* we ought to do and *why* we ought to do it (the problem of moral justification), I focus on the problems of *how* we can become *motivated* to do environmental good (the problem of moral motivation); what kind of *knowledge* we need for this (the problem of moral epistemology); and what the relation is between these problems of moral motivation, moral knowledge, and the problem of *modernity*. I will argue that our inability to change our lives and social, political, economic, and technological institutions is partly but importantly due to misconceiving and "misliving" our relation to our environment as people who are still deeply *modern*. In particular, this book questions how we usually think about "nature", "environment", "virtue", and "technology". It questions conceptions and ways of thinking that we inherited from modern-rationalist but also modern-*romantic* thinking. After critically reviewing a broad range of possible responses to the problem of environmental motivation—a journey from Plato and Augustine to Rousseau and Thoreau, but also lessons from contemporary analytic philosophy and empirical psychology—this book argues for a non-Stoic and non-modern, especially non-romantic environmental ethics that moves away from our normative focus on *either* detached reason and control (Stoicism and Enlightenment reason) *or* the natural, the emotional, and the authentic (Romanticism), *both* of which turn out to be disengaging and alienating modes of thinking and doing. Instead, it centres on the notion of skill, in particular skilled engagement with the environment: engaged, embodied, "care-full", and habitual activity that affirms our "environmental" nature. I will argue that what we need now is not so much more knowledge of environmental theory and environmental facts, better management, more self-control, or more warm feelings for "nature", but a different, more practical and active relation to our environment, which involves better know-how rather than more know-that: we need *better environmental skill*. We have to acquire the art of environmental living.

I will show that this concept of "environmental skill" enables us to answer the problem of moral motivation construed as a gap between knowledge and action. The problem arises due to the kind of knowledge that is assumed in this problem definition: theoretical knowledge is not enough and itself creates the gap; instead, we need know-how, which is by definition not detached from action and experience but produced by it. If we assume the latter meaning of knowledge, the explanation for our environmental inaction and demotivation is that we do not *really* "know" what to do unless we skillfully engage with our environment. Thus, when it comes to environmental ethics this understanding of environmental knowledge and motivation provides (1) a way to avoid alienation from our environment and (2) a way to "become motivated by moving" rather than by something external, such as theoretical knowledge. Moreover, the concept of environmental skill also suggests a different way of thinking. It recommends that we reject both the disinterested, objectivist aspect of modern science and the naturalism of Romanticism as detaching, alienating modes of thinking and doing; it involves different assumptions about the relations between humans and their environment, and different understandings of the relations between skills, virtues, moral sentiments, and technologies. While I will draw attention to reasons why moral-environmental change is difficult, I will show that this approach has implications for the way we live: for the way we walk in "nature", but also for the way we deal with issues such as health, food, animals, energy, and climate change.

1.3. APPROACH AND POSITION IN THE LITERATURE

The book draws on a number of philosophical sources and traditions to support its main thesis. Engaging with phenomenological (Heidegger and Dreyfus) and pragmatist ideas (Dewey), but also with literature on Romanticism, with the work of Rousseau and Thoreau, with contemporary 'environmental virtue ethics' (see for instance van Wensveen or Cafaro), and with thinking about manual skill and craftsmanship (Pirsig, Sennett, Crawford, Dreyfus and Kelly), the book shows how existing thinking about nature is often still highly romantic and how the proposed approach tries to overcome this way of thinking. This delivers not only a more adequate description of our basic existential relation to our environment and of different ways of *perceiving* our environment, but also gives us a conceptual tool that is normatively and practically relevant. By revealing different ways of *actively* relating to our environment and by encouraging us to develop environmental know-*how* and to exercise environmental virtue understood in terms of skill, it promises an environmental ethics that practically explores new possibilities and that, with its emphasis on skill as well as concrete and embodied know-how, asks us to do things in a way that *moves* us, makes us care, makes us more "environmental", and thereby lets us, and our environment, flourish.

Evidently this is not the first time that anyone has questioned modern ways of thinking or used a transcendental approach to think about "nature."

4 *Introduction*

However, when it comes to environmental philosophy, usually this project is limited to questioning scientific and technological ways of thinking and doing. Romanticism is often left out of the picture. This is understandable: if we perceive the world through romantic glasses, we do not see the glasses themselves. With its focus on the "natural", the "authentic", and "the wild" (including the very idea of "rewilding"), modern environmental philosophy—including Thoreau—is deeply romantic. This book diagnoses this blind spot and reflects on how we can remove it.

Moreover, due to our Romanticism we often set up a divorce between "environmental" issues and questions concerning "technology", which is reflected in the gap between academic fields that deal with these problems. This book is different: It makes a much-needed connection between environmental philosophy and philosophy of technology. It rejects those views in philosophy of technology that think of technology in terms of a "system" or in terms of (a specific kind of) rationality that dominates "nature". Instead, it associates technology more with the ancient term *techne*, which is not aimed at disinterested understanding (*episteme* as *theoria*) but concrete (ways of) making and doing. The book does not view *techne* as a kind of lower activity, as Aristotle did, but moves beyond Aristotle's freedom/necessity dualism, which presupposes a detached human subject. Thus, the book does not only question our talk about "nature" but also our talk about "technology"—which many assume to be external to us and external to the active and practical ways we relate to our environment. It replaces the human-technology and human-nature dualisms with the notion of "environmental skill" and with what I call, in a Heideggerian idiom, "acting-in-the-world".

This non-dualist, or at least less-dualist, approach also reconnects the environmental "crisis" (which seems to be "out there") with the crisis of meaning and value (which seems to be a matter of the "inner"). It retrieves the concept of alienation and takes seriously feelings of alienation, but in contrast to the earlier tradition in philosophy of technology and in environmental ethics, it offers a different definition and solution to the problem: Alienation is not about "the system" or "technology" that threatens us and destroys nature and the natural as well as human nature and value and meaning (as in Heidegger but also Frankfurter Schule and Habermas); rather, alienation concerns the more concrete and practical ways in which *we* relate to the environment. This implies, among other things, that we become more, not less, responsible when we adopt a non-modern approach.

I use the term "non-modern" to distinguish my approach (1) from efforts that seek to overcome the modern by reverting back to pre-modern technologies and ways of life—a tendency which is present in the works of Heidegger, Dreyfus, Illich, and Borgmann—and (2) from "post-modern" thinking, which may well succeed in exploring the non-modern, but which is heavily focused on discourse and text, thereby neglecting the material dimension and its related skills and *techne*. With its focus on environmental

Introduction 5

skill, this book develops an approach that avoids a romantic environmentalism and a nostalgic philosophy of technology and that seeks to redress the balance between *techne* and *logos* when it comes to the techno-logical aspects of environmental thinking and practice.

Furthermore, by moving beyond an ethics of control and management, the book also achieves distance from what it now reveals as a superficial critique of society and of how we generally relate to our environment: anti-consumerism understood as a response to lack of control. The environmental crisis has to do with consumerism, for sure, but in an anti-Stoic move the book argues that (1) the problem is misconceived if the problem with consumerism is defined in terms of lack of control of desires (or *too much* desire) rather than a failure to connect with things—a failure to adequately connect to the environment—and that (2) the solution of more self-control tends to aggravate the environmental crisis rather than solve it, since it re-enforces the attitude and the kind of thinking and acting Heidegger called 'technological' and promotes an ideal of autonomy (detachment, total control) that is theoretically inadequate and practically and environmentally destructive.

Finally, the book is sympathetic to environmental virtue ethics (see, for example, van Wensveen, Sandler and Cafaro), but distances it (1) from the Stoic tradition (including perhaps Stoic Christianity and, for example, Carson's plea for restraint in *Silent Spring*), which over-emphasizes virtues that have to do with self-control, such as temperance; (2) from the Romanticism inherent in for example Thoreau's and Leopold's work (e.g. celebration of the wild); and (3) from (interpretations of) Aristotelian thinking about virtue that put too much emphasis on theoretical knowledge and neglect contingency and pluralism. The ethics of skill argued for in this book avoids promoting restraint if that amounts to detachment and disengagement, and criticizes the romantic rejection of the artificial. Moreover, arguing against the more theoretically oriented dimension of Aristotle's ethics, the book emphasizes that (developing) virtue is a matter of practical skill and habit rather than a matter of character, attitude, or theoretical knowledge (e.g. definition of virtue as principles or rules how to act). It thus emphasizes the practically oriented dimension of Aristotle and of the virtue ethics tradition. Environmental virtue is neither "internal" (character) nor "external" (acts) but concerns how we relate to our environment as beings-in-relation, as environmental beings.

1.4. OVERVIEW OF THE ARGUMENT

The book will move through a number of ways of understanding and answering the problem in order to pave the way for a new direction in environmental ethics. Each time a particular view is considered, I will first articulate why it might be considered an attractive response to the

6   *Introduction*

problem, and single out the observations and insights that must be saved and endorsed. Then I will raise my objection(s) and point out limitations (without necessarily entirely dismissing the view in question) and suggest a different response, the implications of which are then more fully developed and elaborated in the last chapters of the book. Thus, there is a "negative" and "positive" moment in the book, but development of the positive view starts already in the first chapters. Let me give an overview of the argument.

In **Part I**, I start with discussing *psychological* conditions of possibility for environmental change: What explains our lack of "green" motivation? To answer this question, I try to learn from ancient and modern thinking about motivation and knowledge and from contemporary psychology. In **Chapter 2** I use mainly philosophy—in particular, ancient Greek philosophy—to construct a number of moral-psychological problem definitions and explanations. I start with the Socratic view that knowing the good is sufficient for a virtuous life and argue that if this means "theoretical" knowledge then this view is not very helpful: There has been enough instruction about what is environmentally good, but this knowledge has not produced much more environmental good. I review a number of ancient and modern explanations for the gap between knowing and choosing the good, including weak will and lack of self-control, "environmental evil," turning away from environmental good, and mindless work and consumption by "environmental zombies"—"environmental evil" turns out to be more banal than first assumed.

In **Chapter 3** I review contemporary psychological explanations for the lack of environmental motivation. I discuss theories of intention and behaviour, motivation, and self-regulation. In the specific literature on environmental psychology, I pay particular attention to the role of direct experience. However, in the next chapters I take distance from most philosophical and psychological explanations and pay more attention to the social-collective, political-ideological, and especially cultural-philosophical dimension of the problem. Perhaps the stress on self-control is itself part of the problem. Maybe the problem is not a lack of reflection, but the *wrong kind of* thinking. And why is it that our contemporary culture tends to neglect the role of direct experience in morality?

My answer to these questions is provided by my discussion of the relation between environmentalism and modernity in **Part II**. I argue that contemporary environmentalism is still very modern, and that in order to further understand it and find a solution to the motivation problem we need to discuss the problem of modernity. In **Chapters 4** and **5** I show how problematic modern thinking is for guiding environmental ethics, how this kind of *cultural-philosophical* condition of possibility limits our possibilities to change things. In particular, I argue that contemporary environmentalism is deeply shaped by Enlightenment rationalism and Romanticism. This Janus-faced modern outlook limits our thinking in at least two ways.

Introduction 7

On the one hand, environmentalists draw on science to show what is going on ("the facts") and often politicians propose technological solutions. However, this approach is problematic: Enlightenment reason promotes the control and technological manipulation of nature, but this has become a source of existential, social and moral alienation: We feel that the modern world has no meaning or value. And as Marx and Heidegger have argued, the result of this way of thinking is that we treat nature as a standing-reserve (Heidegger 1977) and become alienated from one another (Marx 1844 and 1867). On the other hand, we try to solve this problem by anti-reason, by re-enchanting "nature" with our love, and by living in a more "natural" and "authentic" way. Environmentalists value the "wild", that is, what is untouched and unpolluted by humans. We start walking in nature to reconnect with it: this is the romantic solution, rooted in, for instance, the work of Rousseau and Thoreau, and alive in the current yearning for "the wild" and "wilderness". At first sight, this romantic response seems to solve the problem of environmental motivation: If we loved nature, we would become motivated to protect it, especially if it is our Mother Earth. If we were more *authentic* and *natural*, nature could be liberated from the corrupting influences of science and society. But I will show that at closer inspection, romantic thinking is also a modern way of thinking, which is dualist and (therefore) in practice often amounts to a detached attitude and a lack of real involvement and engagement in one's environment. I also show that conservative and liberationist politics do not escape the modern approach to environmental problems.

In **Part III**, therefore, I explore ways to go beyond modern thinking in environmental philosophy. In **Chapter 6** I show how we can move beyond thinking in terms of "nature" and beyond a dualistic view of the relation between humans and their environment. After discussing Heidegger's critique of modernity and showing that it still has a romantic dimension, I argue that a non-modern view holds that the world was never disenchanted in the first place (Szerszinsky), that we should not presuppose that it was first a blank slate on which we ascribed meaning (Ingold), but that we were and are *always already related to our environment*: there is no separate "nature" (and indeed no separate "human" in this sense). As Berleant puts it in his participatory environmental aesthetics: 'There is no inside and outside' and the environment cannot be objectified since it is 'continuous with the participant' (Berleant 2005, pp. 13–14). In other words, we are environmental by nature.

Then I argue that in order to really move beyond a modern view of our environment, we have to better understand how alienation works and avoid both contemplative mysticism and fatalistic non-activity. First I suggest that in so far as we think and act modern, we are involved in a kind of "dialectic" process of self-alienation. Then I argue that a mysticism that is absorbed in contemplating the unity of everything may actually be at the expense of real involvement with the world. When Heidegger recommends *Gelassenheit*,

8 Introduction

therefore, this attitude of letting-go (or indeed the Taoist concept of *wuwei*) should not be interpreted as inactivity but as a kind of flow without sense of self and without too much *logos* (or at least no meta-logos). Can we find a way of thinking and doing that avoids control-oriented science and technology and is "environmental", yet not romantic or mystical (at least not mystical in the sense articulated here), but rather very practical and material?

This is what I attempt in **Chapter 7**, in which I start developing a non-romantic environmental ethics as an "ethics of skill", the nexus of which is the concept of "environmental skill". First I revisit Socrates' argument. Perhaps knowing the good equals doing the good, but in a different sense than Socrates assumed: We can only get real knowledge of good by means of skilled activity rather than by means of theoretical contemplation. I will argue that becoming more environmentally good requires us to actively and skillfully relate to, and engage with, our environment. By drawing on work by Dreyfus, Borgmann, Sennett, Crawford, and others, I show that disengagement is the (modern) problem; active and skillful engagement, the solution. I also further distinguish my approach from Romanticism by "re-reading" Rousseau and Thoreau. However, I note that becoming more "environmental" in this sense is not entirely a matter of choice, since modernity continues to shape the conditions of possibility of our thinking and doing. We cannot (fully) control the change. In order to *find* (rather than create) a better relation to our environment, therefore, we need patience. Changing habits takes time. We need a "slow" environmental ethics, an ethics we need to grow into rather than instruct and enforce.

In **Chapter 8** I further develop the notion of "environmental skill" by engaging with the virtue ethics tradition—in particular, by responding to proposals for an 'environmental virtue ethics' (Cafaro). However, I take distance from the standard interpretations of Aristotelian virtue within virtue ethics, which tend to emphasize reason and deliberation, and firmly link virtue with skill. I elaborate this interpretation by discussing a Humean interpretation of virtue, which I argue is better equipped for this purpose since it pays attention to moral sentiment, to the relation between natural abilities (skills) and virtue, and to the role of context, circumstance, and contingency in the moral life. It also opens up a more pluralist understanding of virtue than Aristotle's, and can deal with what is sometimes called "the situationalist challenge for ethics".

In **Part IV** I further spell out the implications of this "environmental skill" approach for ethical, political, and technological practice. I argue that an "ethics of skill" should not (only) make overly general and abstract claims, but carefully analyze the phenomenology of specific practices in order to show which ways of doing and thinking are alienating and what possibilities there might be for better engaging with our environment. Then I give some examples. In **Chapter 9** I discuss walking versus working in nature to explore how this analysis could be done. I argue that walking in "nature" is not necessarily good; other activities may be environmentally better and, if we want to walk at all, what matters is *how* we walk and do other things: Does a particular activity and *way* to act promote skilled engagement with our environment? And what is the role of technology? What are good walking and wayfinding? In **Chapter 10** I discuss what "environmental skill" and "environmental virtue" mean in other "environmental" domains: health care, food and eating, relations with animals, energy, and climate change. I show how much our practices in these domains and our thinking *about* these issues are still captivated by modern thinking. I show how anthropology can show us a less modern approach to these issues, and criticize Heidegger's view of energy and modern concepts such as planet management. I coin the notion of *Umwelt-Vergessenheit*: We forgot that we are environmental beings and represent our environment as a thing, as external "nature."

I also argue that this non-modern approach to environmental ethics has consequences for thinking about politics. It questions (1) the liberal assumption that politics should be neutral on substantial issues (it promotes a particular conception of the good life) and (2) the nationalist assumption that politics should mainly take place at the level of the nation state (it rejects the romantic focus on "the people" of "the nation"). Instead, an ethics and politics of skill aims at both personal and societal growth and a participatory approach to democracy (see also Dewey), which is less alienating than the current systems. Moreover, I argue that modern environmentalism is torn between a universalist, science-oriented, technocratic, Baconian side and a romantic particularist, community-oriented, democratic side, and show that we might be able to go beyond this tension by understanding expertise and community in a different, non-modern way. I argue for situated, but also cross-political engagement, which is "local" and "global" at the same time due to new technologies and related skills.

In **Chapter 11** I say more about the implications of "environmental skill" for thinking about technology. I conclude from the previous chapters that if the main problem is a kind of "environmental alienation" and if we have to try out ways to more intensely engage with our environment, this ethics of environmental skill should not be understood as implying a romantic rejection of technology (as many old-style environmental philosophers and philosophers of technology did), but as a proposal to evaluate specific ways of "*techne*", specific ways of skillfully-technologically relating to the world. I argue that technology can also disclose different worlds and—especially important with regard to the problem of motivation and alienation—that it can also open up new opportunities for skilled engagement. I discuss new information and communication technologies (ICTs) and their relation to environmental ethics. Responding to Dreyfus' suggestion that the internet is necessarily alienating, I offer a more non-modern and non-dualist approach to the use of ICTs, which allows for a more nuanced and richer analysis of the problem of how we should relate to our environment and how technology shapes this relation, and which tries to avoid putting so much normative

10 Introduction

weight on the modern-romantic distinction between natural and artificial. Furthermore, I use Illich's concept of 'convivial tools' to further develop an "environmental skill" view of technology. I argue that instead of rejecting "technology" and embracing a romantic view, we should help to develop *different* technologies and skills that establish a different relation to our environment, that make us more environmental.

In the concluding chapter, **Chapter 12**, I summarize my contribution to environmental ethics, but stress that it should not be presented, in a very modern way, as a "new" or "alternative" vision or concept that should then be "applied". But how *should* it be understood? I further discuss the problem of moral-environmental change, given the pervasive influence of modern thinking on our way of living. Is change possible? Drawing on my work on moral status, I argue that our thinking about the environment depends on a range of conditions of possibility, which limit the room for moral change. The extent to which we can move towards an environmental ethics as an ethics of skill and, more generally, towards a different, more engaged relationship with the environment, depends on the way we talk about the environment (language), the way we live together (society and culture), the way we relate to our bodies, our relationships with materiality and technology, and the forms of spirituality that influence us. If and in so far as these ways of thinking and doing are still modern, we are still constrained by a modern form of life and hence by modern environmental thinking and doing. We cannot simply "step out" of it. Thus, it is neither sufficient nor desirable to propose the concept of environmental skill as constituting a blueprint for a better world and a better (environmental) ethics that then needs to be "applied" or "implemented"; rather, as suggested at the end of Chapter 7, we need to grow into a new form of life. I suggest that environmental ethics is a kind of craft and an art, and that the coming into being of a new, non-modern environmental ethics is not a matter of conceptual design but more comparable to birth. Therefore, I argue, the philosopher's task is that of a non-Socratic, or at least not all too Socratic *midwife*: it is our task to accompany the birth of new environmental practices by enhancing environmental (meta-)know-how, thus contributing to the growth of "environmental skill".

NOTE

1. Consider some milestones in the history of environmental awareness: the publication of *Silent Spring* in 1962; the 1972 report *The Limits to Growth*, commissioned by the Club of Rome; the rise of Greenpeace and other green non-governmental organizations in the 1970s and especially in the 1980s; the 1987 Brundtland Report (which put 'sustainable development' on the agenda); the reports of the Intergovernmental Panel on Climate Change (for example, the 1995 report, which influenced the adoption of the Kyoto Protocol in 1997); more recently, Al Gore's presentations and film *An Inconvenient Truth* (2006) and a number of United Nations climate change conferences— for example, in Durban, Doha, and Warsaw.

Part I

Environmental Motivation and Knowledge

Ancient and Modern Lessons from Philosophy and Psychology

2 The Moral Psychology of Environmental "Sin"

INTRODUCTION

It is easy to blame *others*—in particular "politics" and "business"—for not being "green" enough. Of course it would be good, for instance, if there were more political support for green living. There is a consensus among environmentalists that the current generation of politicians fails to create and implement policies that could make a real difference in this respect. Protests motivated by these ideas seem entirely justified. But blaming politicians for the environmental problems we have does not really address the central problem identified in the first chapter: the problem of environmental motivation. Why is it that *we* are not motivated enough to change our lives? Rather than blaming others, we could start with evaluating our own lives. And *why* do most people continue to vote for politicians who do not and will not promote green living, and hence get the politicians they "deserve"?

In this part of the book, I will review a number of psychological explanations for the lack of environmental motivation. This will require me to engage with both ancient and contemporary moral psychology—including environmental psychology. Let me start in this chapter with ancient thinking about morality, knowledge, and motivation. While attention to "environmental" issues (under that description) is relatively recent, there is a long history of philosophers who tried to understand lack of moral motivation. Let me use ancient Greek and Christian thinking in order to construct a number of problem definitions and explanations of the gap between what we believe we should do and what we (fail to) do.

2.1. IGNORANCE ABOUT ENVIRONMENTAL GOOD

A first explanation of our lack of environmental motivation might be that we lack knowledge of environmental good. If people vote for the "wrong" kind of politicians and support the "wrong" kind of policies, so this explanation goes, it is because they are ignorant about what environmental ethics demands from us. What we need, then, is to instruct people about

14 *Environmental Motivation and Knowledge*

environmental ethics: about moral principles (modern approach) and about what environmental virtue is (ancient approach). With sufficient moral knowledge, so we might hope, people will do what is environmentally right, live in an environmentally good way, and support rather than threaten the development of a "green" *polis*.

This approach to moral knowledge has roots in the ethics of Plato as articulated in the Socratic dialogues. Those who argue today that we need more knowledge about environmental good may share with Socrates the following assumptions:

(1) Virtue is a matter of knowledge;
(2) Knowledge by itself does motivate action; and
(3) Moral knowledge (virtue) is theoretical knowledge.

In this book I will question these assumptions, at least if "knowledge" in assumption 1 and 2 is understood as theoretical knowledge, and explore its implications for environmental ethics. Let me first outline Socrates' view.

In the *Protagoras* (Plato 1997b) Socrates discusses with Protagoras the question of whether virtue can be taught. What kind of knowledge is moral knowledge? Socrates first denies that virtue is teachable, and articulates the Athenian view that public deliberation can be done by everyone and does not require a particular kind of expertise. In 'technical matters' we need a 'craftsman', whereas in politics 'anyone' can become wise (319b–e). With regard to environmental matters, this view implies that we do not need a special expertise when it comes to making individual or collective decisions concerning the environment. We can leave the 'technical matters' to others.

But then, later in the dialogue, Socrates agrees with Protagoras that virtue is an expertise based on rationality and calculation. He and Protagoras agree that moral expertise is 'the art of measurement': Whereas 'the power of appearance often makes us wander all over the place in confusion (. . .) the art of measurement would save us' (356d–e), which is 'nothing other than arithmetic' (357a). Here it seems we *do* need a special kind of expertise. As Cooper rightly observes in his introduction to the dialogue:

> In fact, Socrates shows himself to be much more an ally of Protagoras on the question of the nature of human virtue than at first appears. He is deeply committed, more deeply indeed than Protagoras, to Protagoras' initial claim that virtue is a rationally based expertise at deliberation and decision.
>
> (Cooper 1997, p. 746)

Thus, according to Socrates this moral expertise requires knowledge, but it is not a practical craft. It is a kind of theoretical knowledge and, more precisely, a matter of rational calculation. On this point Protagoras agrees. And Protagoras and Socrates share this assumption with contemporary environmentalists to the extent that they rely on theoretical expert knowledge to back up their normative claims. According to them, the point is to know certain things about the environment (e.g. about ecology), and on the basis of this scientific expertise, which goes beyond appearances and is based on measurements, we (experts or those who rely on experts) can make good environmental decisions.

Moreover, if and once we have this kind of moral knowledge, then Socrates thinks it is impossible that one does not act in accordance to it. He argues against the view of 'most people' (352d), of 'ordinary people' (353a), who 'maintain that most people are unwilling to do what is best, even though they know what it is and are able to do it' (352d). He endorses the view that 'if someone were to know what is good and bad, then he would not be forced by anything to act otherwise than knowledge dictates' (352c). He even thinks that it is 'absurd' to suppose that 'a man, knowing the bad to be bad, nevertheless does the very thing, when he is able not to do it, having been driven and overwhelmed by pleasure' (355b).

Of course Socrates would not deny that we are sometimes driven by pleasure and (therefore) do bad things. For example, today being "driven" by pleasure seems to play a role in the mass consumption of meat and electronic devices, which have "bad" consequences for the environment. But Socrates would deny that we can describe this problem as a matter of *knowing* the good but *doing* the bad. For Socrates, such a person never knew the good in the first place. Being "overwhelmed" by pleasure turns out to be a form of ignorance—'ignorance in the highest degree' (357e). Self-control is important for Socrates, of course (see also Chapter 7), but self-control is not a matter of (a strong) will but of knowledge: 'To give in to oneself is nothing other than ignorance' (358c) and 'no one goes willingly toward the bad' (358d). Doing the bad is a mistake. For environmental ethics, this view means that if we act in environmentally unfriendly ways, we do so because we are ignorant about environmental good.

I think the latter view is far less common today. I will show later that modern ethics and contemporary psychology offer other explanations. But the view that what we call today *scientific* knowledge is needed for environmental good and environmental virtue is widely shared.

Moreover, some might even hold a Platonic view. If we combine the Socratic view with Plato's theory of Forms (in the *Republic*), we might say that what matters morally-epistemically, in Socrates' view, is *seeing* the good. The *kind* of knowledge we need is theoretical knowledge as a kind of seeing: we need a correct *vision* of the good, which means moving away from appearance. Theoretical knowledge as vision and contemplation (*theoria*) enables us to do good.

Applied to environmental matters, this Platonic view implies that we need "environmental vision": a vision of environmental good. In modern-scientific terms, this becomes: a vision of the current state of the environment, of a better environmental future, and a method for calculating

16 *Environmental Motivation and Knowledge*

the environmental future. What is needed is better theory, in the sense of more in-sight and fore-sight, and more environmental assessment and calculation. Today most of us are in the cave. We only see appearances; we have not yet seen the environmental truth and we have not been taught to calculate. Those who know the good and those who know how to calculate need to educate the leaders of the *polis*, the politicians (as philosopher-kings), and if they have true environmental *vision* we can trust them to lead us. Environmental experts should rule the people.

A democratic version of this view might run as follows: We have to educate *all* citizens in order to make sure that they will do what is best for others, for themselves, for the city, and indeed *for the environment*.[1] Such a Socratic environmental education would involve courses in environmental measurement, calculation, and assessment (say, what we would now call environmental *science*), but also philosophical inquiry into the nature of environmental good, which would be very similar to the kind of questioning Socrates does in the dialogues: He does not want to hear about practices and experiences of good, but wants to know what is *universal* in them in order to arrive at the *nature* or ultimate Form of the good. Similarly, we might do "environmental ethics" by writing a philosophical essay on the nature of environmental good, inquiring what people mean by environmental "good" when they say that something is "good" for nature, "good" for the environment, "good" for animals, "good" for climate, etc.

In sum, a Platonic/Socratic approach to the problem of environmental motivation explains the problem by pointing to our moral ignorance of environmental good, and recommends moral knowledge—in particular, theoretical knowledge as vision and "calculation"—to remedy the problem. This may include at least three kinds of "theoretical" exercises, which are inter-related: rational assessment of the state of the environment, vision of and insight into environmental good, and philosophical inquiry into the nature of environmental good.

In later chapters I will question the Platonic/Socratic assumption about the *kind* of knowledge we need, but let me first focus on Socrates' argument that the problem of moral motivation is a matter of knowledge at all. What does this argument imply for my initial problem formulation? In a sense, the Platonic/Socratic position implies that *there is no problem of motivation*—at least not in the way I defined the problem in the introduction—but only a problem of moral *knowledge*. If knowing the good is sufficient for a virtuous life, as Plato and Socrates argue, then how *could* there be a gap between moral knowledge and moral action? Once we knew environmental good, there would be no problem of motivation. Socrates—at least towards the end of the *Protagoras*—thinks virtue *can* be taught. For environmental ethics, this implies that if we instructed people about environmental good, then they would act in environmentally virtuous ways.

Is this true? There has been plenty of instruction, yet this has not produced much environmental good. Today many people are not ignorant, or

The Moral Psychology of Environmental "Sin"   17

at least *no longer* ignorant about environmental problems, and we have methods of calculation and assessment, we have an environmental science and we have modern moral philosophy. But apparently knowledge, or at least theoretical knowledge, is (at least) not sufficient for environmental good. For example, Al Gore has been teaching 'an inconvenient truth', but in contrast to what we would expect from Platonic/Socratic theory, this "truth" has not motivated us to radically change our lives. Many reports have been published by (inter)governmental and non-governmental bodies and organizations (for example, the Club of Rome report in 1972 or the 2007 Intergovernmental Panel on Climate Change report), but the numbers, "calculations", and assessments have done little to change our policies and our lives.

How can we explain this? In modern thinking we usually accept that, contrary to what Socrates argued, there *can* be a gap between (a) knowing the good and (b) doing the good. But even in antiquity this gap was recognized by other philosophers, for example—and most famously—by Aristotle. In the next sections I will turn to the Aristotelian problem and review (other) ancient and modern explanations for the gap between knowing the good and doing the good.

2.2. WEAK WILL AND LACK OF SELF-CONTROL

A traditional, ancient Greek explanation for the gap between knowing the good and doing good is weak will (*akrasia*) or lack of self-control, which I will treat in this section as referring to the same problem. With regard to environmental ethics, this explanation means: We know environmental good, but we fail to *do* good because our will is weak, because we lack self-control. What does this mean?

As we have seen, in the *Protagoras* Socrates denies that there can be such a thing like weak will, saying that 'no one goes willingly toward the bad' (358d). For Socrates, a person who acts badly is ignorant about good. But human experience—in Socrates' view, the experience of 'ordinary people'—is quite different, and environmental matters are no exception. As Aristotle points out in Book VII of the *Nicomachean Ethics* when he writes about *akrasia* and responds to the Socratic position, the common view is that we often know that what we do is wrong, but put aside our rational judgment because of our "passions", our lack of restraint: 'the incontinent man, knowing that what he does is bad, does it as a result of passion' (VII.1, 1145b12). The real trouble for environmental ethics, it seems, is not a lack of knowledge about environmental good, but a failure to *will* and do what is good for the environment because of a lack of self-control. We know environmental good, but we fail to restrain ourselves. It seems that the main problem is excess consumption of oil, food, and other things, and the moral-psychological explanation is a lack of individual and collective

18   *Environmental Motivation and Knowledge*

self-control. Moreover, consumerism boosts this by telling us that we can satisfy every desire and buy everything. This makes it harder for us to exercise restraint and self-control. In other words, it makes us *addicts*.

To understand this problem and to explore what can be done about it, let me return again to the history of philosophy, in which we can find an influential moral-psychological current that splits the human psyche in two parts: One part makes us do what is good or rational, the other part want to keep us from doing good and is irrational.

We can find this idea already in Plato. For example, in a famous part of the *Phaedrus* (245c–249d) Socrates compares the soul to a chariot pulled by two winged horses. One is noble and represents rationality and morality; the other is 'the opposite in breed' and represents the irrational passions and appetites. The charioteer tries to avoid that the horses go different ways; he must make sure that the chariot (the soul) arrives at the truth. (Here Plato seems to acknowledge that there can be a gap between knowing and doing, due to the passions.)

The Greek and Roman Stoics further emphasized the rational self-control that was already praised by Plato and Aristotle. They tried to achieve a psychological state in which they were free from attachment to external things and people. They argued that we should be independent from them, since dependence also brings with it the risk of loss and of misery. The Stoics tried to reach immunity for misfortune by means of *askesis*. Their aim was detachment and *apatheia*: to be 'without passion'. The passions are a kind of disease and must be eradicated. Reason is the medicine. Applying reason to emotions is a kind of therapy, indeed what Nussbaum has called a 'therapy of desire' (Nussbaum 1994). We should control our emotions and follow reason, the *logos*. Virtue means having a will that is in agreement with Nature, which means again perfecting *logos* (Greek) and *ratio* (Latin). Living in harmony with nature does not yet have the romantic meaning we tend to attach to it today; for the Stoics, it meant living in harmony with a rational universe. Again this ideal of self-control and self-discipline presupposes a divided self: a reasonable part or "true" self which tries to live in accordance with logos, with Nature, and therefore must suppress its "passionate" part, the bodily part which is *external*, which is not "me", since not in accordance with my rational nature and not in harmony with the Logos of the universe.

In modern times, philosophers have tried to express their ideas in less metaphorical and literary ways than Plato and the Stoics did, but the idea of a divided person remains influential. Harry Frankfurt, for example, provides insight into the phenomenon of what he describes as a divided will. He has famously argued that what distinguishes humans from animals is our capacity to *reflect* on our desires and form a desire concerning these desires, which he calls 'second-order desires' (Frankfurt 1971, p. 6). We may have a first-order desire (not) to do something, but then we may also desire not to want this first-order desire. If I am free, I decide which desire I want to be effective, which desire I wish to identify with. If I am an addict, by contrast, my will remains divided and I act upon desires I have not identified with. (Here identity seems key rather than rationality, but Plato and Frankfurt share the idea of a divided person.)

In this tradition, good is linked to freedom: If the good part of us "wins", we are deemed to be not only good but also free; that is, we are what we are supposed to be as humans. This is how Isaiah Berlin describes the idea in his famous article 'Two Concepts of Liberty':

> I wish my life and decisions to depend on myself, not on external forces of whatever kind. (. . .) I wish to be a subject, not an object; (. . .) I wish to be somebody, not nobody; a doer—deciding, not being decided for, self-directed and not acted upon by external nature or by other men as if I were a thing, or an animal, or a slave incapable of playing a human role (. . .)

> (Berlin 1958, p. 203)

Berlin also famously warns that this conception of 'positive liberty' and dividing up the self can easily be misused by others—for example a dictator—to tell us what is best for us and perhaps even to coerce us to do what (the dictator says) accords with the rational part of us—thus making us less, rather than more free (see also my remarks below).

Nevertheless, when it comes to understanding the problem of moral motivation, splitting up the psyche seems to have a lot of explanatory value. Consider again the problem of environmental motivation. Using the Platonic/Socratic view of the *Phaedrus* (but not the *Protagoras*), we might explain the problem now as our failure to maintain control over our divided psyche, in particular our failure to restrain our passions and appetites, which pull us away from what we rationally ought to do. And with Frankfurt, we could explain the problem as our failure to identify with the right kind of desire and to make it an effective desire, 'one that moves (or will or would move) a person all the way to action' (Frankfurt 1971, p. 8). Do we sufficiently reflect on our first-order desires such as the desire to eat a lot of meat or the desire to always use a car for transportation? Do we ask if we really want to have this desire? Do we ask if this is our true self that wants these things? Or are we addicted to meat, oil, and comfort, failing to be moved by the "green" desires we really want to have? Are we in this respect even what Frankfurt calls 'wantons', beings that do not care about our will at all? Consider the two kinds of addicts Frankfurt describes in his article:

> One of the addicts hates his addiction and always struggles desperately, although to no avail, against its thrust. He tries everything that he thinks might enable him to overcome his desires for the drug. But these desires are too powerful for him (. . .). He is an unwilling addict, helplessly violated by his own desires. (. . .) The other addict is a wanton.

20   Environmental Motivation and Knowledge

> His actions reflect the economy of his first-order desires, without his being concerned whether the desires that move him to act are desires by which he wants to be moved to act.
>
> (Frankfurt 1971, p. 12)

If we think the problem of environmental motivation is a matter of lacking self-control, these discussions and distinctions are very helpful and allow a more refined analysis of the problem. Why, exactly, do we lack self-control? Is it a failure to be rational, is it a failure to identify with the right kind of desires, or both? And if we are not motivated to act environmentally because we cannot make our desire for environmental good effective, are we like the addict who (nevertheless) struggles against his own desires (the unwilling addict), or are we often more like wantons, unconcerned with what we want?

Given what I said before, the most plausible explanation within this framework seems to be that our failure to act environmentally good is not due to us being wantons, since we *are* concerned with the environment, and not due to a lack of rational capacity (we know what we should do), but to a 'higher-order' failure to act upon the knowledge and concerns we have by restraining our appetites (our first-order desires) and to make the right kind of desires effective.

However, there are several problems with these explanations. First, they raise Berlin's worry. How can we avoid the implication that the unwilling addicts we apparently are should not only be told but also *coerced* to do what is environmentally good, "helped" to become environmentally better people? Should we avoid this consequence? The problem is the following. On the one hand, if the unwilling addict cannot "overcome" her desires by her own efforts, then it seems that *some* kind of intervention from "outside" is necessary to end her struggle. On the other hand, it would be better to avoid coercion for at least two reasons: (1) for the sake of (what Berlin would call negative) liberty, which is at least *also* a value, whatever environmental values there may be and (2) for an epistemological reason: how can those who tell others what to do be so sure that they know the "environmental truth"? It seems that we should be very cautious about this route, to say the least.

In order to deal with the liberty concern, one might propose what we may call "environmental *nudging*". Influenced by Thaler & Sunstein's book (2008), one could argue for 'libertarian paternalism' and apply this solution to the problem of self-control with regard to environmental matters: People should be 'free to do what they like' but they should be 'nudged' in the right (here: more environmentally good) direction. Thaler & Sunstein claim that 'it is legitimate for choice architects to try to influence people's behaviour in order to make their lives longer, healthier, and better' (Thaler & Sunstein 2008, p. 5). Similarly, one could try to influence people's behaviour in order to improve the environment. I disagree with the authors that people should

The Moral Psychology of Environmental "Sin"   21

always freely choose what they like (we also need environmental regulation, etc.), but their proposal is interesting since it avoids Berlin's objection. People are not forbidden to live other kinds of lives, but in effect their behaviour is altered. This is *manipulation*, surely, but since people can in principle make other choices, it does not count as coercion and seems to respect their liberty. It is an external intervention that will help the unwilling addict, whose desires for the bad kind of things are discouraged. Moreover, since people's choices and behaviour are anyway always already influenced, as Thaler & Sunstein rightly say (p. 10), why not influence their choices in an environmentally good direction? We could create environments at work, at home, and elsewhere that support environmentally good behaviour. Even if nudging may be not enough (we might need measures that are also restrictive, such as environmental laws), it seems that this kind of soft manipulation must be encouraged when it comes to promoting environmental good.

However, both the ethics of self-control and what we might call the ethics of benevolent manipulation (which includes nudging) neglect the problem I touched upon before: how we can know the truth, how we can know which direction is good, how we can know which desires are good? It is good to keep in mind that self-control and environmental nudging presuppose that one already knows what is environmentally good (and that there is *one* environmental good, *one* best way of life). We are asked to be strong and, if necessary, to use the crutches given to us, but how decisive can we be and how justified can manipulation be if we lack knowledge? Knowledge of environmental good needs to be assumed. *If* we have the knowledge, *then* these pieces of moral psychology and moral engineering can help us to describe our failure to act and give us some normative guidance—even if very thin—on how to solve the problem. But what kind of knowledge? Theoretical, Socratic knowledge? I will have to return to this question later in the book. Let me first point out two further difficulties.

One is a more deep-seated one, which will only become fully clear in the next chapters, but which I shall mention already. Both self-mastery and nudging-type manipulation are forms of control. But when it comes to our relation to the environment, control may well be part of the problem rather than the solution, since it assumes a detached view of humans and (the relation to) their world, and promotes the manipulation of nature: the nature "outside" (mastery of nature, nature is forced, used and abused for our purposes) but also the nature "inside" (the choice architect designs the economy of our desires). Although "being human" may always involve taking *some* kind of distance (e.g. in reflection) and although some manipulation of our environment may be unavoidable and not necessarily bad, the overemphasis on choice, will, and control in our Western culture—including in the history of ideas—is problematic with regard to environmental ethics (see Parts II and III).

Finally, so far I have assumed that most of us are concerned with the environment, have at least a (first-order) desire to protect the environment, and do only environmentally bad things because we are either ignorant people (first

22   *Environmental Motivation and Knowledge*

section; I rejected this explanation) or "addicts" who struggle against their bad inclinations and who would rather be good, if they could only be strong, self-controlled persons. Thus, I have assumed that there are no bad intentions involved. But is this assumption tenable? Are we all good-willed with regard to the environment? Is there is no such thing as "environmental evil"?

2.3. ON THE ORIGIN OF ENVIRONMENTAL SIN
AND THE PROBLEM OF CONVERSION

Is there a sense in which we can say that there is "environmental evil"? It is undeniable that there are people who willingly and knowingly do "bad" things to the environment. They know what is right but they do not act right, they know how to live better, "green" lives, but they do not redirect their lives accordingly and they do not intend to do so. Again there is no lack of moral knowledge, but the intentions and the acts are not right and the lives are not environmentally virtuous. This is not a problem of self-control or mastery of one's desires; if it is a matter of will at all, it is matter of "bad" will or "evil" will. How can this happen? And what can be done about it?

To discuss this problem, let us turn to Augustine, one of the most influential philosophers and theologians in the history of Christianity and indeed in the history of the West. Augustine's answer—in the *Confessions* (397–398) and in other writings—is that people who do wrong things and lead bad lives do not *choose* evil, since that would suppose, as the Manichaeists did, that on the one hand there is good (God) and on the other hand there is evil, and that we have to choose between them. Augustine rejects such a dualist moral metaphysics. Rather, his view is that if people live bad lives they have *turned away* from God and from the good. Surely, he still assumes a dualistic view of the will. He writes in the *Confessions*:

> So these two wills within me, one old, one new, one the servant of the flesh, the other of the spirit, were in conflict and between them they tore my soul apart.
>
> (VIII.5/p. 164)

But Augustine does not understand this struggle as a battle between good and evil, but rather as a turning away from God and good.

> For love of your love I shall retrieve myself from the havoc of disruption which tore me to pieces when I turned away from you, whom alone I should have sought.
>
> (II.1/p. 43)

Similarly, one could say that someone who willingly and knowingly lives an environmentally vicious life has turned away from environmental good,

The Moral Psychology of Environmental "Sin" 23

rather than having chosen environmental "evil". This approach seems to avoid a dualist metaphysics.

But what can make one turn back to the good? Interestingly, Augustine thinks that even if some kind "strength" is required to return to the good path (compare: self-control), we cannot get this strength from ourselves alone, we need God. In Augustine's words:

> You listen to the groans of the prisoners and free us from the chains which we have forged for ourselves.
>
> (III.8/p. 66)

Moreover, Augustine's own conversion, which he describes in the *Confessions*, also relies on external help from God. After all his inner tensions, he takes the singing of a child to be a command from God to open up the Scriptures and read. He reads a passage from Paul (against lust) and is converted. Then he thanks God: 'You converted me to yourself' (VIII.12/p. 178).

Thus, if there is such a thing as environmental "sin", then an Augustinian solution to the problem would not rely on individual choice (alone) but would always require external help; we need a kind of "grace" that helps us convert. But it remains unclear who or what can help us in a "secular" culture. To speak in a somewhat Nietzschean and Heideggerian fashion: Which god can save us if we erased all gods from our horizon?

Yet even if today, when we might reject any "religious" view of moral psychology and might believe that there is no god who can give us "grace", it is interesting to see what happens when we frame the issue of environmental motivation as a problem of "conversion" and consider the view that a conversion to a better way of life is not merely a matter of individual will-power and strength of will, as modern thinking says, and that even if it is a matter of "strength", that such a strength does not have its source in ourselves alone. If this is true, then perhaps we—individuals but also humanity at large—cannot just change our lives and our societies in a more "green" or "environmental" direction merely by *wanting* a change and by means of more control, such as more self-control and more political control. We need to consider the role of *others* (perhaps not God but fellow human beings), of society, and of culture—and related to these: the role of *language*. Is environmental change possible if the way we speak about the environment is itself a barrier to change? But what can words do to change things? Augustine's conversion raises the question if "the word"—here very concretely the act of reading—is enough to change a life. It seems to me that when it comes to environmental matters, it is not. We read books, but reading is not enough. In any case, more needs to be said about *logos* and language in relation to morality and environment. I will return to these issues in later chapters.

In addition, it might be instructive to relate some of the (other) Christian moral-psychological metaphors to the problem of environmental motivation. Many people in the West live in what we may call a *post-Christian*

24 *Environmental Motivation and Knowledge*

culture, and this means that our moral psychology is still influenced by that culture—whether we like it or not. For instance, if we "sin" by eating (non-biological?) meat or by using a car (for a short distance), we might get feelings of "guilt". Depending on the underlying Christian tradition, this feeling of guilt might result in individual blame or self-blame, or give rise to the sentiment that it was wrong to act in this way, but that we can be forgiven. Either way, if we use this kind of language, we think in a post-Christian manner about our conduct.

Moreover, environmental "sin" might also be understood as a kind of "original sin". This narrative goes as follows. "Originally", "in the beginning", all was well with Nature. There was harmony between man and nature. But now this original harmony is broken. After the environmental Fall, we pollute and we are sinners. (And to this story an apocalyptic part can be added: We will destroy the Earth and all will be destroyed.) If this kind of thinking is at work, it implies that "environmental sin" has at least the following three features. First, environmental "sin" is a *collective* problem, not just an individual one. If there is environmental "guilt" at all, then *we* are (all) guilty. Our societies and our communities have a particular relation to nature. Second, this also means that environmental "sin" is *historical*. We inherited the world from our ancestors, and we also inherited the way(s) we treat nature. While this may not release us from moral obligations towards "nature", it also calls into question the emphasis on individual responsibility in contemporary environmental ethics: "Yes, we are responsible for present and future generations, we sin, but the *past* generations have sinned too, and it is because of *their* (original?) sin that we now sin and suffer, that we are in this predicament". Third, applying the concept of "original sin" to environmental matters also means that a *mythology* can be used to explain the "origin" of the environmental "evil". For example, we could re-interpret the biblical story of the Fall as a story about our "Environmental Fall": "We have eaten the fruit of modern knowledge, and now we are environmentally cursed. We are banished from the Garden, where we lived in harmony with Nature. But then we used science and technology to break that harmony. This was the environmental Fall. Now we are heavily punished for our Baconian sin. Alienated from the Tree of Life, we have to spend our lives in misery. We wanted to be like God, but we became the servants of the Machine." (Note that there is also a romantic interpretation at work here—see later in this book.)

Furthermore, pre-Christian myths can be used to understand the problem and give meaning to our environmental condition. We might think of ancient Greek myths such as the myth of Prometheus or the myth of Icarus, which can be used as tools in our efforts to understand our relation to nature and to technology. For example, Prometheus stole fire from the Olympic gods and was punished for his *hubris* by Zeus, and this myth can be interpreted as suggesting that our relation to technology is a kind of hubris, which will be (is being?) punished by the gods. The explanation offered in my chapters on modernity can also be interpreted as introducing a (new) myth: The environmental Fall happened when we entered modernity; today we inherit this kind of "original sin" from our ancestors.

Thus, even in a so-called "secular" culture, religious concepts, metaphors, and myths—for example Greek or Christian—can be part of our hermeneutic effort to better understand current environmentalist thinking and therefore also why we lack environmental motivation and why changing our lives is so difficult. In particular, this brief discussion suggests that such change may not only require individual, contemporary, and scientific efforts, but may also require attention to the collective, historical, and mythological dimension of our relation to the environment and to technology. Of course we can and must discuss whether these metaphors and myths are good ways to understand ourselves. Perhaps we do not *want* to be Christians, not even post-Christians or post-Augustinians (which does not mean we can easily get rid of the moral psychology of sin). But even if we reject Christian or "religious" explanations, it is worth discussing these issues: If we want fundamental change, we first need to become more aware of how our cultural history continues to shape our thinking about the environment. Once we have a better collective self-understanding, we can then try to change our thinking and begin to alter things.

Nevertheless, when it comes to individual moral psychology, we may still feel that the use of religious vocabulary is often too strong in the case of environmental wrongdoing and vice, especially since many environmentally relevant acts can hardly be described as "choosing evil": most people do not intend environmental wrongdoing or environmental vice at all. Even if we use the term "sin" in cases of environmental vice, this usually refers to a lack of self-control in the more mundane Platonic/Socratic or Frankfurtian sense described in the previous section. In these cases, the Augustinian explanation is less relevant and we might want to stick to the explanations already offered.

However, there is also another interesting route to understanding the lack of environmental motivation at the individual level. In the previous section I focused on the case of the 'unwilling addict'. But Frankfurt also mentioned another category: the wanton. If we still want to do justice to the intuition that some deeds are much worse than others and indeed constitute something that deserves the name "evil" considering its devastating consequences, but at the same time avoid a heavy, cumbersome metaphysics ("religious" or not) and pay attention to the everyday aspects of environmentally relevant moral psychology, then we could connect Frankfurt's concept of the wanton to Hannah Arendt's thinking about evil.

2.4. THE BANALITY OF ENVIRONMENTAL EVIL

Perhaps most of us are neither unwilling addicts nor purposeful and wiling evildoers when it comes to environmental ethics. Usually we are not tortured

26 Environmental Motivation and Knowledge

(or: we do not torture ourselves) by the psychological struggles that mark these moral-psychological experiences. Most of the time, at least, we are not like the drug addict or like Augustine, who know and feel that they should live a different kind of life, but fail to get clean or to convert—going through a tormenting inner struggle and maybe even seeking help. Perhaps environmental "evil" is more *banal* than that: Maybe the main problem is that we simply *don't think about it*. With regard to environmental matters we are often *mindless* consumers and workers, wantons rather than people with evil intentions. We are like young children who already know the right and the good, but forget about it when they are playing. Moreover, there is another sense in which we are like young children: We easily do what others do and what we are told to do; our social environment has a large influence on us.

Contemporary psychology has of course something to say about this, but let me first complete my tour of (ancient and modern) philosophical views.

Both explanations for evildoing—mindlessness and conformism—have been addressed by Hannah Arendt, one of the most lucid and relevant philosophers of the past century. She emphasized in her work that we should *think* and used the phrase 'the banality of evil' in response to Eichmann's process (Arendt 1963). Arendt argued that Eichmann was not a 'monster' and did not display guilt; rather, he was an ordinary person who did his duty, obeyed orders and the law. In that sense, the evil he did was 'banal'.

Arendt's claim is often associated with social-psychological experiments that show a tendency "normal" people have to obey authority and even to be cruel under certain conditions, for example the Milgram experiment (Milgram 1963) and the Stanford prison experiment (Zimbardo 1982). There are also experiments that show our tendency to conformity—for example, the experiment Solomon Ash conducted (Ash 1952, 1956). Although people from collectivist cultures show higher levels of conformity (Bond & Smith 1996), in "individualist" societies there is also a rather strong tendency to conform. Ash showed that group pressure can even affect one's visual perceptions, and that conformity is especially likely to occur in a situation when the majority that expresses an opposing opinion is large and when one is alone against a majority, without a fellow dissenter.

We might also consider Heidegger's claim in *Being and Time* (1927) that we tend to think and do what 'one' thinks. In this way, our lives are guided by 'one' (*das Man*) rather than being authentic. Various philosophers have also criticized (public) "opinion" for being opposed to reason, autonomy, and authenticity (see also Enlightenment and the romantic tradition as discussed later in this book). Thus, one may be "self-controlled" in the sense of standing by one's opinion, but this is not the kind of self-control we want, since the opinion may be false. As Aristotle writes in Book VII of the Nicomachean Ethics: 'the incontinent man has not knowledge when he is mastered by his pleasures, but opinion' (VII.1, 1145b35–36) and that 'if continence makes a man ready to stand by any and every opinion, it is bad, i.e. if it makes him stand even by a false opinion' (VII.2, 1146a16–19).

The Moral Psychology of Environmental "Sin"   27

Arendt's solution to this problem is the same as that of the Enlightenment philosophers, including Kant: *Think* for yourself! We lack courage to use our reason and our wisdom.

Thus, if lack of environmental good and environmental motivation is due to the "mindless" way we work, organize, manage, produce, and consume things, to our habit to just do what others tell us and to our tendency to conform (especially in the situation described by Ash), then the challenge is to tackle this "banal" problem. If we administrate and manage "nature" as part of our "banal" activities, then according to this view *this* is what needs to be changed: We need to *think about what we are doing.* Otherwise we keep on doing what others do and what others tell us, and this is bad for the environment and bad for us.

But how "mindless" are we really, given that many of us express a concern for the environment and are well aware that what we do in our daily lives influences the environment?

On the one hand, it is probably true that (1) many people do not think very often about the environment in the course of their daily activities and that (2) even people who are sympathetic to "environmentalist" politics and ethics are not aware of the problem all the time, are often "forgetful" in this sense.

This forgetfulness can be re-interpreted in Aristotelian terms. If we forget, we are like the beast-like, unrestrained, incontinent persons Aristotle describes in the *Nicomachean Ethics* when he talks about *akrasia* (Book VII, Chapter 1, see also my earlier quote):

> the incontinent man, knowing that what he does is bad, does it as a result of passion, while the continent man, knowing that his appetites are bad, does not follow them because of his reason.
>
> (VII.1, 1145b11–14)

We might know the good, but our passions keep us away from *activating* this knowledge: we are not 'using it' (1146b32), not 'exercising it' (1146b34). This is what Aristotle calls 'the case of the man drunk or asleep' (VII.3, 1147b6) and his account explains how it is possible to act 'incontinently' with knowledge (VII.3, 1147b19). This view implies that when we fail to do environmental good in spite of knowing it, we are asleep and incontinent. We fail to use our reason.

On the other hand, it seems to me that usually, at least, well-educated people in the West are wide awake. Maybe the problem is not so much that people do not think at all, but rather that they indulge in *the wrong kind of thinking*. Perhaps we are even *educated* into that wrong kind of thinking. Perhaps we are imprisoned in an *ideology*.

Such a view would concord with Haslam and Reicher's response to Arendt. They argue that "evil" deeds are done by "ordinary" people, as Arendt thought, but contrary to Arendt they say that these "ordinary"

28 *Environmental Motivation and Knowledge*

people did what they did because they identified with an (evil) ideology. They conclude:

> People do great wrong, not because they are unaware of what they are doing but because they consider it to be right. This is possible because they actively identify with groups whose ideology justifies and condones the oppression and destruction of others.
>
> (Haslam & Reicher 2008)

This suggests that our inquiry into the problem of environmental motivation must not remain content with the psychological explanations reviewed so far, but must turn to examine how ways of thinking—in particular, ways of thinking that are engrained in our politics, society, and culture—influence environmentally relevant ideas and practices. This examination will be my next task in this book. In Parts II and III, I will connect the problem of environmental motivation to the discussion about modernity. I will also say more about politics. (And I will also return to the ancient view of virtue when I say more about "environmental virtue ethics" in Chapter 8.)

However, let me first further review some of the lessons from contemporary psychology—including environmental psychology—about motivation and self-regulation in order to sketch a more comprehensive and more up-to-date picture of the problem at the individual, psychological level of analysis. Moreover, such studies are not only helpful to understand what goes wrong but, so it seems, may also contribute to a solution: While psychological processes such as conformity can work *against* pro-environmental behaviour, knowledge from these studies may also be used to *support* pro-environmental behaviour. For example, what we know about group pressure might be used to conclude that participation in an environmentalist group and community would help environmentally "mindless" individuals to live in a different way. But if such participation is encouraged or even arranged and controlled from above, is this a good or even an acceptable way to treat individuals? Should we manipulate people in this way? (Think also again about objections to "nudging".) In the next chapter I will need to say more about this problem.

NOTE

1. Note that I write 'democratic version' since, in contrast to what many readers of Plato such as Popper seem to assume when they focus on the anti-democratic side of the argument, the principal Socratic problem here is not *who* should rule but what kind of moral *knowledge* is needed for ruling—whoever rules. Once this moral-epistemological problem is settled, one can then combine it with a democratic or a non-democratic view. Furthermore, of course the Socratic/Platonic view does not include environmental good, only human good. A Socratic environmental ethics, therefore, would have to make an argument that connects both kinds of good—which I believe 'environmental virtue ethics' has done (see Chapter 8 in this book).

3 Lessons from Contemporary Psychology

INTRODUCTION

In the previous chapter I mainly discussed ancient Greek and Christian moral psychology, but I also made some bridges to modern thinking and contemporary psychology. For example, I related ancient Greek views to the work of Harry Frankfurt, and I mentioned psychological studies of obedience and conformity. In this chapter I will further use contemporary (empirical) psychology in order to shed light on the problem of environmental motivation and to explore what might be done to remedy it. Empirical psychology, including a subfield called 'environmental psychology' and the related field of environmental education, offers a range of explanations for the gap between environmental knowledge and environmental action (which they conceptualize as "behavior"). Let me review some of this work in order to further prepare my argument about environmental skill and engagement in the later chapters, which will focus less on the individual and more on our (modern) culture.

3.1. PSYCHOLOGY

3.1.1. Intention and Behaviour

The problem of motivation as formulated in the beginning of my book assumes that we have good intentions. But intentions are not enough. In psychological literature we can find studies of a phenomenon known as the intention-behaviour gap (Allan 2008), which confirm that intentions do not reliably predict behaviour (Sheeran 2002)—we might intend to behave environmentally friendly but in fact act differently—and try to explain this gap. Why do we often fail to stick to our good intentions? So-called Social Cognitive Theory (Armitage & Connor 2000, p. 176; Bandura 1986) says that whether or not behaviour follows intention depends on the extent to which someone believes she is able to perform the behaviour (self-efficacy) and on the belief that the behaviour will bring about a desired result (outcome expectancies). The latter factor seems very relevant in the case of

30 *Environmental Motivation and Knowledge*

pro-environmental action in relation to global environmental problems such as global warming and climate change: many people believe that whatever they do, it does not matter—it does not help anyway. The former factor is also called 'perceived behavioral control' by the theory of Planned Behavior (Azjen 1991): Whether we behave in a particular way or not depends on the extent to which a person believes she is able to perform the intended behaviour. For example, we may believe it is better not to eat meat, but at the same time we may also believe that we could never switch to a vegetarian diet.

Studies that extend the theory of Planned Behavior have added other factors, such as salient beliefs, past behaviour and habit, moral norms, self-identity, and implementation intentions, that is, concrete plans for acting upon one's good intention (Connor & Armitage 1998). For example, I might believe that I should not use a car too frequently, but if my habits include car driving and if I fail to make concrete plans to reduce my car driving, there will be no change in my behaviour. With regard to the problem of implementation, Kuhl's Theory of Action Control is also relevant: He argues that in order for action to take place, a 'motivation' system and an 'action' system need to be activated; the action system takes care of the execution of the plan (Kuhl 1987). Another theory is that the will is like a muscle, and hence can be trained. Exercising small amounts of discipline over time in a particular domain increases discipline in all areas of life (Baumeister et al. 2006; Oaten & Cheng 2006a, 2006b). This seems interesting for environmental ethics: If we want to overcome what Aristotle called our 'incontinence', then maybe it helps to exercise self-discipline in other domains not directly related to the environment, such as sport or health.

In fact, these theories have been mainly applied in other domains, such as health and sports, but there is no reason why they should not be relevant to environmental behaviour. If we summarize the results of these psychological studies, there seem to be two kinds of factors involved in the intention-behaviour gap: one kind has to do with what a person thinks, believes, etc., whereas another kind has to do with habit and exercise—which are not necessarily reflected upon, but which may be at least as important as the former in relation to the problem discussed in this book. I started from the observation that on the cognitive side of things there are no big problems: We have the knowledge, beliefs, intentions, and so on. What may be lacking with regard to environmental matters may well be the same as what has been shown to be lacking with regard to health matters: sufficient exercise and the right kinds of habits. The main problem then is not that we do not know that we live in an unhealthy or environmentally bad way; the problem is that we fail to change our habits, that we fail to make even small changes to our lives.

3.1.2. Motivation

In my formulation of the problem so far I used the term "motivation". There is, of course, a vast literature about motivation in empirical psychology. What

Lessons from Contemporary Psychology   31

is motivation and which factors shape our motivations? Motivation is something that makes us do things—things we aim at, things we plan. Many psychologists would say that what motivates us are attitudes, which in turn are made up of knowledge and beliefs. Could it be that we have the wrong attitude vis-à-vis the environment, and, if so, how can we change our attitude?

According to the Elaboration Likelihood Method (Petty & Cacioppo 1986) people's attitudes can be influenced via two routes: a central route, by which a person receives a message that is given full cognitive attention, and a peripheral route, which relies on superficial cues such as the attractiveness of the person conveying the message or a funny slogan. In the latter case, the message gets much less cognitive attention. Needless to say, the peripheral route is often used in advertising. Interestingly, if the central route is successful, the shift in opinion is more persistent. Thus, it would be great if people were convinced by environmental arguments. However, I started from the observation that often this does not work. So what *does* work? Shall we promote environmental ideas by combining them with, say, an attractive woman (to use an example from car advertising)? Maybe this is not what we want, but it is worth looking at how advertising works (or is supposed to work).

The Elaboration Likelihood Method relies on conscious processing of a persuasive message. But there are also non-conscious ways in which attitudes can change. Again, advertisers have made use of these findings. For example, researchers found that when people are exposed multiple times to the same stimulus, they will tend to like this stimulus (Zajonc 1968). This is called the 'mere exposure effect'. In environmental matters one could try to repeat the message, for instance. However, this may also work against the aim: People might get tired and bored of the repetition. Perhaps this has happened to some extent during the past two decades, in so far as the environmental movement has repeated the same message.

Another phenomenon is the 'overjustification effect': When people are awarded (e.g. paid) for a task, they assume that the task itself was not worthwhile, whereas when they do a task without reward they convince themselves that the task what worthwhile. (Enzle & Ross 1978). This suggests that it would be better for their motivation if people did pro-environmental things voluntarily, rather than receiving money for it (e.g. from the state). A related effect is 'cognitive dissonance': people like to think of themselves as persons whose behaviour is in line with their ideas, and if they think their behaviour is not in line with their ideas, they might change their ideas (Festinger & Carlsmith 1959). This suggests that doing the right thing may lead to intending the right thing. If we want to change people's environmental attitudes and motivation, it might be a good idea to try to have them *do* pro-environmental things and then hope that they will bring their attitude in line with their action (and hope that this attitude is lasting).

This is an interesting route: It starts from behaviour rather than from beliefs. In the section on environmental psychology later in this chapter, I will

32   *Environmental Motivation and Knowledge*

further discuss how experience rather than information and "intellectual" methods can change attitudes and motivate. Note that this need not happen in a "sneaky", non-conscious way; as I will show below, it may well require people's capacity to interpret what they're doing and give meaning to what they're doing. Moreover, it seems important that this happens in a way that does not infringe on, and is not seen as infringing on, people's freedom. Studies found that persuasive methods can have adverse effects, particularly when people have the feeling they are 'being told what to do' (Ringold 2002) and when the message uses language such as "You must" or "You cannot" (Quick & Stephenson 2008). (This may also be a problem with philosophical normative theories that use the language of "ought." I will return to this issue when I say more about the advantages of the virtue approach in comparison to deontological and consequentialist theories.) Another objection against telling people what to do is provided by Kaplan (2000): People are not only likely to resist what they are told what to do; telling people what to do also 'ignores the possibility that there may be significant local variants in how best to achieve a particular goal' (p. 505). Kaplan recommends that we instead reject the assumption that man is a 'passive organism' and embrace a view of the human as an animal that attempts 'to comprehend, to make sense of its world' and that is 'addicted to exploring, to discovering, to finding out' (p. 505). (This image fits well the pragmatist view of the human, which has also inspired my own thinking here and elsewhere.)

Psychologists also distinguish between different kinds of motivation. A well-known distinction is the one between intrinsic and extrinsic motivation. Intrinsic motivation means that the activity is pursued for its own sake, whereas extrinsic motivation means that the motivation lies in an external reward or punishment. Environmental ethicists would like people to be intrinsically motivated, of course. It would be better if people were intrinsically motivated to act in a pro-environmental way, with no need for external pressure. Extrinsic motivation is seen as belonging to a lower stage of moral development (see the work of Kohlberg and Piaget—but I will not say more about this here). It is the way we treat children: We give them rewards or punishments. Unfortunately, it is also the way nation states tend to treat their citizens: by means of (external) regulation. We can make environmental laws, for example, but this means again that people are told what to do. These measures seem to assume that intrinsic motivation is either not there or not strong enough in most people. This is a very pessimistic view of the human, which I hope is false. It seems to me that we have the capacity to be intrinsically motivated, including when it comes to environmental matters. The question is then: How can we strengthen this intrinsic motivation? (The answer I will provide in this book is that we can strengthen it by means of skillful engagement with one's environment.)

Of course it may well turn out that not every pro-environmental action is pleasant, and if this is the case then extrinsic motivation is not necessarily bad: A person may do things she does not like to do, but do it because she has an environmental goal she wants to reach (identified regulation) or because the behaviour is congruent with her self-image (integrated regulation). For example, if we want to become an environmentally better person, this may motivate us—albeit externally—to engage in pro-environmental action. But how external is this relation between personality and action? (Later I will say more about how I understand (environmental) virtue ethics.) And why would pro-environmental behaviour *not* be intrinsically motivating? Maybe the problem is, again, that people who are not motivated lack sufficient experience with it and hence have not felt the intrinsic motivation and the joy that is related to it. I will return to the issue of direct experience in the section on environmental psychology (and to the issue of pleasure in Chapter 8).

There are also other factors that can motivate. Fear, for instance can motivate people into action (Ruiter et al. 2001). We are all familiar with doom scenarios for our planet, which at first sight do seem to have some motivational force. However, I see at least two problems with this route. First, motivation by fear is a form of extrinsic motivation, which is less desirable as a method to address adult citizens (if it is desirable at all to apply the method to children—nowadays educators prefer rewards). Second, even if people are scared, they may not act if they have the feeling that they are not able to change the problem. This is again the self-efficacy problem (see again the theory of Planned Behavior) and in motivation studies it is captured by the term 'a-motivation': If people believe that their action does not produce the desired outcome, that it does not matter, they will not be motivated to act. Thus, a doom scenario does not help if no concrete solutions are offered (and this is often the case). In sum, using fear is not only morally problematic but is also not necessarily very effective.

What *does* seem to help, however, is watching the (pro-environmental) behaviour of others. We do not only tend to conform with group behaviour (see my previous remarks about this), we also *learn* by imitation. According to Bandura's Social Learning theory, learning happens in a social context. We learn a behaviour by watching others perform it. Bandura and McClelland call this 'modeling' (Bandura & McClelland 1977). For example, a study has shown that children behave in a more aggressive way if they have watched an adult kicking and punching a doll (Bandura et al. 1961). Watching the behaviour of others offers people a kind of direct experience with the behaviour. The presence of others "doing the right thing" may be a vital factor in changing environmental behaviour. (I will return to this issue in the section on environmental psychology.)

There are other factors relevant to the problem we are discussing. For example, one can have conflicting attitudes. Environmental psychologists Kollmuss & Agyeman (2002) give a personal example: They want to see their families in Europe, but at the same time they have a strong attitude against flying because it is a cause of global warming. Another factor is the "cost" of a behaviour: Diekmann and Preisendörfer (2003) found that if

34 *Environmental Motivation and Knowledge*

the cost of environmental behaviour gets too high, the connection between attitude and behaviour becomes weaker. Costs are also related to the social and economic circumstances of people. I will say more about environmental psychology below, but let me summarize that it seems that people "balance" environmental values with other values. But is this kind of "moral accounting" an appropriate method for environmental ethics? (In the next chapters I will say more about the "management" approach to environmental (and other) issues as embedded in modern thinking and modern culture.)

More generally, there are many contextual factors involved (Stern 2000) in environmental motivation. For example, social norms are important, since (as already mentioned) people copy the behaviour of others. This means that the social norms embodied in the popular media (e.g. soap operas, entertainment shows) or in one's social network can motivate. If we want to change environmental behaviour, it seems, we have to change society.

3.1.3. Self-Regulation Skills

One of the problems already discussed in the previous chapter is self-control and related terms such as "continence." In contemporary psychology the term 'self-regulation' is used: a 'process by which people seek to exert control over their thoughts, their feelings, their impulses and appetites and their task performances' (Baumeister et al. 2006). It is clear that self-regulation, by itself, is something that improves our lives. A famous empirical study is the so-called 'marshmallow' experiment (Mischel et al. 1989) about delay of gratification. Children were given the choice between getting one marshmallow now, or waiting for some time to receive two marshmallows. Children who managed to wait for the bigger reward turned out to be more successful later in life. Self-discipline also helps in academia, athletics (Jonker et al. 2009), and in other fields of life. *If* self-control is good for environmental living (an assumption which can be criticized: I already began to question it in the previous chapter and will continue to do this in the later chapters), we want to know how to strengthen this capacity.

In the psychological literature we find some advice on how to make self-regulation successful. This concerns not abstract principles but very concrete and specific tricks and skills. In the marshmallow study, for example, some children covered their eyes in order not to be exposed to the image of the tasty marshmallow. Others sang songs to distract themselves. In health psychology we find several successful self-management strategies (Kitsantas 2000): goal-setting (e.g. losing 10 pounds), self-monitoring (keeping track of one's performance), social assistance seeking (seeking help from others, e.g. a support group), information seeking (e.g. a book on how to diet successfully), environmental structuring (keep temptation to a minimum, ban the bad food—see also the marshmallow study), and time management (planning time for exercise). Could one also identify very concrete skills and strategies for environmental behaviour? The answer is positive, I think, and it seems that some of those skills and strategies would at least be similar to those of health psychology. For example, if I want to train myself to bike to work rather than take the car, then it helps if I set a clear goal (for example 4 days a week I take the bike), if I keep an eye on what I in fact do (or fail to do), if I tell others so they can remind me if I forget, if I read about how others deal with their oil addiction, if I do not make my car easily available, and if I plan time for biking to work (otherwise I might use the excuse that I don't have time to bike).

An important difference with health problems, however, is that I may not immediately and directly experience the benefits to the environment (only the benefits to myself—in case of biking). The "reward" of the behaviour is at least distributed between me and the environment. This need not be a problem for motivation. For instance, if an environmentally friendly activity is pleasant, there is no problem for motivation since the pleasure is motivating. It is only a problem when the activity is not pleasant (e.g. biking in the rain) because then there is no immediate reward. But why should the joys of life be like eating a marshmallow? I may still have delayed gratification and joy—for example, because I feel good after biking and feel healthy in the longer term.

Sometimes the advice from psychologists is *very* concrete and surprising. For example, experiments in cognitive science have shown that strengthening the muscles increases our will-power (Hung & Labroo 2011). This does not only add support to the thesis that the mind is embodied, it also shows again that will-power is *very much* like a muscle (Baumeister et al. 2006) and that so-called "mental" or "psychological" strategies are more *bodily* than we think. For the problem of environmental motivation, this means that it might also be helpful to engage in activities we do not usually associate with "doing something for nature" and that it is worth finding out more about the kind of "training" and "skills" we need, with "training" and "skills" understood as having a significant bodily aspect. Perhaps becoming more environmental is not only a change in the mind but also a change in the body. Doing physical exercise (which of course is also an exercise of the mind) could well be part of the solution.

Most of the studies summarized here are from general psychology or other fields of psychology. Since the 1970s there has been a subfield of psychology that is explicitly focused on problems related to the environment: environmental psychology. Let me now pay specific attention to their insights.

3.2. ENVIRONMENTAL PSYCHOLOGY: DIRECT EXPERIENCE AND MEANING

Environmental psychology offers a number of frameworks that explicitly try to explain the gap between the possession of environmental knowledge

36 *Environmental Motivation and Knowledge*

and pro-environmental behaviour. In their overview of the literature, Kollmuss & Agyeman (2002) describe how rationalist models from the early 1970s, which 'assumed that educating people about environmental issues would automatically result in more pro-environmental behavior', were proven to be wrong: In most cases knowledge and awareness did not lead to pro-environmental behaviour (Kollmuss & Agyeman 2002, p. 241). Changing behaviour and habits is very difficult. The authors sum up many explanations for the gap between knowledge and behaviour, most of which we already met in the section on general psychology: for example, the person's feeling that he or she cannot bring about change through his or her own behaviour (consider for example the feeling that I, as an individual, cannot do anything to remedy climate change—see also again what social cognitive theory says about outcome expectancies), so-called 'situational factors' (e.g. social pressure) and cultural norms, lack of pro-social and altruistic behaviour, a person's values and attitudes, economic factors, and resistance against non-conforming information (see Festinger's famous theory of cognitive dissonance—for example, Festinger & Carlsmith 1959). One explanation mentioned by Kollmuss and Agyeman, which has not yet been discussed but is especially relevant for the argument I will make in the later chapters, relies on a distinction between direct versus indirect experience:

> Direct experiences have a stronger influence on people's behavior than indirect experiences. In other words, indirect experiences, such as learning about an environmental problem in school as opposed to directly experiencing it (e.g. seeing the dead fish in the river) will lead to a weaker correlation between attitude and behavior.
>
> (Kollmusss & Agyeman 2002, p. 242)

Perhaps one of the main problems with environmental motivation is that our environmental knowledge is mainly indirect. Another way of saying this is to point to the "non-immediacy" of many ecological problems. Most environmental degradation is not immediately experienced by most people—for example, the accumulation of greenhouse gases or the loss of species. There is also often a time lag between our behaviour and its effects, and we are not very good in perceiving incremental changes. And even if the damage is translated into perceivable information, this does not guarantee our emotional involvement (Kollmuss & Agyeman 2002, p. 253; Preuss 1991).

From Kollmuss and Agyeman's overview we can gather that many studies in environmental psychology support the idea that environmental knowledge and awareness is not enough to make us behave in environmentally friendly ways, and one type of explanation has to do with *the kind of knowledge* we usually have of the environment: we usually lack direct, immediate experience of the environment and its degradation (or, for that matter, its improvement). This includes a lack of emotional involvement, which renders it less likely that a person will engage in pro-environmental behaviour, although even *with* emotions there is no guarantee that we will

Lessons from Contemporary Psychology 37

actually do something. After experiencing negative feelings, a person may refuse to accept reality or emotionally distance herself when frequently exposed to bad news (e.g. a scientist or a philosopher). And if a person has the feeling that he or she cannot do anything to change the situation (see one of the factors mentioned above), the result may be apathy and resignation (Kollmuss & Agyemann 2002, p. 255).

Note that this also explains why the feeling of environmental "guilt" (discussed in the previous chapter) is not sufficient to move people into action. We may feel guilty about doing bad things to the environment, but if our response to this negative emotion is that we then distance ourselves or if we feel we cannot change much, the moral force of our emotion is weakened and we continue to "sin".

Work in environmental education seems to confirm the important role of direct, vivid and emotional experience. For example, a study that interviewed environmentalists about significant life experiences found that environmentalists often report that being in nature as a child was a formative experience and convinced them to care about the environment (Chawla 1999). The study concludes that 'important as school-based instruction may be—environmental educators need to seek ways to foster the type of out-of-school experiences that figure so saliently in environmentally committed people's memories. The author therefore recommends '(a) preservation or creation of neighbourhood natural areas to ensure that informal experiences of nature are an accessible part of children's everyday lives, (b) outreach to parents to encourage them to serve as role models of care for nature, and (c) support for a variety of community organizations where children can find adult and peer role models as well as opportunities for collective action' (Chawla 1999, p. 25). Hungerford and Volk (1990) also found that from the numerous individuals with great environmental sensitivity towards environmental issues they studied 'only a few reported the importance of educational courses or books' (p. 264).

Responding to and in explicit accordance with Kollmus & Agyeman, another study found that 'emotional involvement and experience are central to sustained pro-environmental values and behaviour' and claims that 'it is essential that pro-environmental behavior change initiatives work with experience and not simply continue to assume that information alone stimulates such change' (Maiteny 2002, p. 305). Maiteny argues that direct experiences shape a 'deep' kind of involvement with nature, giving people a powerful drive to act. However, the author also stresses that it is not only experience as such that does the work here; the way people give meaning to their experiences and their lives is also important. He argues that when we want to change bad environmental habits, such direct and meaningful experience works better than intellectual information, external regulations, incentives, and/or anxiety:

> intellectual information about environmental problems is inadequate on its own to stimulate behaviour change. (. . .) Experience is more likely

38 *Environmental Motivation and Knowledge*

to motivate imperatives to break environmentally damaging behaviours (or 'bad habits') in everyday life that arise from *within* persons. Intellectual activity alone is less likely to trigger this.

(Maiteny 2002, p. 304)

Thus, again direct experience is held to be crucial for pro-environmental behaviour change, not only by psychologists who study people, as it were, from a distance (e.g. in lab experiments), but also by scholars who take seriously people's own self-understanding as meaning-giving beings and who engage in descriptive phenomenological research in order to attend to people's consciousness (in this case, people were asked to tell the story of the sources of their commitment and about attempts to change lifestyle). This suggests that *interpretation*, and therefore *culture*, plays an important role in environmental change. In the next chapters we will need to delve deeper into this.

Note that not all environmental psychologists emphasize direct experience. For example, the Value-Belief-Norm theory of Stern (2000) starts from values, defined as predispositions that make certain *beliefs* more likely—beliefs which are held to influence norms and behaviour. Beliefs here include worldviews about the role of humans on the planet, the threat of environmental conditions, and whether actions might alleviate environmental threats. But for those of us who try to understand how one can *have* the right kind of beliefs and yet fail to act, the evidence for the importance of direct experience is an interesting avenue worth exploring further.

Note also that the emotional experience of people is often connected to particular places. Vaske & Kobrin (2001) found that an emotional connection with a particular natural place correlates with environmentally responsible behaviour. If people use a natural place for outdoor activities such as hiking, they develop an emotional connection with that place. This inspires concern for the environment and promotes environmentally responsible behaviour. More generally, environmental education studies show that if one wants someone to develop an affective relationship to the natural environment, outdoor activities are essential. For example, a study found that pupils who were personally experienced in outdoor activities had a stronger empathic relationship to nature than those who were not (Palmberg & Kuru 2000).

Based on this overview of the literature, we can conclude that according to contemporary environmental psychology the problem is complex and involves many factors, and that one of the most important factors concerns the directness or immediacy of environmental experience—an experience which may be connected with particular emotions, is always interpreted, and is linked to places (in particular in the outdoor environment). It seems, therefore, that in order to close the gap between knowledge and action, we would need more direct experience of the environment, including emotional, interpretative, and meaning-giving involvement, and—taking into account another lesson mentioned before—the feeling and experience that we can change something. Abstract knowledge of the environment is not enough; we need personal experience and engagement.

What we also need, it seems, are others. For example, 'role models' are mentioned in the literature. Consider also again the 'modeling' theory mentioned in the previous sections, which is also about exemplars. In the next chapters I will return to the importance of direct experience and exemplars. (For instance, exemplars will turn out to be important within a virtue ethics understanding of the problem.) Perhaps attending to the role of direct experience and example can help us to tackle what Kollmuss & Agyeman see as the strongest barrier to pro-environmental behaviour: old behaviour patterns—in other words, *habits*. The authors write:

> Anyone who has ever tried to change a habit, even in a very minor way, will have discovered how difficult it is, even if the new behavior has distinct advantages over the old one.
>
> (Kollmuss & Agyeman 2002, p. 241)

This is not only true for doing something about smoking and other unhealthy behaviour; it is also true for changing environmental behaviour. However, such "individual" problems are not merely individual; they are related to problems of our culture and our society. This is also true for environmental behaviour, beliefs, and attitudes. In the next chapters I will say more about this societal-cultural aspect when I relate the problem of the gap between environmental knowledge and environmental action to some problems associated with modernity. Furthermore, so far I have not said much about *character*. For environmental virtue ethics, which will be part of the account of "environmental skill" I will develop, this is crucial.

Part II

The Janus Face of Modern Environmentalism

Enlightenment and Romanticism

4 Enlightenment Reason and Liberation Politics

INTRODUCTION

The environmental movement is inspired by at least two related cultural-philosophical and cultural-historical movements: the Enlightenment and Romanticism. Both are *modern* ways of thinking and doing, which shape our practices and our existence, including how we relate—in perception and action—to our environment. In order to understand our lack of motivation to act and live in a more "green" way, we first have to understand the glasses through which we look at the world—indeed, the way we construct that world. For instance, what is the "nature" we wish to protect? What is our relation to "nature"? And is perhaps the way we look at "nature" part of the problem of environmental motivation?

In this part of the book, I connect what may seem an "inner" and individual psychological problem (Chapters 2 and 3) to a deeper cultural and existential issue that concerns our relation to the world: the problem of modernity. It is now time to further analyze the grounds that makes possible the kind of environmental thinking that is so common and that seems so attractive to the good-willing green mind, but risks remaining morally-motivationally impotent. In this chapter I will say more about the modern way of relating to the environment and highlight how it was approached in Enlightenment thinking. Drawing on a well-established tradition of criticism of modernity I will articulate what is problematic about this approach. I will also show that modernity and the Enlightenment still shape the framework for the discourse about environmental politics, in particular the discussion between environmental conservatives and environmental liberationists. Then, in the next chapter I will say more about the romantic face of modernity and its implications for how we think about the environment.

4.1. THE STUDY, MANAGEMENT, AND MANIPULATION OF NATURE

Contemporary environmentalism is heir to the Enlightenment face of modernity for at least two reasons: It is based on science and it promotes the manipulation of nature. Let me explain this.

44 *The Janus Face of Modern Environmentalism*

Faced with charges of being "soft" or "utopian", contemporary environmentalism often presents itself in the form of reasonable arguments based on "facts"—that is, on "hard" scientific knowledge. As Dobson says in his book on green political thought:

> modern green politics turns out to be based on a self-consciously hard-headed assessment of the unsustainability of present political and economic practices—it is remarkable, indeed, to see the extent to which the success of modern political ecology has been mediated and sustained by scientific research.
>
> (Dobson 2000, p. 11)

In addition, as we have seen in the previous chapter, contemporary environmentalists may dream of a better world indeed, but their vision of the environmental future is informed by rational argument and philosophical principles, such as concepts of liberty and equality. Consider again Singer-style arguments for animal rights: They appeal to reason and principles (e.g. equality) and are meant to persuade people via the use of argument. And as Dobson also notes, green recognition of the (intrinsic) value of the natural world is not only based on intuition, but is also influenced by 'rationalist attempts to account for such value' (Dobson 2000, p. 11).

The high reliance on a scientific basis by contemporary environmentalism can be illustrated by observing the discourse on sustainability and climate change. Normative (political and ethical) claims that we should take political and personal action in response to the problem of climate change are based on several premises, the truth value of which is highly dependent on scientific research: (1) we can meaningfully talk about a "global" climate and about "climate change", (2) climate change is significant, (3) significant climate change has undesirable consequences for humans and for non-humans and the environment, (4) current climate change is partly and significantly due to human activities, and (5) we can (still) do something to counter the effects of climate change and influence climate change. To the extent that they wish to present themselves as reasonable and (scientifically) credible, so-called climate skeptics will have to doubt the scientific basis of these claims; in other words, they will have to directly engage with the results of scientific research, or even conduct such research themselves. Greens present themselves as people who take seriously scientific knowledge.

Similarly, arguments for a more sustainable economy and a more sustainable way of living are based on scientific assessments of biological systems and (their relation to) economic systems, demography, etc. Sustainability is scientifically *measured*. We produce reports, indicators, benchmarks, audits, standards, indexes, and certification systems. Ecosystems are studied in terms of 'ecosystem services' (see also later in this chapter) and they are managed on a scientific basis: Environmental management is based on environmental science and (conservation) biology. Economic analysis studies nature and its "services" as an economic "externality". New technologies

Enlightenment Reason and Liberation Politics   45

are being developed that are more sustainable since they consume less resources. Efficiency of energy use is improved, waste is reduced—all by means of scientific research and technological development.

Another example of the link between environmentalism and science is the discussion about moral status. Although the mainstream arguments for moral status differ significantly about the precise justification of moral status (e.g. deontological versus utilitarian arguments), they all share the assumption that the moral status of an entity depends on its (ontological) properties such as consciousness and the ability to suffer (see, again, Singer). But how do we know if an entity has consciousness, and if so, what kind of consciousness? How do we know about *any* property of entities? Again environmentalists and animal liberation activists must rely on science for their arguments: In modern society, they better make sure that their claims about the ability of a particular animal to suffer are based on hard science, rather than appearance. (See also the Socratic argument about truth.)

Moreover, as these examples show, environmental action is usually not passive at all, but involves active intervention and manipulation of nature. Nature is also manipulated when animals are fed, moved, or even captured to avoid massive starvation or extinction, or when land is managed as a "nature reserve" or when it is "rewilded". Environmentalists inherit from modernity the wish to control, to be master of our environment.

In this sense, the roots of modern environmentalism are the same as the roots of the scientific and technological interventions in "nature" criticized by environmentalists: early modern science and its desire for mastery—perhaps even its scientific-utopian pretentions. This seems plausible since the roots of what Pepper calls 'technological' environmentalism are to be found in early modern thinking and in the scientific revolution (Pepper 1986), which has a strong utopian orientation. Perhaps we could say that, to the extent that greens shape their concerns in scientific terms, they share with the modern Baconian scientist the desire for a kind of 'New Atlantis'—albeit an "eco" version of it. The environment—"nature"—is conceived of as something external to us that we have to study, protect, and transform.

Indeed, environmentalists design policies and landscapes. Nature reserves have to be managed. Nature is not really "left alone" but is also shaped according to what we think nature should be, and this is based on science or on romantic intuition (see the next section and chapter). Nature is both metaphorically and literally *constructed*. "Wild" nature is created. We intervene in animal lives. We make "natural" products (again see the next section and chapter for understanding this paradox). We police nature, animals, and people to attain our environmental goals.

Consider visions of 'rewilding' North America. Several authors argue that, given the scientific knowledge we now have of ecosystems, more needs to be done than just protecting a few areas (e.g. in the form of national parks or wilderness reserves). Conservationist Dave Foreman proposes that we 'work on very large landscapes, probably continental in scope' and create a wildlands 'network' that is 'based on the scientific approach of rewilding'

46 *The Janus Face of Modern Environmentalism*

(Foreman 2004, p. 4). And in his commentary in *Nature*, Donlan has proposed a plan to 'restore animals that disappeared 13,000 years ago from Pleistocene North America', a vision he thinks is 'justified on ecological, evolutionary, economic, aesthetic and ethical grounds' (Donlan 2005). In other words, ethical and aesthetical arguments are not enough: They need to be supported by the sciences if they are to appeal to the science-oriented modern mind.

4.2. PROBLEMATIC OBJECTIVIST MODERNITY

To show how *modern* this approach is, and to show what may be problematic about the *Enlightenment* side of modern environmentalism, let us consider how this interventionist and science-oriented environmentalism and conservationism raises a number of philosophical problems related to the issue of scientific modernity and Enlightenment rationalism.

First, knowing the "facts" is not enough. What Pepper had already observed in the 1980s, when the environmental movement was growing, is still true today:

> a study of the facts alone seems to lead nowhere. Scores of books have been written about these facts—of chronic imbalances in population/resource ratios, of ecologically damaging technology, of wasteful consumption patterns (. . .). Yet one can legitimately argue that little change of a truly *fundamental* nature has been achieved by the environmental movement (. . .) The spread of detailed knowledge about how man degrades and threatens his own planet has not of itself produced the likelihood of serious or permanent remedial action.
>
> (Pepper 1986, p. 3; Pepper's emphasis)

Heavy reliance on scientific research and rationalist argument might be *convincing* and we might change our *beliefs* about nature and about what we ought to do, but it is doubtful that "reason" and "factual" knowledge provide sufficient conditions for *doing* the environmentally right things and for *living* environmentally good lives. It seems that these beliefs and that knowledge do not and did not make us into environmentally *virtuous* persons. In other words, we encounter again the problem of moral motivation set up in the first chapter. It seems that great work has been done in the area of *justification* (for example, by Singer in the area of animal ethics, or work on 'deep ecology') but at the end of the day, the problem of *motivation* has not yet been solved. This puts the future of the environmentalist project in jeopardy, however *justified* that project might be.

Furthermore, when it comes to Enlightenment modernity, it seems that in so far as environmentalism puts on a rationalist and scientific Enlightenment face, the *Humean*, "moral sentiment" side of the Enlightenment (see

Enlightenment Reason and Liberation Politics 47

also Smith) is neglected. Hume famously argued that reason *alone* cannot move us to action; rather, moral evaluation depends on sentiments (moral approval and disapproval) and is aided by the faculty of sympathy (today we would say: empathy), which makes us aware of the sentiments of others (Hume 1739/40). A Humean environmental ethics, therefore, would shift the emphasis from (theoretical) knowledge and rational argument—which are necessary but not *sufficient* for environmental right and good—to what we may call "environmental sentiments". This can be interpreted in different ways, but all interpretations will rely on feeling as a motivator. For example, it might be understood as saying that we need a kind of environmental empathy: an expansion of our moral imagination and our moral emotions to non-humans and to "nature". Then we should not so much use our *reason* to expand the circle of moral concern, as Enlightenment rationalism and, in ancient times, the Stoics recommend, but rather stretch our imaginative and emotional capacities.

Although this recommendation needs not to be interpreted in a communitarian way, it might be taken to mean that we should imaginatively and emotionally participate in a global community of humans and non-humans. For instance, Callicott, who has recognized the importance of the psychological dimension of environmental ethics, has used Hume and Smith to argue that an environmental ethic is only possible if we are motivated by affection for what Leopold called the 'biotic community' (Callicott 1989). His point is not anti-science; on the contrary, according to Callicott it is the "is" of scientific findings, in combination with social feelings, that get us to the "ought" of preserving the biotic community:

> Leopold urges us to the conclusion, (3) we ought to "preserve the integrity, stability, and beauty of the biotic community." Why ought we? Because (1) we all generally have a positive attitude toward the community or society to which we belong; and (2) science has now discovered that the natural environment is a community or society to which we belong, no less than the human global village.
>
> (Callicott 1989, p. 127)

But do we have such feelings? Do we necessarily have a positive attitude (1) to the human community and, if so, (2) do we necessarily extend this feeling of "belonging" to the "biotic community"? Callicott seems to assume so, but what he says in the name of "we" only seems to refer to environmentalists—and only those who have those specific kind of community feelings:

> The intrinsic value we attribute to individual human beings and to humanity expresses only our feelings for co-members of our global village and for our human community.
>
> (Callicott 1989, p. 153)

48   *The Janus Face of Modern Environmentalism*

But even if we had those feelings, what is the precise relation between feelings and reason then? Are emotions enough for moral motivation and action? And *should* we rely on environmentalist sentiments only?

These are interesting questions within the lines of 18th- and 19th-century thinking, and, for instance, Hume himself seems to have a more nuanced view than is usually ascribed to him, giving also a role to reason (see, for instance, Russell 2013). However, I believe we need to take further steps. Although I share Callicott's attention to the question of moral motivation and although I am sympathetic to the Humean-Smithean philosophical tradition, in the next section and in the next chapters I will attempt to move beyond the rationalism-feeling discussion with regard to the problem of moral-environmental motivation. In the next chapter I will question what I take to be the romantic face of modern environmentalism, which over-emphasizes feeling, and later, in Chapter 7, I will use the notion of skilled engagement to suggest a different, non-dualistic and non-romantic kind of moral psychology that seems more useful to environmental ethics.

Indeed, criticizing scientific modernity and rationalist Enlightenment does not necessarily require taking a sentimentalist position, let alone a romantic one (see the next section). Let me therefore first consider "cool" criticisms of modern thinking, which criticize modernity without relying on sentiment. Therefore, before discussing romantic environmental feelings and before moving on to what may be regarded as more "exotic" criticisms of modernity (e.g. Heidegger later in this section or mysticism in Chapter 6), let me start with "non-sentimental" thinking about modern science.

As I already mentioned, rationalist Enlightenment thinking—and environmental ethics that stands in this tradition—tends to focus on justification rather than motivation. This problem can be further analyzed by using a well-known distinction made in modern philosophy of science: the distinction between the context of discovery and the context of justification, used for example by Popper (1934). According to this kind of thinking, there is on the one hand the actual process of discovery, in which scientists may use their intuition, imagination, emotions, or whatever helps them to make progress with their research (this may even include pure luck), and on the other hand rational, logical justification, which (re-)describes the process in terms of theory, hypothesis, empirical testing, falsification, etc. This distinction has a normative cousin: According to modern moral philosophy, the process of moral *motivation*, in which feelings, imagination, etc. may play a role (or are even necessary), *should* be clearly distinguished from, and kept separate from, the task of moral *justification*, which is a non-emotional, objective, rational matter.

If we apply this distinction to the problem of environmental motivation, the modern approach implies that it may well be true that people need feelings, empathy, intuition, and so on in order to be motivated to act (for example, feeling empathy for animals that are badly treated or having the intuition that we are all part of the same "Mother Nature"), but the modern rationalist Enlightenment philosopher will insist that this has nothing to do, and *should* have nothing to do, with the question whether or not our acts, including speech acts—for example, the ascription of moral status—are *justified*, which is an objective and rational matter, relying on objective moral principles and valid arguments. Such philosophers would think that environmental ethics, as a philosophical and normative ethics, should be concerned only with justification, not with the "empirical" question of what actually motivates people to act more environmentally friendly.

However, these distinctions are very problematic, to say the least. As is well known, the distinction between context of discovery and context of justification has been criticized by subsequent developments in the philosophy of science (see for example Kuhn and Feyerabend) and, later, by 'science studies' and 'science and technology studies' (STS). While in principle such studies could understand themselves as limiting their inquiry to the 'context of discovery' (thus remaining within the modern dualistic framework), it has turned out that many scholars in this area have taken a constructivist, sometimes non-modernist stance. Their point is not merely that we should pay more attention to the 'context of discovery', but that *the very distinction* is flawed. They question the positivist "objectivity" claim: They argue that there are no pure facts divorced from values; there is no "justification" separate from the process of 'discovery'. For example, Bruno Latour has argued not only that we should study science in action, which involves a network of actors and 'actants' (all kinds of artefacts), but also that we should question the way modern science understands itself. In *We Have Never Been Modern* (1993) he shows how various dualisms were literally produced—created—by the (early) modern scientists using material artefacts and created by philosophers using modern concepts, but that such processes of 'purification' have never been entirely successful, and that in this sense we have never been modern. In other words, discovery and justification were never separate, there never was such a thing as objective science.

These constructivist criticisms apply to environmental ethics in at least two ways. First, they suggest that we question the distinction between the problem of motivation and the problem of justification, and hence question modern environmental *ethics* in so far as it presupposes this distinction. For this book, it means that we have to clarify and re-frame the main problem. This book is not about moral-environmental motivation *as opposed to* or *as distinguished from* moral-environmental justification; instead, the problem of what we ought to do and of what the "good life" is, environmentally speaking, is seen as intrinsically bound up with the question regarding motivation. This means that, as we will see in Chapters 7 and 8, the solution I offer to the problem of motivation ("environmental skill") must not be understood as being a "merely empirical matter", a "psychological" matter, or a "merely descriptive matter", but has a strong normative dimension and is not only "psychologically" or "mentally" relevant but has direct practical, bodily, and material implications: It questions such modern distinctions

50   *The Janus Face of Modern Environmentalism*

(e.g. inner/outer[1], mind/matter, soul/body etc.) and implies a view of how we should best act and live, of what good "green" living is (I will argue that better "environmental" living is a more engaged, involved way of living).

Second, in so far as environmentalists claim to base their claims on "objective" science, their claim is vulnerable to the constructivist objection: the way scientifically oriented environmentalists frame their cause and their opponents ("irrational") rests on a positivist, objectivist outlook, which is a very modern way of seeing things, but also a deeply problematic one. If environmentalists rely on science, they *also* construct (for example, they construct *their* "nature")—indeed, all participants in the environmental debate construct, there are no objective facts, no neutral evidence. They do not hold the "objective" truth (based on science) as opposed to their opponents, who are "subjective", "irrational", "religious", etc. All participants construct their views in particular ways, and although some ways are *better* than others (constructivism does not imply that 'anything goes'), they cannot be *a priori* framed as better by referring to them as "objectively true", and they have to be defended on other grounds.

This way of understanding science also explains why "science" can be both supportive of environmentalist concerns and detrimental to the environment at the same time. Science can save "nature" and destroy "nature", and it can also give us opposing messages with regard to environmental good. This thesis of the non-neutrality of science answers a question that may be asked by those who wish to rely on "facts": 'How can this "science" which we have grown to respect for its precision, its unambiguity and its neutrality give us these two quite opposing messages at the same time?' (Pepper 1986, p. 10). The answer is that science is not neutral at all—that, in a sense, there are many "sciences."

This implies that when we look for example at the debate about climate change, there can be *different*, opposing views of the issue, which are both the result of science. Typical for this kind of debate is that facts and values are mixed, and this is not "bad" but unavoidable—it is present in *all* ethical and all ethical-environmental issues, which are neither merely ethical nor merely scientific but should be called ethical/scientific issues—if we must continue to use these terms at all. Scientists cannot be "objective"; to present what they do as such presupposes the separation of humans (scientists) from their environment ("nature"). But, as Latour suggests (1993), to believe and defend this separation requires active *purification*: "facts" are separated from "values", "nature" is separated from humans—that is, from the environment in which we are already involved. Similarly, environmentalists, in so far as they are modern, often assume that there is a kind of "pure" nature. (This is true for the rationalist Enlightenment branch but also for the romantic branch—see the next chapter.) But with Latour we should question this kind of construction of the environment. In *The Politics of Nature* (2004), he argues—in line with *We Have Never Been Modern*—that in modernity nature and science (facts) are separated from

Enlightenment Reason and Liberation Politics 51

human culture and society (values), but that this ignores how "nature" is socially constructed. He argues that spokespersons should speak for otherwise unrepresented, mute non-humans (by which he means things and I would add: animals and living nature).

Thus, our modern "nature" talk is the result of a process of purification, by which we detached ourselves from our environment: we separated the human world from the non-human world. In *We Have Never Been Modern* Latour shows how this process of purification already started with early modern thinking and science. Similarly, Pepper shows how Galileo, Descartes, Bacon, and others constructed science as "objective" (and I would add: "nature" as external), thus distinguishing it from what he calls 'natural magic':

> The basic tenets of natural magic were (. . .) that the universe is an organism, fully alive and active. It was permeated with influences, forces, and correspondences that linked everything in nature, man included, to everything else, forming a multi-dimensional network that was not only material but also mystical and spiritual. (. . .) Consequently natural magic was opposed to any suggestion that a distinction had to be drawn between man and nature, as subject and object, as a precondition for understanding nature; the contrary was the case. The natural magician had to recognize that he was in inextricably part of the nature he was studying.
>
> (Pepper 1986, p. 53)

Thus, when environmentalists talk about "nature", they presuppose a conception of the environment that was fabricated by the same science they often blame for environmental evils (see also the next chapter on Romanticism). Descartes and other moderns separated the human subject from the world, from the sensual.

This illusion that we are detached from our environment, uninvolved in the world, has already been criticized before: There was already criticism of modernity before Latour, both "within" modern thinking (critical theory inspired by Marx, but also Romanticism) and on the fringes, if not also outside modern thinking (Heidegger). Environmentalists have an ambiguous relation to these criticisms and indeed to modernity, or at least particular kinds of modernity. Let me explain this.

Within modern thinking there has been a romantic reaction to rationalist Enlightenment thinking (see the next chapter), but Critical Theory, inspired by Marx, has also criticized the rationalist face of the Enlightenment. Philosophers such as Adorno, Horkheimer, Marcuse, Habermas and (today) thinkers such as Feenberg are not against rationality, but have criticized what they call *instrumental* rationality. As Horkheimer and Adorno argued in *Dialectic of Enlightenment* (1947): By becoming instrumental reason, reason has become controlling rather than liberating and emancipating; in this

52 The Janus Face of Modern Environmentalism

way, Enlightenment turned into its very opposite. Horkheimer and Adorno had in mind the control of people; their context is totalitarianism and the rise of mass culture. But one could also apply it to the relation between humans and their environment: By means of instrumental reason, humans have dominated, oppressed "nature". Similarly, one could use Habermas' distinction between 'lifeworld' and 'system' to frame environmental problems as being the result of the 'colonization' of 'nature' by the 'system'.

The upshot of this direction of thought is not that we need to move beyond modernity, but rather that we need a *different*, 'alternative' modernity (to use Feenberg's term, Feenberg 1995). Indeed, this application of Critical Theory still remains within the boundaries of modern thinking: "Nature" is still something external, something conceptually distinguished and practically separated from the human. Thus, Critical Theory does not criticize modernity, and not even Enlightenment, but "merely" a particular *form* of Enlightenment—a "perverse" form of it, or indeed its very opposite—and a particular form of modernity. But in principle they still fully endorse the value of modern reason and the Enlightenment ideal of emancipation, which both presuppose a dualistic conception of the relation between humans and world.

This modern thinking has been questioned by Heidegger, who argued that we are always already involved in the world. He coined the concept 'being-in-the-world' to articulate his view that we cannot have an objective standpoint (Heidegger 1927). Moreover, he also questioned our modern-technological way of thinking, which treats everything (non-human) as a 'standing reserve' we can use for our purposes (Heidegger 1977). Applied to the question regarding the environment, this epistemological conceptual framework (the perception of the world as external to me versus humans that are always already involved in the world) and ethical conceptual framework (treatment of non-humans as standing-reserve versus a non-instrumental, engaged relation to the environment) offers a powerful critique of modern environmentalism, which presupposes a "nature" in which we are not involved and which we can (or even have to) manipulate. Indeed, the most central environmentalist term itself, "nature", is questioned by Heideggerian thinking (as it is by Latour's non-modern thinking). Tim Ingold, an anthropologist influenced by Heidegger, warns in his excellent book on the perception of the environment about the confusion of the term "environment" with the term "nature":

> the notion of environment (. . .) should on no account be confused with the concept of nature. For the world can exist as nature only for a being that does not belong there, and that can look upon it, in the manner of the detached scientist (. . .). Thus the distinction environment and nature corresponds to the difference in perspective between seeing ourselves as beings *within* the world and as beings *without* it. (. . .) We have, then, to be wary of such a simple expression as 'the natural environment', for in thus conflating the two terms we already imagine

Enlightenment Reason and Liberation Politics   53

ourselves to be somehow *beyond* the world, and therefore in a position to intervene in its processes.

(Ingold 2000, p. 20)

The epistemological and ethical aspects of the Heideggerian view are inter-related: to treat "nature" and "natural" beings as "resources" presupposes a way of perceiving our environment as something external to us, something in which we are not involved. Again this way of perceiving has roots in the scientific revolution. Garner summarizes:

The central feature of the scientific revolution (. . .) was the separation of man from nature and the belief that humans could understand and control it. From this, it is a short step to the position, rejected by ecocentrics, that the world was made for human use; that it only has meaning and value in relation to our needs.

(Garner 1996, p. 37)

This explains how it is possible that non-environmentalists sometimes talk about "nature" in economic-scientific terms—for example, as a kind of goods or even as providing "services". The Wikipedia entry (2014) on 'ecosystem services' reads:

Humankind benefits in a multitude of ways from ecosystems. Collectively, these benefits are known as **ecosystem services.** Ecosystem services are regularly involved in the provisioning of clean drinking water and the decomposition of wastes.

Thus, the environment is framed as a collection of 'natural ecosystems' that provide services to humans. The ecosystem is perceived as what Heidegger would call a 'standing reserve' of goods and services. Yet this kind of thinking is often used by both greens and those who oppose them. Environmentalists, in so far as they are *modern*, share the same modern outlook. This is so because they share the same *language*. As Curtis White has argued, scientific thinking has become part of the language of environmentalists:

There is an idol even in the language we use to account for our problems. Our dependence on the scientific language of "environment," "ecology," "diversity," "habitat," and "ecosystem" is a way of acknowledging the superiority of the kind of rationality that serves corporate capitalism. (. . .) We use our most basic vocabulary, words like "ecosystem," with a complete innocence, as if we couldn't imagine that there might be something perilous in it.

(White 2007, pp. 14–15)

According to White, the acceptance of this kind of *logos* makes environmentalists collaborators. Caught up in the language of science and

54   The Janus Face of Modern Environmentalism

bureaucracy—languages that 'have legitimacy in our culture' (p. 16)—they neglect languages that speak of nature in different terms (e.g. poetic or spiritual terms; White mentions Emerson and Thoreau here—but they are also modern in their own way, as I will show later), blame external powers such as corporations, and fail to examine their own lives.

This leaves us with the following paradox, which is highly illustrative of the ambiguous relation between environmentalism and modernity. On the one hand, environmentalists *seem* to concord with criticisms offered by Critical Theory (instrumental rationality) and Heidegger (treating everything as a 'standing reserve'), at least in the sense that they also question particular kinds of rational and technological interventions. But this is only a superficial reading of the more profound criticism Heidegger in particular offers. Indeed, on the other hand, to the extent that they rely on science and technology to justify their arguments and to manage and actively transform the environment, environmentalists risk being vulnerable to the same criticisms offered by Critical Theory and especially by Heideggerian critique: If and in so far as they rely on scientific "facts" and their mission to actively protect and restore "nature", environmentalists treat "nature" as something that can and must be understood by using science and that can and must be controlled by technological means. As long as they understand what they are doing in scientific and managerial terms, their "environmental" thinking and their "environmental" practices remain locked in what Heidegger called the 'Enframing' or what Habermas called the 'System'.

Of course some environmentalists may reply that they take distance from the "cold" view of nature offered by science, that they "love nature", and that *they* do *not* want to intervene in "nature". But all the same that "nature" is perceived as something "external", something we can or cannot transform, something we can intervene in or not, something we can turn to or take distance from. To develop this point I will discuss another branch of modern thinking, which might be seen as the flip side of rationalist Enlightenment and which is still highly influential today, both within and outside the environmentalist movement: Romanticism. This will be the theme of the next chapter. But let me first say more about the modern and Enlightenment side of *political* discussions about the environment.

4.3. ENLIGHTENMENT POLITICS OF NATURE: SUV CARS AND THE REVOLUTION

4.3.1. Introduction

Our inquiry into the problem of moral-environmental motivation has, among other things, attended us to the epistemic basis of this motivation: What kind of knowledge is necessary and sufficient to move us into environmental action? Socrates and modern science presuppose that there is truth independent from the observer: a truth which we can view by means

Enlightenment Reason and Liberation Politics   55

of contemplation and reasoning (Platonic vision) or which we can find by means of scientific experimentation. This suggests that we need environmental and moral experts who can guide us to better lives and better societies. But our knowledge of nature and of environmental problems is never "objective", not even if we are "experts" or "scientists"; the "facts" are always colored by our way of seeing. We interpret and give meaning to our observations and to the information we receive, and we do this from within a larger social-cultural field. This field includes *political* thinking. If we want to understand the problem of environmental motivation, then it is also important to discuss how the main political traditions frame environmental problems and motivate or demotivate environmental action.

In the previous section I have argued that in Western cultures and societies, the dominant way of thinking and of relating to nature can be characterized as "modern" and "Enlightenment." This is also relevant to political thinking. In this section I will show how political discussions about the environment also take place within a playing field defined by Enlightenment modernity.

I will first discuss political thought that tends to discourage environmentalism (conservatism and neo-liberalism); then I will analyze *liberationist* movements as responses to that way of thinking (including a liberationist form of conservation thinking). I will also distinguish these ways of political thinking from their *metaphysical* cousins, to which they may be related in various ways: I will sketch an opposition between metaphysical conservatisms and metaphysical anti-conservatisms—for example, biospheric egalitarianism. I will also pay attention to the special position of Marxist thinking, which is politically liberationist but tends to be metaphysically conservative, unless interpreted in a different way. Finally, I will note that the liberationist reactions do not only have problems of their own, but are also problems that are typical of modernity, which render them problematic in a deeper way. This will enable me to reconnect the discussion about environmental politics to the discussion about modernity—a discussion that I will continue in the next chapter.

4.3.2. Political and Metaphysical Conservatism

Historically, modern political conservatism was a reaction against liberal political forces that aimed at changing social and political institutions. Opposing radical change and revolution in the 17th and 18th century, they were often reactionary: They wanted to restore the situation to pre-revolutionary or even pre-modern times. But in the past two centuries conservatism, rather than aiming at restoration, has usually aimed at keeping things as they are. With regard to the problem of environmental change, both forms of conservatism are relevant. (Note that conservatism might also take on a romantic form—see the next chapter.) Let me discuss political conservatism in the following sense: I will use the term "conservatism" to

56 *The Janus Face of Modern Environmentalism*

refer to political currents—especially but not only present in "conservative" political parties—that oppose substantial social and political change. In particular, we must examine the conservative opposition to *environmental* change.

First it must be noted that there are aspects of conservative thought that seem to support environmentalist politics and thought, or at least a particular kind of environmentalist politics and thought: *conservationist* environmentalism. Both (conservative) greens and conservatives may agree to "leave things as they are", including the natural environment. They may also find themselves united in their celebration of the local and (hence) in their opposition against globalization, which is perceived as a major cause of environmental degradation and climate change. (This can be interpreted as a romantic response, which I will discuss in the next chapter.) Furthermore, Garner mentions an interesting reason why, which also explains anti-green sentiments in current right-populist movements in Europe:

> Greens, like conservatives, are skeptical of the human capacity to comprehend a complex, interconnected world and are therefore persuaded to leave things as they are.
>
> (Garner 1996, p. 52)

This is an important problem and at least one reason why *all* of us may have difficulties acting in (more) environmentally friendly ways. Solving this moral-epistemological problem is key to solving the moral-psychological problem of motivation: We need more and better knowledge, and in Chapter 7 I will present my answer to the question of *what kind of knowledge* we need.

Nevertheless, in spite of these similarities between "green" and conservative thinking, today many people who call themselves environmentalists or (in politics) "greens" do not want to "leave things as they are" and will find themselves in opposition to conservative thought on various crucial aspects. Most importantly, most political environmentalists (let me call them "greens" here to stay in line with the literature) want substantial if not radical social and economic change. Although they may promote local action, they tend *not* to oppose globalization as such, but *a particular kind of* globalization—one informed by neo-liberal thinking. In this sense they have a global perspective (see also Eckersley 1992, pp. 176–177)[2], but one that is critical of free-market globalization. This social-economic position renders environmentalism at least *compatible* with the concerns of Marxism-inspired protests and with the goals of what is known as 'the Occupy movement' (in so far as these goals are clear).

If we look at current right-wing parties and right-wing coalitions in Europe and in the U.S., we observe an entanglement of conservative and neo-liberal thinking. Conservatism on so-called "ethical" and "environmental" issues is often combined with arguments for de-regulation and free competition in

Enlightenment Reason and Liberation Politics   57

economic affairs. The latter position does not advocate leaving social and economic institutions as they are, but rather seeks to *reform* them to reach their goals, for example by lowering taxes and by eroding social protection. But this reformist socio-economic stance has also implications for the environment: Such policies usually mean less environmental protection. Perhaps we could even say that, as Eckersley has argued, free-market liberalism itself is responsible for environmental degradation (Eckersley 1992, pp. 22–23). Furthermore, greens who support conservation do not usually mean that things should be literally left as they are. In practice conservation implies more change than "leaving things as they are": For example, conservation is often understood as restoration to a previous state or the creation of new "wild" nature, so-called *rewilding*, all of which require active and significant human intervention. And many greens argue for an expansion of "nature" areas and an expansion of environmental protection—for example, more legal means to protect nature and to protect animals. In these senses, green thinking is not conservative but "progressive".

Thus, one barrier to environmental change is that some of us are influenced by political conservatism and neo-liberalism, which are generally opposed to environmental change or—especially if they join forces in political coalitions—even actively promote environmental change *in the wrong direction* by leaving social and environmental matters to the market. If today "the right" is a significant and influential political force, this helps to explain why many of us do not act in an environmentally friendly way or even in an environmentally bad way. Even if we charitably assume that most of these people are not *environmental zombies* (of course some clearly are, see also the banality of the oil-thirsty SUV car or of eating without thinking—say, thoughtless driving and thoughtless eating) and cannot be called wantons because they *do* reflect on the desires they want to have and perhaps even on the world they want to have, they act in environmentally wrong ways and live in a way that is not environmentally good at least partly because they are influenced by the wrong kind of (political) thinking. They think; they are not zombies or wantons, but their thinking is "bad" thinking, moral-environmentally speaking.

Yet even if we take a more "progressive" perspective and argue for societal change, this does not guarantee fundamental *environmental* change since we might be influenced by a deeper, moral-metaphysical kind of conservatism shared by nearly all modern political ideologies: If we assume that there is a hierarchy of beings, with humans on top, then we might be politically "progressive" but *metaphysically* conservative. Influenced by our Christian and Aristotelian heritage, we might care about the environment but still assume that humans are morally superior to animals or to "nature". In other words, in spite of being progressive in other ways, we might remain conservative in the sense that we remain anthropocentric: We might want to change *human* society, but we are not prepared to change our moral world order.

58 *The Janus Face of Modern Environmentalism*

Metaphysical conservatism is often coupled with political conservatism. Conservatives usually take a (post-)Christian perspective and see humans as guardians or stewards of the earth, thus presupposing that humans have a higher moral status than the rest of nature (Goodin 1992, p.6), and there is little doubt that 'conservative ideologies are essentially those of a human-oriented ideology' (Pilbeam 2003, p. 507). But this coupling is by no means a logically necessary one. Human-oriented thinking and anthropocentrism are shared by most major political movements and maybe even by the more "shallow" forms of political environmentalism. Liberals and Marxists, for instance, reject political conservatism but are usually metaphysically conservative: They want a better society and better lives, but what they mean is a society of *humans* and *human* lives. Traditionally, many modern political movements did not even consider treatment of animals. Today, this has somewhat changed, partly because of pressure by green political parties. There is a sense in which green thinking has become "mainstream". Today, all political parties say something about animals and the environment. However, there are huge differences in the extent to which people and political parties are actually committed to pro-environmental change and action. Moreover, even if politicians say that they strive for better environmental protection and better animal treatment, this is still far removed from accepting more radical, deep-ecological ideas. For example, it is one thing to argue for sustainability, for less pollution and for controlling climate change, but this might be aimed at improving the condition of humans mainly (and indeed at ensuring the survival of the human species), without much regard for non-human beings and the environment. Moreover, like conservationist thinking, mainstream environmental thinking seems to assume that humans are and should be master of their surroundings—indeed master, guardian, and steward of the earth.

Note that liberalism and Marxism are not *necessarily* committed to a strong anthropocentric metaphysical and moral position. For example, the animal liberation movement is committed to a (more) egalitarian moral ontology, and Benton has offered an interesting and original interpretation of Marx, which brings out the naturalist side of Marxism and argues that humans and (other) animals have much in common (Benton 1993).

The political battle between conservatism versus (left and right) liberalism is a familiar Enlightenment feature. In the next section I reconstruct what we may call the (neo)*Enlightenment* response to environmental conservatism, which comes in branches of the liberal tradition broadly construed.

4.3.3. The Liberation of Animals and Nature

One radical answer to political conservatism with regard to the environment can be (re)constructed as a new form of liberalism, which seeks to liberate animals and nature from human interventions. Revolutions have liberated poor men, slaves, and women from misery and abuse; now we have to liberate animals and "nature" from humans. Sometimes this call is taken literally, as when activists "liberate" farm animals. More generally, there is a political and ethical movement called 'animal liberation' which promotes the protection of animals, and which is not necessarily as radical as, for example, the Animal Liberation Front or other activist organizations but also understands itself in terms of *liberation*.

Typical for the liberal tradition is that moral claims are made in terms of rights or related concepts. Most animal liberationists say that they want to protect *animal rights*. Philosophical advocates of the animal liberation view include Peter Singer (see his influential 1975 book *Animal Liberation*—although he only accepts the term 'rights' if those rights are based on interests understood within a utilitarian framework) and Tom Regan (1983). Although their justifications differ (utilitarian versus Kantian, deontological), both thinkers stand firmly within the liberal Enlightenment tradition. The "only" difference is that they expand their circle of moral consideration from humans to animals and (sometimes) the natural environment. This potential was already present in Enlightenment thinking. For example, Bentham already argued against suffering of animals (e.g. in animal experimentation) and complained that their interests have been neglected in legislation (Bentham 1789). His criterion "Can they suffer?" has been taken up by Singer and the animal liberation movement. Their radicalism is the radicalism of Enlightenment thinking: Rational argument shows us that (in this case) humans share the capacity of suffering with animals, and only "the hand of tyranny" can withhold the rights that are based on this. Liberation from oppression is then mandatory. Improvement of the condition of men, women, slaves, and animals is based on rational inquiry and scientific investigation, which should end tyranny and prejudice.

Although conservationists do not usually put their view in terms of liberation, and might have affinities to both political and metaphysical conservatism (see above), their actual position may also be (re)framed as aiming at a kind of "liberation": a liberation of "nature" from human hands. Protecting a piece of nature could be described as giving to nature what Isaiah Berlin famously called 'negative liberty' (Berlin 1958): a freedom from interference. In this sense, while pieces of land cannot have "rights" according to standard liberal thinking (land is not a moral agent—liberals such as Berlin would never agree to this use of the term liberty), we can be said to have a duty not to interfere with (parts of) nature. This is not only a matter of "hands off"; the more active aspect of this doctrine then implies the restoration of nature already "spoiled" and "violated" by human intervention as an act of liberation. If this involves a kind of "guardianship" or "mastery" at all, it is that of the guardian-liberator or master-liberator, who has authority to remove *human* intervention but does not transform nature (note that this position is problematic and perhaps not cogent, since there *is* intervention anyway, even and especially in case of "rewilding").

60 The Janus Face of Modern Environmentalism

Next to liberty, animal liberation thinkers also appeal to another revolutionary Enlightenment principle: equality. For example, Singer argued for 'extending the basic principle of equality to nonhuman animals' (Singer 1975, p. 2). With this position, Singer once again put himself in the liberal tradition, which historically has broadened its circle of moral concern and cherishes the principle of equality. Viewed from this perspective, (classical) liberal and (shallow?) socialist views are not fundamentally different, since as liberal Enlightenment currents they both aim at giving liberty and equality to those who have a right to it—even if they disagree about who is included in the latter category.

Singer's appeal to the principle of equality also suggests that there is an even more radical answer to *metaphysical* conservatism: biocentrism and other brands of metaphysical egalitarianism, which hold that all beings are equal. For example, Næss (1973) has argued that the fight against pollution and resource depletion is aimed at making people in developed countries more healthy, whereas 'deep ecology' endorses 'biospheric egalitarianism': All living beings have intrinsic value, independent of how useful they are to humans. Since then there has been much discussion about what such a principle implies. What does it demand from us? What does it mean to respect the intrinsic value of all living beings? And from the perspective of the problem of moral motivation one may well ask: Who acts on this principle? Who *can* act on this principle? Can we *possibly* act in accordance with this principle? (There is a discussion about this in the literature—for instance, in response to Naess—and "ought implies can" is a famous Kantian principle that is discussed in moral philosophy.) The latter questions are important with regard to the problem of environmental motivation, since if a principle is inconsistent or inapplicable in practice, it cannot (sufficiently) motivate environmental action. As we have learned from psychology, whether or not behaviour follows intention depends on the extent to which someone believes she is able to perform the behaviour. If it is not even clear what kind of action is required, let alone how one could do it, then the good intentions of this form of egalitarianism remain impotent.

Yet there is a more fundamental problem with the moral principles of liberal Enlightenment thinking, which goes beyond the "left/right" or conservatism/liberalism distinction with regard to environmental politics, beyond philosophical questions about principles (utilitarian/deontological) or their interpretation, and beyond empirical-psychological considerations, but rather has to do with the *modern* character of this kind of ethics and politics, at least in so far as it prescribes moral-environmental principles. Liberationalism and conservatism assume that humans and "nature" can be separated, that there is a more "natural" condition possible, in which nature can be in its "pure" state, unpolluted by the human. As an environmental ethics, liberationist thinking (and indeed conservative thinking) presupposes that we are "first" disconnected from the world and "then" have to act in it, according to or not according to a particular principle. How relational and

Enlightenment Reason and Liberation Politics 61

"environmental" is this thinking really? And how consistent is it, given that it calls for more control and intervention in order to halt control and intervention? In the previous chapter I already discussed the relation between modernity and environmentalism, and argued that in so far as environmental ethics presupposes modern ways of doing and thinking (in particular, dualistic rationalist ways of doing and thinking), it is alienating and is itself part of a larger form of culture and life that hinders, rather than fosters, the development of moral-environmental motivation and environmental action. It turns out now that both conservatist and liberationalist politics are fuelled by modern ways of thinking and have this alienating effect. Their reasoning and their principles (liberationalist green thinking) and their resistance to change (conservative green thinking) are well-intended, but are unlikely to generate fundamental alterations to our way of living and to what we do to the environment if they do not address the problem of modernity. For example, it does not help much to demand the liberation of animals and the end of their suffering in factory farms as long as the modern mechanisms of thinking and doing that make possible this slavery and abuse remain out of sight. Consider the modern language we use and the modern technologies we use: This language and these technologies make animals literally and materially into objects for our use and consumption, into what Heidegger called a 'standing reserve'. "Before" the Enlightenment philosopher arrives at the crime scene with his principles and his demands, there is already a configuration of humans, animals, words, and machines in place that defines the relations. Before the philosopher argues for the "intrinsic value" of nature, "nature" has already been set up as something that is separate from the "human," "cultural" world. Before the environmentalist argues that we should "leave nature alone", we have already set up the environment as a "standing reserve" for our scientific experiments and technological transformations by means of our language, our culture, our material doings. Unless we better understand how this works and attempt to change *that*, we have only the limited power of (Enlightenment) discourse. We have appeals to great principles and values, we have moral imperatives, we have protests and we may even have some "liberation" actions. But the modern world remains in place, including its dualistic categories (e.g. human versus nature) and its very own political dialectic of oppression and liberation, of conservative and progressive thinking. The philosopher's thinking is often part of this setup, and usually remains within its boundaries. To question this modern horizon does not imply giving up critical thinking and philosophical reasoning and skepticism, but rather re-directing this criticism, reasoning, and skepticism to a deeper level, where we can find a more fundamental form of corruption and disease, where there is a deeper kind of unfreedom—one we have imposed on ourselves and on our thinking, one that has already grown and spread such that we can no longer fully control what happens. This operation may well hurt, since it touches the intestines of our culture and the way of life that has become *our* nature. But unless we

62 *The Janus Face of Modern Environmentalism*

are prepared to do it, we remain in chains and we will continue to violate the "environment" and cause suffering to the animals we say we care about. In the modern world, we are at once the people who storm the Bastille and the people who guard the standing order. We apply our rationalist and liberationalist thinking to environmental problems, but we fail to see that this very thinking and the actions it inspires are part of the problem. At a deeper level, the philosopher who asks "Can they suffer?" is complicit with the torturers she accuses. At a deeper level, the animal liberator and the farmer are part of the same game; they are collaborators in so far as they work together to continue to bring into being the modern stage of their battles.

To bring profound environmental change, therefore, we need to try to think beyond modernity (see Part III of this book). However, let me first discuss a response to the rationalist side of modernity that developed within modernity and within Enlightenment itself: Romanticism. If we want to better understand contemporary environmentalist thinking and its "motivation" problem, we need to know more about this branch or dimension of modern thinking, which is and has been at least as influential as rationalist and liberationalist thinking in shaping our beliefs and attitudes about the environment.

NOTES

1. There have been several 20th-century philosophers who have questioned the inner/outer distinction—for instance, Wittgenstein regarded the distinction as a 'picture' that is part of our modern language.
2. Part of the explanation why contemporary environmentalists take a more global perspective may be that greens usually live in (large) urban environments, which promote a less 'local' or 'provincial' perspective. As Pilbeam writes: 'whilst traditionalist conservatism is rooted in a 'parochial' rural perspective, modern environmentalism is typically an urban ideology' (Pilbeam, 2003, p. 505).

5 Romantic Feeling for Nature

INTRODUCTION: ROMANTICISM, FEELING FOR NATURE, AND AUTHENTICITY

When I mentioned the possibility of a Humean response to the problem of moral-environmental motivation, I already suggested that one could turn to an environmental ethics that emphasizes feeling rather than rationality. One could take the view that the reason why people are not sufficiently motivated to act in more "green" ways has not so much to do with lack of rational thinking about the environment, but with lack of *emotional* involvement. We know a lot about environmental matters, but we do not sufficiently *love* nature, *care* about animals, *feel* for the environment, etc. Moreover, some of the work in environmental psychology suggests that emotional involvement and emotional connection (e.g. to outdoor places and in outdoor activities) could be motivating. One may conclude from this moral-psychological work (Humean and contemporary) that what is missing in modern environmentalism is a sufficiently important role for feeling. We know the science, the statistics, the numbers, but an environmentalism based on this does not motivate since it is too bloodless. What we need, it seems, is environmental emotion, care, and *passion* rather than objective observation, calculation, and control.

Historically, the turn to feeling—understood as being *opposed to* rationality—was a key part of the *romantic* reaction to rationalist Enlightenment, which fled to the emotional and the irrational in response to what was experienced as an over-emphasis on reason and rationality. Moreover, it was felt that science and modern society had alienated us from "nature" and from the "natural" and had made it difficult, if not impossible, to live in authentic ways. In order to better understand modern environmentalism and, indeed, *contemporary* modern environmentalism, we should not only look at its science-oriented face, but also study its romantic roots.

Romanticism, which Berlin called 'the greatest single shift in the consciousness of the West that has occurred' (Berlin 1999, p. 1), has many (related) features and it is not my purpose to give a definition or to be comprehensive here; I select two (groups of) features or themes that are very

64   *The Janus Face of Modern Environmentalism*

relevant to the question of environmental motivation and environmental ethics: (1) re-enchantment and love of nature and (2) love of the *natural* and the authentic. I will briefly say something about the former feature and then discuss the latter theme in more detail by exploring links between Rousseau, Thoreau, and contemporary environmentalism.

5.1. THE RE-ENCHANTMENT OF NATURE

The starting point of Romanticism is the idea that science and technology have purified the world of meaning. It assumes that we are in the nihilistic situation Nietzsche later described in *The Gay Science*: 'Do we not feel the breath of empty space? Has it not become colder? Is it not more and more night coming on all the time?' (Nietzsche 1882/1887, pp. 181–182). Science has left us a cold universe without gods and spirits. The task of Romanticism then is to re-enchant[1] nature, to re-fill it with spirit, with feeling, indeed with our love. "Nature" then becomes not the objective "universe" of science, but a living whole full of feeling and spirit. "Nature" is something we have been separated from by rationalism, and now it is time to return to nature and to value emotions over reason. In contemporary environmentalism we can also find a more "emotional" and "spiritual" current, which usually borrows from various religious traditions to support the idea that nature and natural beings are not "systems" and "machines" but have spiritual value, are sacred.

For moral-environmental motivation, this romantic re-enchantment view implies that what people need in order to act environmentally good, is not so much scientific knowledge but also and especially sufficient spiritual feeling and imagination. They need to be able to *sense* what is good for Mother Nature, they need to be able to envision a world full of sacred beings and places, and they need to be able to perceive the divine in nature.

However, to the extent that it proposes active re-enchantment rather than recognizing value and spirit that is already "given", Romanticism does not so much reject the scientific, objectivist view of the environment but *presupposes* it: It is only if we assume that science and technology have created a meaningless, spiritless and valueless world, that we can then claim that we want to give meaning to it, re-enchant it, and re-value it (see also the beginning of Chapter 6). In fact, the disenchantment thesis is highly questionable: Several authors have argued that religious thinking, sensitivity of the sacred, etc. is still present today—even in a technological culture (see, for example, Coeckelbergh 2010).

Moreover, the romantic current has been largely colonized by economic rationalism. As Jenkins remarks:

> Romanticism's imagining of, and yearning for, a mythical pre-modern, un-rationalized past perfect remains influential. It is also, these days,

commoditized, routinized and organized, if not thoroughly rationalized. It is big business. Industries such as cinema, television, and heritage are major contemporary conduits of the romantic theme.

(Jenkins 2000, p. 19)

Consider also ecotourism, markets with biological food, New Age, etc. "Back to nature" is no longer reserved for the (un)happy few, it is widely available in the form of commodities and services. In this sense, too, Romanticism is not the antithesis of modernity but is very much part of it.

Let me discuss a related feature of Romanticism in order to better understand (its influence on) contemporary environmentalism, its problems as a *modern* way of thinking, and—ultimately—its failure to move us into action.

5.2. THE NATURAL AND THE AUTHENTIC: ROUSSEAU, THOREAU, AND CONTEMPORARY ENVIRONMENTALISM

A second important feature of Romanticism—historical and contemporary— is the preference for *nature* and the *natural*—and, related to this, the valuing of authenticity. In order to explore this theme and relate it to modern *environmentalism* I propose to focus on Rousseau and, to a lesser extent, on Thoreau.

5.2.1. Walking with Rousseau

Jean-Jacques Rousseau (1712–1778) is sometimes called the father of the romantic movement, not only because of his influential sentimental novel *Julie, ou la nouvelle Héloïse*, but also, at a less superficial level, because of his insistence that we return to nature and become more *natural* and authentic. This idea can be found throughout his writings. Consider for example his argument in his *Discourses* and in the *Émile* (1762a) that humans are good by nature but are corrupted by society and by science, or his stress on authenticity in his *Confessions* and in the *Reveries of the Solitary Walker* (published posthumously in 1782b). Rousseau's writings are interesting in various ways, but in order to get a flavor of his Romanticism with regard to nature, let us turn to the *Reveries*, where we find key romantic themes that have influenced many generations of romantic nature *lovers*, including Thoreau and many environmentalists today.

A first important feature of the romantic is the desire for *authenticity* and, related to that, a focus on the self and a turn away from society. The *Reveries* starts with the words 'I am now alone on earth, no longer having any brother, neighbor, friend, or society other than myself' (Rousseau 1782b, p. 1). Rousseau writes this at the end of his life; he felt hated by his fellows. But there is more to these words than the loneliness of an old man

66 *The Janus Face of Modern Environmentalism*

and his personal bitterness of being rejected by society. In light of the rest of his work, we know that he also *values* being removed from society. He finds in his own self the tranquility and the peace he lacked when he was in the turmoil of society. He is 'tranquil at the bottom of the abyss, (. . .) unperturbed, like God Himself' (p. 5). In a neo-Stoic spirit, he *loves* it when he reaches a state of mind in which 'everything external is (. . .) foreign', since such external objects only 'distress' (p. 5). He writes: 'I find consolation, hope, and peace only in myself' and devotes himself to 'studying myself'—in this sense the *Reveries* are indeed 'the sequel to the severe and sincere examination I formerly called my *Confessions*' (p. 5). "Knowledge" then means not scientific knowledge, but knowledge of oneself. Rousseau is not concerned with others, not with society, and perhaps not even with the natural environment (see below), but with his own soul; he wants to know *his own nature*. Thus, he wants to be natural, and for Rousseau to be natural is—among other things—to be a-social. As many other romantics, he turned to nature and self in order to turn away from the social.

This romantic turn to the self is different from the Socratic dictum that we should know ourselves, which Socrates interpreted as a recommendation to control ourselves (see Chapter 2). Here Rousseau turns to *his own* soul in the sense of an individual, unique self, which should be allowed free expression. His technique of the soul[2] is not a technique of self-control, but a different one, which both stimulates passion and restrains passion. Let me explain this.

The technique of the soul Rousseau uses is *walking*. Rousseau keeps 'faithful record' of his 'solitary walks and of the reveries which fill them' in order to 'be what nature willed' (p. 12). The *Reveries* has no "chapters" but 'Walks'. And "nature" plays a key role in this romantic technique of the soul: The turn away from society is followed by a turn to nature as a *walk* in nature, which creates the conditions under which the romantic can find his true self, can become natural again. Rousseau: 'It is only after having detached myself from social passions and their sad retinue that I have again found nature with all its charms' (Rousseau 1782b, p. 119). He seeks 'refuge in mother nature' in order to 'escape the attacks of her children' (p. 95). In nature, Rousseau can look within himself for all the 'nourishment' his heart needs (p. 12–13). He enjoys a 'natural temperament quite purified of all irascible passions' (p. 90). Thus, "natural" passions are promoted, whereas "social", "unnatural" passions are restrained[3].

Walking alone, Rousseau does not only find peace in the sense that he is removed from society, but he also has 'moments of rapture', 'ecstasies' (p. 13) related to being immersed in nature. He writes that he made himself 'one with the whole of nature' (p. 95). When he was on the island Saint-Pierre in the Bienne lake (Switzerland), he felt happy and spent many hours walking in forest and field. But he was also far less active. He would indulge in his reveries on a boat or on the lake bank: 'While they were still at the table, I would slip away and go throw myself alone into a boat that

Romantic Feeling for Nature 67

I rowed to the middle of the lake when the water was calm' (p. 66). Then he would stretch out and enjoy his reveries. Thus nature—here especially water—was a means to reach his state of happiness.

As Babbitt has argued in his classical study *Rousseau and Romanticism* (1919), Rousseau's reveries were new, at least in the following sense. Although in Hellenistic philosophy (for example, Stoicism) and, we might want to add, in Renaissance thinking, we also find an inclination to 'affirm the ultimate identity of the human and the natural order', the 'melting of man into outer nature' and the celebration of the wild was new. Whereas the ancients would 'have a positive shrinking from wild and uncultivated nature' (Babbitt 1919, pp. 269–270), Rousseau experienced this wild nature in a very different way.

Consider, for instance, how we climb a mountain today, which is influenced by Romanticism: Whereas before Romanticism mountainous areas would be regarded as a problem (not suitable for farming activities, difficult to access and a nuisance to travellers), now it is our romantic solution to the modern problem of authenticity. In the mountains we can find "authentic" nature, "real" wilderness. In the mountains we can find our "authentic" self, too. This was new at the time Romanticism emerged. Even when Petrarch ascended Mt. Ventoux in a quasi-romantic manner, he remained a Christian. As Babbitt reminds us, Petrarch opened Augustine's *Confessions*. And on his way down, Petrarch reflected on the vanity of human wishes, concluding: 'How earnestly should we strive, not to stand on mountain-tops, but to trample beneath us those appetites which spring from earthly impulses' (Petrarch). The romantic hiker, by contrast, wants to stand on tops. She wants the *extreme*, the ultimate, the summit.[4]

(Ironically, the same romantic way of thinking has often led us to try to recreate the wild: the artificial creation of nature. Consider the English garden with its artificial landscape and artificial ruins, or "re-wilded" nature areas today. Can we escape the artificial? Can we escape . . . the human? I return to the question concerning technology in due course.)

Today's environmentalists—and maybe most of us—are Rousseauist in the sense that we want "natural" and "authentic" experiences and products. We also walk to leave behind the city and to get back in touch with ourselves and with "nature". We want "pure" nature, unpolluted by human intervention. Consider also McKibben's Rousseauistic complaint about what he calls 'the end of nature', which starts with a yearning for a humanless world:

> Almost every day, I hike up the hill out my back door. Within a hundred yards the woods swallow me up, and there is nothing to remind me of human society (. . .); it is a world apart from man.
>
> (McKibben 1989, p. 47)

McKibben then argues that today man is everywhere, that there is no nature left, and that planet earth is now seen as a space ship, a machine, something

68 *The Janus Face of Modern Environmentalism*

to be managed (p. 166). (He fears that soon Thoreau will make no sense—I will discuss Thoreau in the next section.) He does not want 'something that looks a lot like nature but isn't' (p. 180). He wants the real thing, that is, the *natural* thing.

Advertisements for holidays and food seem to be directed to the romantic in us: increasingly we want "natural" things and we only want the real thing, the authentic stuff. Authenticity has become a term that is always used in a positive sense, as Potter notes (Potter 2010, p. 6). Authentic means "good". In response to the realization that modern life is 'pleasant' but not 'meaningful' (p. 266), we 'seek the authentic in the jeans we buy, the food we eat, the vacations we take, the music we listen to, and the politicians we elect' (p. 264). We want to be authentic, we want to be natural. Paradoxically, these romantic desires have created a food industry and a tourism industry that artificially, scientifically, and technologically creates "natural", "pure" experiences and products.

We do this partly because we want to have nature in an easy way: We buy naturalness and authenticity in the travel shop, in the supermarket, and in the nature reserve; we do not really want to do much effort for it. It has to be *available* (see also Borgmann's critique as discussed later in this book). We are eco-consumers and consumers want their stuff fast and easy.

5.2.2. Walking with Thoreau

In Thoreau, who has influenced many contemporary environmentalist thinkers, we can find an attitude and practice that is very close to Rousseau's. For a start, Thoreau was also a "nature *walker*" in the full Rousseauistic sense. His *Walking* (1862) starts with the following famous words:

> I wish to speak a word for Nature, for absolute freedom and wildness, as contrasted with a freedom and culture merely civil—to regard man as an inhabitant, or a part and parcel of Nature, rather than a member of society.
>
> (Thoreau 1862, p. 1)

This is not only Romanticism in its pure form; it is also Rousseau *pur sang*, or at least the romantic side of Rousseau (he also has an Enlightenment side—see below). Nature is contrasted with society, and life outside society is recommended. Leaving for a walk in nature means leaving society, even family and friends. Thoreau writes:

> If you are ready to leave father and mother, and brother and sister, and wife and child and friends, and never see them again—if you have paid your debts, and made your will, and settled all your affairs, and are a free man—then you are ready for a walk.
>
> (Thoreau 1862, p. 2)

Romantic Feeling for Nature 69

Indeed, like Rousseau's walker, Thoreau's walker is a *solitary* walker. He asks us to 'shake off the village' (p. 6) and compares his walking with that of 'the old prophets and poets' (p. 8), which is free from the business of men. He says in a way that clearly displays the dualist thinking of Romanticism:

> Let me live where I will, on this side is the city, on that the wilderness, and ever I am leaving the city more and more, and withdrawing into the wilderness.
>
> (Thoreau 1862, p. 12)

He seeks 'the Wild' (p. 17) in the West of his country, and anywhere really where there is 'wildness' (p. 19): This can be real place—'Give me the ocean, the desert, or the wilderness!' (p. 20)—or an imagined one: 'In literature it is only the wild that attracts us' (p. 22) and 'Genius is the light which makes the darkness visible' (pp. 22–23). It is literature's task to give 'expression to Nature' (p. 23). And since 'all good things are wild and free' (p. 25), he even suggests, in a true liberationist spirit, that we liberate the domestic animals: He would love 'to see the domestic animals reassert their native rights' (p. 25). He praises instinct, and draws the conclusion that humans should also be(come) natural, return to Nature, which he calls our 'mother' (p. 27).

> I would not have every man nor every part of a man cultivated, any more than I would have every acre of earth cultivated.
>
> (Thoreau 1862, p. 28)

He also argues that such freedom is necessary to acquire knowledge. We have accumulated 'a myriad of facts', we 'have eaten hay long enough', but we know nothing (pp. 29–30). Thoreau suggests that becoming more natural also implies become more *knowledgeable*. But what kind of knowledge does he mean? If we want to address the problem of environmental motivation, finding an answer to this question is crucial.

Let me first say more about Thoreau's view. In *Walden* (1854) we find a similar romantic, and indeed very Rousseauist message: Turn away from society and live in the midst of nature. Like Rousseau's *Reveries* and *Confessions*, *Walden* starts from Thoreau's own, solitary self: 'I should not talk so much about myself if there were any body else whom I knew as well' (Thoreau 1854, p. 3). Thoreau wants to live 'in the midst of Nature', alone but not 'lonesome' (p. 131). In *Walden*, too, we find a praise of reverie:

> I love a broad margin to my life. Sometimes, in a summer morning, having taken my accustomed bath, I sat in my sunny doorway from sunrise till noon, rapt in a reverie, amidst the pines and hickories and sumacs, in undisturbed solitude and stillness, while the birds sang around.
>
> (Thoreau 1854, p. 111)

70   *The Janus Face of Modern Environmentalism*

Like Rousseau, Thoreau links his reveries to water, a symbol of the romantic purity he is after: Walden Pond, 'remarkable for its depth and purity' (p. 175) and 'too pure to have a market value' (p. 199), lends itself to a reverie practice surprisingly similar to what Rousseau used to do on the lake when he was living on the isle Saint-Pierre:

> having paddled my boat to the middle, and lying on my back across the seats, in a summer forenoon, dreaming awake, until I was aroused by the boat touching the sand, and I arose to see what shore my fates had impelled me to.
>
> (Thoreau 1854, p. 191)

Both Rousseau and Thoreau trust themselves to nature. The romantic takes a bath in nature. Being "natural" is always the criterion of the good life. Thoreau recommends that we become 'simple and natural', such as the Canadian wood-chopper he got to know (p. 144); we have to 'link' 'to Nature again' (p. 175). He wants to be like 'fisherman, hunters, woodchoppers, and others, spending their lives in the fields and woods' since they are 'part of nature themselves' (p. 210). But his love of the wild goes further. He wants to eat a woodchuck, not because he is hungry, but because he is hungry 'for that wildness which he represented' (p. 210). He even wants to live 'as the animals do' (p. 210).

Thoreau compares his quest for the wild to the exploration and mastery of new lands—in the West of his own country but also elsewhere. In a passage that is overly romantic (but at the same time also shows the Janus face of modernity—see below), Thoreau writes:

> We need the tonic of wildness. (. . .) At the same time that we are earnest to explore and learn all things, we require that all things be mysterious and unexplorable, the land and sea be infinitely wild, unsurveyed and unfathomed by us because unfathomable. We can never have enough of Nature. We must be refreshed by the sight of inexhaustible vigor, vast and Titanic features, the sea-coast with its wrecks, the wilderness with its living and its decaying trees, the thunder cloud, and the rain (. . .). We need to witness our own limits transgressed.
>
> (Thoreau 1854, p. 318)

But as in Rousseau, the Romantic's voyage is also an *inner* travel. Thoreau asks us to 'be a Columbus to whole new continents and worlds within you', where we are the 'lord of a realm' and must 'explore the private sea, the Atlantic and Pacific Ocean of one's being alone' (p. 321). The romantic explores and enjoys "outer" and "inner" nature.

Hence it is understandable that *Walden* has become, in Updike's words, 'a totem of the back-to-nature (. . .) mindset', a message welcomed in 'a time of informational overload', 'ubiquitous electronic entertainment' and of an 'ever more demanding work-place' (Updike in Thoreau 1854, p. ix), and an antidote

Romantic Feeling for Nature 71

to consumerism (p. xvii). To the contemporary romantic, the 21st century is at least as 'restless, nervous, bustling, trivial' as the 19th-century Thoreau describes (p. 329). The turn to nature allows us to escape that difficult world, with its artificial things and its artificial people; we find peace in nature and in our inner self. We believe that by living a simple and (preferably) solitary life we can become authentic, real, and natural. Thoreau's *Walking* and *Walden* are both deeply romantic and *Rousseauist*; so are we.

I have already argued that, in spite of appearances, Romanticism is still modern. The next question is then: Is Romanticism necessarily anti-Enlightenment?

5.2.3. Romanticism and Enlightenment

Rousseau (like Thoreau) was not only and not always engaged in romantic reveries; he also had a scientific mind. For example, he had a great interest in botany. He loves plants not only since the 'brilliant flowers, diverse colors of the meadows, fresh shady spots, brooks, thickets, greenery' etc. 'purify' his 'imagination' and thus make him forget about social matters (p. 97), but also because he is interested in them as a *scientist*—in particular as an Enlightenment botanist. When he visits 'charming places' he also stops from time to time 'to look at plants in the vegetation' (p. 13). He also wrote a *Dictionary of Botanical Terms*.

Writing dictionaries is of course a typical Enlightenment preoccupation. Many Enlightenment thinkers were writers and scientists; there was no sharp division between "humanities" and "natural sciences". Rousseau was not only a (pre)romantic; he was also an Enlightenment thinker. Romanticism is not really anti-Enlightenment but its complement. In Rousseau, the two faces of modernity meet. For instance, Rousseau shared the modern and Enlightenment aim to create a better society, and he uses reason to argue for a social contract. His philosophical and scientific work is very different from, say, the writings of 19th-century romantic figures. Rousseau believed in the power of feeling, but at the same time also in the power of reason.

This explains why Rousseau can be read as a romantic, but also as an Enlightenment "philosophe". As Hulliung has pointed out in *The Autocritique of Enlightenment* (1994), Rousseau has even been interpreted as anticipating Kant (by Cassirer—see below). These very different readings are possible because modernity itself has these two sides. In Rousseau we find the Enlightenment and at the same time a critique of it. In Rousseau we thus find a modern paradox that persists until today. Modern environmentalism is at the same time representative of what we may call a "green Enlightenment" movement, which seeks to make the world more "green" by using reason and science (e.g. arguing on the basis of ethical principles and facts, thinking and acting "global"), and a "green Romanticism", which emphasizes feeling for "nature" and which seeks "authenticity" (persuading by emotion, thinking and acting "local").

72   *The Janus Face of Modern Environmentalism*

Similarly, Thoreau was as much an Enlightenment thinker as a romantic. As Updike pertinently remarks in his introduction to *Walden*:

> Readers new to Walden may be surprised at the high proportion of its energy given to empirical exploration and demonstration. The romantic Nature-celebrant wears the polished spectacles of Franklin and the *philosophes*.
>
> (Updike in Thoreau 1854, p. xx)

Indeed, Thoreau also *observes* nature and uses scientific instruments such as a thermometer (p. 299). He even thinks of nature as *illustrating* 'the principle of all the operations of Nature' (p. 308). Here nature does not give us 'the tonic of wildness' (p. 318) and it is not allowed to remain 'mysterious and unexplorable' (p. 318); it is no longer 'living poetry' (p. 309). Instead, nature becomes a matter of 'operations' and 'principles'. It is not a living whole but a mere illustration, a symbol of abstract principles and scientifically explainable operations.

The roots of Thoreau's Janus face, and, more generally, of modern environmentalism's Janus face, can be traced back to Rousseau, who studied nature and dreamt in nature. This is also the case for their views on the "natural" and self-control. We must correct, if not reject, Babbitt's picture of Rousseau as an unrestrained dreamer. A key part of Rousseau's thinking (and indeed of Thoreau's) is influenced by Stoicism and hence puts more emphasis on self-control than one might expect (see also Coeckelbergh 1999). If the romantic part of Rousseauist thinking asks us to be "natural", the Stoic part interprets this nature as a demand not to want too much and even to *control* one's imagination. Natural passions are fine, but they easily become artificial passions. He writes in the *Emile* that we should not increase our needs too much, since 'he whose needs surpass his strength, be he an elephant or a lion, be he a conqueror or a hero, be he a god, is a weak being' (Rousseau 1762a, p. 81). And in Book III he is even more explicit about the danger he sees in our 'passions':

> From where does man's weakness come? From the inequality between his strength and his desires. It is our passions that make us weak, because to satisfy them we would need more strength than nature gives us. Therefore, diminish desires, and you will increase strength.
>
> (Rousseau 1762a, p. 165)

Rousseau thinks that we should 'diminish the excess of the desires over the faculties' (p. 80) and believes that it is problematic that our imagination 'excites and nourishes the desires by the hope of satisfying them' (p. 81). He therefore argues for *restricting* our imagination:

> The real world has its limits; the imaginary world is infinite. Unable to enlarge the one let us restrict the other, for it is from the difference

Romantic Feeling for Nature 73

between the two alone that are born all the pains which make us truly unhappy.

(Rousseau 1762a, p. 81)

Moreover, Rousseau also sees a problem if we too often get what we want. The teacher wants to avoid that the pupil's desires 'grow constantly due to the ease of satisfying them. . . Without being God, how will you content him?' (Rousseau 1762a, p. 87).

Here Rousseau's view is much closer to the views I discussed in Chapter 2: the ethical demand is to become strong, self-controlled persons, who restrain their passions (today: emotions) and their imaginations. Applied to environmental ethics this reads: Environmental vice is due to a lack a of self-control (including lack of control of imagination, which is stimulated by advertisement and by an education that gives children too often what they want), and it is due to adult people being treated as children, or rather as *spoiled* children: They are too much accustomed to get everything they want—food, devices, it's all *available* (see also Borgmann later in this book). In our society, neither our desires nor our imagination is restrained. As Rousseau writes: 'gluttony is the passion of childhood' (p. 152)—fine for children, but, so he seems to assume, adults should control themselves (even if he thinks that gluttony is at least more natural than vanity).

Rousseau's Stoicism thus comes close to contemporary critiques of consumerism (and indeed to Buddhism). Here he seems far removed from the Rousseau of the *Reveries*. If this is still a romantic view at all, it is Romanticism fused with Stoicism. It is this Stoic-romantic Rousseau who writes in the Emile: 'O man, draw your existence up within yourself, and you will no longer be miserable' (Rousseau 1762a, p. 83). He recommends to train children 'to be as self-sufficient as possible' (p. 119). It is from within this Romantic-Stoic thinking that Rousseau, living at a time when the industrial revolution was only beginning, warns against getting too much dependent on machines: 'Always machines? Who promises you that they will follow you everywhere in case of need?' (p. 133).

Similarly, in Thoreau one can find significant traces of Stoicism (which has its roots in the Socratic stress on self-control)—especially a Christian form of Stoicism. His arguments against luxury and for simplicity can be called "Stoic", but there is also a specifically Christian side to *Walden* that stands in stark contrast to its Romanticism. When in these passages Thoreau recommends 'purity' and 'chastity', he does not want to become "natural" or live like an "animal"; on the contrary, he says that we must *overcome* nature and kill the animal in ourselves in order to become a good Christian:

Chastity is the flowering of man. (. . .) Man flows at once to God when the channel of purity is open. (. . . .) He is blessed who is assured that the animal is dying out in him day by day, and the divine being established.

(Thoreau 1854, pp. 219–220)

74 *The Janus Face of Modern Environmentalism*

Here Thoreau does not endorse sensuality but condemns it: 'whether a man eat, or drink, or cohabit, or sleep sensually', all this must be replaced by chastity. He writes, in a very un-romantic state of mind: 'Nature is hard to be overcome, but she must be overcome' (p. 221). Here the romantic spirit has abandoned him entirely and has been replaced by the self-controlled Christian.

Furthermore, although Thoreau praises reverie, he also says that we can always stand back from our thinking and our actions:

> By a conscious effort of the mind we can stand aloof from actions and their consequences; (. . .). We are not wholly involved in Nature. I may be either the drift-wood in the stream, or Indra in the sky looking down on it. (. . .) However intense my experience, I am conscious of the presence and criticism of a part of me, which, as it were, is not part of me, but spectator, sharing no experience, but taking note of it.
>
> (Thoreau 1854, pp. 134–135)

Similarly, Rousseau's reveries obviously did not prevent him from reflecting on his experience and to be judge of himself. He is a dreamer and a philosopher-writer at the same time.

As Wilkins has argued, Rousseau's Romanticism should not be confused with 'the dark, Dionysian creeds of later-day Romanticists' (Wilkins 1959, p. 666), and although there are many differences between Voltaire and Rousseau, in many ways they were both Enlightenment thinkers, who championed liberty, respected reason, and were, rightly or not, *both* associated with the French Revolution (for example, by Burke).

Another comparison to Enlightenment thinking is also apt: between Rousseau and Kant. I already referred to Cassirer's reading of Rousseau. As Wilkins has suggested, there are good reasons why 'Kant, the celebrated author of *What is Enlightenment?* and the most enduring product of 18th-century rationalism could regard the late Jean-Jacques Rousseau as a kindred spirit and draw inspiration from his work' and why Cassirer could give us 'a bloodless Rousseau' (Wilkins 1959, p. 680). Not only is *The Social Contract* 'nearly a hymn to law and to reason'; with its claim that obedience to a law we prescribe to ourselves is liberty, it is a direct precursor of Kant's moral philosophy. Indeed, in *On the Social Contract* Rousseau equates liberty—that is, 'moral liberty' and true 'mastery'—with 'obedience to a law which we prescribe to ourselves' (Rousseau 1762b, p. 12).

One may also point to links between Rousseau's Deism or "natural religion" and the Deism and beliefs of (other) Enlightenment thinkers. Here it becomes clear again that Rousseau's position can only be fully understood if interpreted within the context of the Enlightenment.

Romantic Feeling for Nature   75

Finally, Rousseau's education in the *Emile* may be directed to raising a "natural" man, but the way Rousseau does this is rather artificial, controlled, and *engineered*. It is often closer to contemporary efforts to manipulate or "nudge" humans into a greener lifestyle—using knowledge from psychology, for example (see Chapter 3)—than it is to romantic celebrations of the natural. Consider Rousseau's description of how the teacher deals with Emile. There is only manipulation; if Emile has a "nature", then it is one that is created, engineered. Based on what he takes to be the teacher's 'deliberate, persistent use of artifice and trickery to assure willing docility', Crocker writes: 'Emile is a (. . .) more complete manual of human engineering, an experiment in capturing hearts, minds, and wills' (Crocker 1968, p. 24). Today we might also use the term "surveillance" for the teacher's constant monitoring of his pupil. The teacher even wishes to control Emile's sexuality: 'The youth must not be let out of sight, day or night, not allowed to go to bed until he is in a state of exhaustion. Even then the tutor should share his bed. (. . .) Rousseau assures us that sexual desire is not a genuine physical need; it is the work of the imagination, which can be controlled' (p. 25). How different is this kind of thinking from that of the 19th-century Bohemian, and indeed from contemporary individualism, which since the 1960s celebrates absolute sexual liberty (let alone that it would recommend the restriction of anyone's *imagination*—a horror to any true romantic liberal).

This paradox in Rousseau's thought can only be understood if we read Rousseau not only as a romantic, but also as an Enlightenment thinker and a neo-Stoic (and hence neo-Socratic), who recommends personal self-control but also *modern* control and educational engineering. He wanted to create better people and a better society (and thought that the latter was required for the former). It may be true that *current* society is corrupt, but Rousseau thinks we can *make* better people and a better society. As he says in Book I of the *Emile*: 'Plants are shaped by cultivation, and men by education' (Rousseau 1762a, p. 38).

Thus, Rousseau did not reject reason in his work, but rather combined reason and feeling in various ways, and did not seem to think that this is contradictory in any way—and indeed neither do many contemporary greens. Babbitt presents a one-sided picture of Rousseau. But we cannot deny that there is a tension between the different aspects of Rousseau's work, and indeed between the Enlightenment strand and the romantic strand in modern thinking.

Modern environmentalism, then, has the same Janus face. On the one hand, it is highly romantic in its emphasis on the natural and the authentic. At the same time, there is also a strong Enlightenment current running through its veins. Its reliance on science, its criticism of consumerism, and its (sometimes utopian) project to change society show a continuation of

76 *The Janus Face of Modern Environmentalism*

the Enlightenment project rather than its rejection. We can conclude that Romanticism is anti-Enlightenment, yet at the same time it is also very much connected to it. We can also conclude that the Janus face of modernity and indeed of modern environmentalism was already present in Rousseau.

5.3. PROBLEMATIC ROMANTIC MODERNITY

Moreover, Romanticism is not only connected to Enlightenment but is also still very modern, and therefore problematic, in at least the following senses, which I will further develop in the next chapters.

First, as I already suggested, it is not clear why the world was ever disenchanted in the first place. In the beginning of Chapter 6 I will refer to Heidegger, Ingold, and Szerszinsky to develop this point and study some paths towards non-dualism, or at least three kinds of *attempts* to arrive at a non-modern environmental ethics (and I will argue that they all (risk to) fail).

Second, it is questionable if "authenticity"—in the romantic sense—exists. It has become a highly suspect term. Many 20th century philosophers have argued that there is no "authentic" self. For example, Foucault has argued that our subjectivity is always shaped in relation to disciplining, and contemporary philosophers of technology have argued that technology is part of what it is to be a human being. Subjectivity is always shaped in relation to our social and material environment. The absolute, non-relational freedom the romantics were after is not possible. We cannot really leave society or reject technology. Moreover, even if we wanted to, we cannot go back to a past when everything was "authentic"[5]; we never lived in an "original" state or a "state of nature."

Furthermore, as Potter has recently argued the search for the authentic is a kind of "trap" since 'if everyone is recognized, then no one is' (p. 267): We all want to be "authentic", but we can no longer distinguish ourselves if everyone is recognized as authentic. Indeed, our search for authenticity is often a kind of vanity and narcissism. In a secular age we search for meaning by focusing on personal identity and authenticity, but our taste for organic produce, ecotourism, yoga, and "authentic" politicians is often a form of status seeking and risks creating self-absorbed individuals (Potter 2010). Thus, it is not only the case that 'the search for the authentic is itself twisted into just another selling point or marketing strategy' (p. 3), since this would not make it misguided *per se*, I guess, but rather the very ideal of authenticity does not make us more environmental at all since, as I now will argue, it removes us from our environment; it is itself alienating.

Indeed, third and most important for the purpose of this book, it is highly problematic that, like Enlightenment rationalism and its Socratic and Stoic precursors, Romanticism also promotes a *detached* attitude. Nature is not really valued for its own sake, but is a kind of projection screen for one's own feelings. The only thing one is really interested in is the self. Consider these observations by Rousseau:

> The countryside, still green and cheerful, but partly defoliated and already almost desolate, presented everywhere an image of solitude and of winter's approach. Its appearance gave rise to a mixed impression, sweet and sad, too analogous to my age and lot for me not to make the connection. I saw myself at the decline of an innocent and unfortunate life, my soul still full of vivacious feelings and my mind still bedecked with a few flowers—but flowers already wilted by sadness and dried up by worries. Alone and forsaken, I felt the coming cold of the first frosts (. . .).
> (Rousseau 1782b, p. 14)

Thus, Rousseau uses (the perception of) his environment entirely *instrumentally*: He uses it as a mirror of his own feeling. He does not see his environment, but *he sees himself* ('I saw myself'). The environment is a projection screen, a mirror. Given this romantic use of the environment as a mirror of the self and its emotions, the myth of Narcissus seems particularly apt to describe the romantic play with nature. Babbitt already noted this:

> The nature over which the Rousseauist is bent in such rapt contemplation plays the part of the pool in the legend of Narcissus. It renders back to him his own image. He sees in nature what he himself has put there.
> (Babbitt 1919, p. 302)

Furthermore, the Romantic's idle reveries are literally care-free. Rousseau strives for 'natural carefreeness'. Romantics "love" nature, but in so far as they are pursuing their reveries, they could not care less about what really goes on in their environment. What matters to them is the "I". The environment, constructed as "nature", is used as a *symbol* of one's inner feelings. What Babbitt says about Chateaubriand (a French romantic writer) fits Rousseau and his contemporary romantic followers:

> Chateaubriand's chief concern is not with any outer fact or activity, but with his own emotions and the enhancement of these emotions by his imagination.
> (Babbitt 1919, p. 278)

Whether or not this reduces Rousseau's relation to his environment to 'mere emotional intoxication', as Babbitt claims (p. 287), or whether or not romantic self-centeredness boils down to 'egoism' (p. 304), it seems right that the romantic "concern" with nature is not really a concern with the environment at all, but with one's *own* "nature", that is, one's own self. In this sense there is indeed a kind of 'hollowness' to 'the Rousseauistic communion with nature' (p. 305).

78   *The Janus Face of Modern Environmentalism*

Babbitt therefore rightly makes a connection to German idealism, in particular Schelling: 'All things are only a garment of the world of spirit' (Schelling quoted in Babbitt 1919, p. 293). We can find a similar idealistic focus on the self in North American idealism—in particular, in Emerson's and Thoreau's 'transcendentalism'.

Like Rousseau, the Transcendentalists in 19th-century New England believed that man is good but that society corrupts the individual. Emerson argued in his essay *Nature* (1836) that we need solitude (p. 13) to achieve 'wholeness' with nature. This "wholeness" must be interpreted from within the Judeo-Christian tradition—in particular, the concept of the Fall. As Schulz (1997) has argued, both Thoreau and Emerson regarded nature as the original home of human beings and believed that with the Fall, the original harmony between man and nature was lost. Humans then try to recreate the original union. For Rousseau and Thoreau the Fall also means that man started to live a life of conveniences and luxuries—something that needs to be undone (Schulz 1997, p. 24). Moreover, based on his idealism Emerson also thought that nature is a *phenomenon*, dependent on our emotions. He writes: 'Nature always wears the colors of the spirit' (Emerson 1836, p. 17). For Emerson, mind was the only reality (Cooke 1881, p. 268). Nature is 'the symbol of spirit' (Emerson 1836, p. 31), with every appearance corresponding to a state of mind (p. 32). At the 'centre' of nature 'the moral law lies' (p. 47). He entertains the 'noble doubt (. . .) whether nature outwardly exists' (p. 52) and claims that nature is a 'phenomenon': Spirit has necessary existence, nature 'an accident and an effect' (p. 54). It is 'an appendix to the soul' (p. 60). Nature also serves our human needs—for example, our desire for beauty. For the Transcendentalists, America was a blank slate on which no European history was put; they could fill it with their emotions. Thoreau was influenced by Emerson and hence is also vulnerable to the objection that his Transcendentalism led him to regard his environment as a mere 'appendix to the soul', a mirror for his 'emotional intoxication'.

Thus, Rousseau's writings stimulated a romantic view of environment, which made "nature" something external to the human, something that is given to the inner self, on which that self could project its emotions. In the 18th century, this way of looking at nature was new. Today, we have problems *not* walking through nature in this way. (I will say more about walking later in this book.)

Fourth, as has been noted with regard to Rousseau's craving for authenticity, the romantic turn to the self also involved a turn away from the social. Babbitt: 'the inner life in which the romanticist takes interest is not the life he possesses in common with other men but what is most unique in his own emotions—his mood in short' (Babbitt 1919, p. 297). It seems that if 'the romanticist tends to make of nature the mere plaything of his mood' (pp. 298–299), she also makes *others* the mere plaything of her mood. The others are the ones who do not recognize her genius, her uniqueness, etc. She is uninterested in the experiences and lives of other people.[6]

Finally, in Rousseau, in contrast to Thoreau perhaps, there is no suggestion that *working* in nature could be good at all. On the contrary, in the *Confessions* Rousseau wrote:

> I know something about the work of nature, but nothing about the gardener's. I devoted the time after dinner entirely to my idle and nonchalant mood and to following the impulse of each instant without any order.
>
> (Rousseau 1782b, p. 254; see also Rousseau 1782a, p. 629)

Rousseau wants to stress here that he knows nature, whereas the gardener only knows the royal garden, something *artificial*. But Rousseau's positive valuation of idleness here and in the *Reveries* has a downside: It assumes that we can get knowledge of our environment without really engaging with it and without *working* in it and with it. Maybe this is the main problem with the romantic attitude to nature in relation to the problem of motivation: It includes no notion of an active relation to the environment. But perhaps such an active relation, such an engagement, is a better, if not the best way to gain full knowledge (not just knowing-that but also knowing-how), a way to really—that is, practically—*care* (with its positive and negative aspects; see also Heidegger's concept *Sorge*), and a way to motivate environmental action. Towards the end of this book I will present a view which focuses on skill and technology, and which is perhaps more in line with a less well-known passage in the *Confessions*, in which Rousseau writes:

> Nothing would have been more congenial to my temperament or more conducive to my happiness than the peaceful and obscure condition of a good artisan (. . .). I could have been a good Christian, a good citizen, a good father, a good friend, a good worker, a good man in all ways. I could have been content with my condition (. . .).
>
> (Rousseau 1782a, p. 42)

In Chapter 7 I hope to explain why I think that this kind of activity could make someone more "environmental" and perhaps, in Rousseau's words, 'a good man in all ways'. In preview of that chapter, it is also good to remark that Romanticism could only emerge and grow as a reaction to the technological and material developments of its time: the scientific and industrial revolution and the urbanization of the 18th and 19th centuries. If we want to understand modern environmentalism and its problems, it is important to keep in mind the relation between modern environmentalism and technological development.

To conclude, Romanticism might be (in a Hegelian sense) the "negation" of the Enlightenment, but it was and is not the negation of *modernity* but rather a particular expression of it. It also has been connected to the Enlightenment. It is a modern way of thinking which, like Enlightenment

80 *The Janus Face of Modern Environmentalism*

rationalism, tends to alienate us from our environment by promoting a detached and anti-social attitude. Both faces of modernity, which are also the two faces of modern environmentalism, promote a way of life that treats the environment as what Heidegger called a 'standing reserve': as a mere means to realize the aims of rational management or romantic reverie. The environment—human and non-human—is treated as a "natural resource" for our food and our activities and as "fuel" for our self-absorbed imagination. Even in the 21st century, the "negation" of *that* kind of thinking and living is still only vaguely discernable at the horizon. In the next chapters, I hope to contribute to articulating a non-modern view, one that is not to be considered as a Hegelian "synthesis" of rationality and feeling or of Enlightenment and Romanticism, but as a view that goes *beyond* this dualism.

In the next chapter I will start with discussing ecological thinking. This is in some ways different from Rousseau's Romanticism and different from Rousseau's thinking in other respects, too. For instance, Rousseau still had a hierarchical view of animals (see, for example, second *Discourse*), whereas ecological thinking is often more egalitarian. There are important differences between Romanticism and deep ecology. But how "deep" is 'deep ecology' really? Does it also go beyond modern thinking? How *modern* is Leopold's idea of a 'biotic community' as expressed in *A Sand County Almanac* (Leopold 1949)?

NOTES

1. I use a term that has been used in response to Max Weber's notion 'disenchantment', which he borrowed from Schiller. According to Weber, science and bureaucracy have made the world secular, understandable, controllable, and manipulated. They have made nature less mysterious.
2. One might also say 'technique of the self'—see also Foucault.
3. This can also be understood as a romantic interpretation of Stoicism; see below.
4. With Babbitt we must note, however, that Rousseau 'did not crave the ultimate degree of wildness'; he was content with his Lake. But we are not; as ultra-Romantics we crave the mountain summit.
5. Arguably this was not Rousseau's aim; it rather serves as a kind of guiding ideal—it remains to be seen how nostalgic he was. As Doorman has argued, he rather wanted a different *future*, and this is indeed the question with regard to the environmental question: What future do we want? Rousseau was an Enlightenment thinker who thought about the future.
6. Note that Romanticism shares this individualism with existentialism, which also turned away from rationalism and from technological culture (Smith 1954, p. 61), but in contrast to Romanticism à la Rousseau, existentialists did not only drop the assumption of an original nature (Smith 1954, p. 55) but also turned away from the environment, which they experienced as threatening. See, for example, Sartre's novel *Nausea*: Even nature becomes a constraint, something that is in the way of the individual's freedom and mind; the root of a tree becomes a problem, a resistance, etc. In this sense, existentialism is the summit of alienation from one's environment.

Part III

Beyond Nature, Beyond Modernity, Beyond Thinking

A Non-Romantic, Non-Modern Approach

6 Beyond "Nature" and Modernity
Towards Non-Dualistic Thinking

INTRODUCTION

Both rationalist and romantic modern thinkers presuppose that science and technology have disenchanted the world: The "optimistic" rationalist welcomes this and the "pessimistic" romantic regrets it, but they share the same assumption. In addition, they also share the assumption that a high degree of individual autonomy is important and possible: The "optimistic" rationalist thinks science and technology empower the individual, whereas the "pessimistic" romantic believes that science and technology threaten the individual's autonomy, but both think that individual autonomy is highly valuable. Moreover, both also see the social as an artificial construct: The "optimistic" rationalist wants to design and engineer the ideal society and the perfect individual, whereas the "pessimistic" romantic rejects society *because* it is artificial, unnatural.

In the 20th century philosophers have started to question these modern assumptions, although they could not always distance themselves from either rationalism or Romanticism. For example, Critical Theory has questioned instrumental rationality and the dominance of the "System" (see, for example, Adorno and Horkheimer, or Habermas), but has defended another kind of rationality instead (e.g. 'communicative' rationality), re-enforcing the early modern and Enlightenment idea of creating a new, better society. And Heidegger has criticized modern technology (Enframing) and has taken important steps towards a non-modern view, yet in his emphasis on individual authenticity as opposed to *das Man*—and indeed in his criticism of technology—he has remained rather Romantic. Let me further articulate and discuss the Heideggerian critique of modernity as a first exploration of non-modern thinking and as an example of how *difficult* it is to move away from modern thinking.

In addition, I will also show how we are trapped in a dialectic of control and nostalgia (we always create "new natures") and briefly explain why I think versions of ecological thinking and mysticism focused on "nature" are not the alternatives to look for when it comes to finding a non-modern relation to our environment.

84 *Beyond Nature, Beyond Modernity, Beyond Thinking*

6.1. THE HEIDEGGERIAN CRITIQUE OF MODERNITY

In spite of its romantic side, Heidegger's work is still very helpful for criticizing modern ways of thinking and hence for criticizing modern environmentalism. For example, in 'The Question Concerning Technology' (1977) Heidegger questions the instrumental view of technology, the view that technology is a mere means. We have the idea that 'we will master it' (Heidegger 1977, p. 5), but rather than a means technology is "a way of revealing" and *modern* technology is a particular way of revealing. It reveals nature as a 'standing-reserve': 'everywhere everything is ordered to stand by, to be immediately at hand' (p. 17). This is what Heidegger calls 'Enframing' (p. 19). Physics 'as pure theory' 'sets nature up to exhibit itself as a coherence of forces calculable in advance', something to be experimented with. Nature becomes 'the chief storehouse of the standing energy reserve' (p. 21). As he says in his *Elucidations of Hölderlin's Poetry*, science tries to develop 'a final world formula which would once and for all secure the totality of the world as a uniform sameness, and thus make it available as a calculable resource' (Heidegger 2000, p. 202).

This scientific mission does not only have consequences for (our view and treatment of) nature, but also for our construction of the human and its position. Heidegger writes that 'man (. . .) is nothing but the orderer of the standing-reserve', the 'lord of the earth', and 'comes to the point where he himself will have to be taken as standing-reserve' (Heidegger 1977, p. 27). If we become this kind of lord, everything humans encounter then becomes their construct:

> In this way the impression comes to prevail that everything man encounters exists only insofar as it is his construct. This illusion gives rise in turn to one final delusion: It seems as though man everywhere and always encounters only himself.
>
> (Heidegger 1977, p. 27)

Thus, modernity does not only involve a particular way of seeing and treating things, it also has anthropological implications. We become the creators and managers of everything. But this also means that we never encounter anything that is not "us". We keep on looking in the mirror. This modern narcissism reminds us of what Babbitt said about Romanticism:

> The nature over which the Rousseauist is bent in such rapt contemplation plays the part of the pool in the legend of Narcissus. It renders back to him his own image. He sees in nature what he himself has put there.
>
> (Babbitt 1919, p. 302)

Both rationalist, controlling modernity and romantic modernity are narcissistic: They both construct the environment in their own image. The

Beyond "Nature" and Modernity   85

environment is *their* "nature". In this sense, *modernity has erased the environment*. The only relation left is a kind of boomerang relation, which always returns to the human, without interaction with the non-human. This is a rather "closed" mode of existence, one which precludes the possibility of the emergence of meaning and which denies the very relationality that makes possible existence as being-in-the-world. We can only exist as environmental beings. If we neglect this, it is at our own peril. Narcissus is not only unhappy; he also dies, since his mirror-looking prevents life-sustaining exchanges with his environment. The boomerang hits us and kills us.

But even if we could avoid this suicidal hermeneutical narcissism, modern thinking and doing is very restrictive in terms of the range of perceptions, meanings, and action options that are available to us. We only see one world: a world that we create and *order*. We become the ones who order (nature) and give orders (to other humans, to animals). In Heidegger's words: Enframing endangers 'man in his relationship to himself and to everything that is' and 'banishes man into that kind of revealing which is an ordering', thereby driving out 'every other possibility of revealing' (p. 27). In other words, modern thinking unnecessarily and undesirably reduces hermeneutic plurality.

This Heideggerian critique of modernity is highly relevant for the critique of modern environmentalism I have been developing: In so far as it is modern, environmentalism is in danger of seeing nature as a 'standing-reserve'—even if it is a standing-reserve we should take care of. Moreover, it is because we see it as a 'standing-reserve' that we have the feeling we *should* take care of it. Even if we do not want to use nature as a storehouse for energy and other goods, we might still see it as a domain over which we are the lord and master—even if perhaps a benevolent lord and a kind master. But if Heidegger is right, we are banished into this way of seeing nature. In so far as environmentalism remains modern, it reveals the environment as a nature to be ordered and to be controlled.

In the next chapters I will discuss how we can get out of this epistemological deadlock. But for now it is important to note that Heidegger's own alternative to this modern mode of revealing is deeply influenced by a nostalgic and romantic view, and is even still *modern* at times. We might think of his nationalism here, of course, but there is also a deeper kind of Romanticism and modernism in his epistemological and ethical work.

First, his epistemology is still modern in so far as it presupposes and sets up "nature" as a separate, external entity—for example, when Heidegger writes that 'the revealing that rules in modern technology (. . .) puts to nature the unreasonable demand that it supply energy that can be extracted and stored as such' (p. 14). This is a criticism of a particular modern way of seeing things, yet it remains modern in so far as it assumes that nature is a separate kind of entity, something external to the human. I will soon suggest ways in which we can think differently about the environment.

Moreover, Heidegger is nostalgic and romantic when he discusses the difference between an old windmill with a coal mine and a hydroelectric power

86 *Beyond Nature, Beyond Modernity, Beyond Thinking*

plant. According to him, the old windmill is not suffering under our unreasonable demands since 'its sails do indeed turn in the wind; they are left entirely to the wind's blowing' (p. 14), whereas the earth is treated as 'a coal mining district' (p. 14) and the river is turned into 'a water power supplier' or into 'an object on call for inspection by a tour group ordered there by the vacation industry' (p. 16). But surely the wind is also used by the old wind mill as resource, as a *wind power supplier*? Heidegger is nostalgic about the old wind mill and about 'the old wooden bridge' that joined the banks of the Rhine river before the power plant was built. Perhaps that bridge *was* more beautiful than the power plant. But he remains within modern thinking when he assumes that we have to choose between either rational thinking or poetic thinking, between technology and beauty. (In the next chapter I will question this assumption by discussing Pirsig.)

Second, as suggested above Heidegger is still deeply romantic in his ethics of authenticity. In so far as he asks us to turn *away* from the social and be an authentic *individual*, he is closer to Rousseau than to any of the ancient Greeks he admires. This is especially clear in *Being and Time*, in which Heidegger warns against the danger of conformity and mass existence. On the one hand, Heidegger argues that being-in-the-world is always a being with others, a *Mitsein* (Heidegger 1927, pp. 111–112). This is part of the non-modern dimension of his social philosophy. The world is always already a social world. On the other hand, there is also a strong individualist, modern dimension to *Being and Time* that has enabled Sartre to develop his individualistic existential philosophy, and which has enabled Olafson to read Heidegger as calling for reclaiming our individual responsibility and 'power of individual choice' (Olafson 1994, p. 63; see also Olafson 1998). Indeed, according to Heidegger, it is not only true that existence is always my own, that *I* exist and that no-one can exist in my place (and no-one can die in my place), but we should also try to achieve *authentic* existence and not let "one" (*das Man*) determine our lives for us. It is this part of Heidegger which Olafson has interpreted in terms of individual responsibility and choice. Although this *strong* individualist reading of Heidegger has been (rightly) criticized (see, for example, Carman 1994), and although Heidegger himself writes in *Being and Time* that 'the self is initially and for the most part inauthentic' (Heidegger 1927, p. 170), suggesting that the inauthentic somehow belongs to (the usual way of) being-in-the-world, it is undeniable that Heidegger shares with romantic thinking an emphasis on authenticity and individuality (if not anti-sociality). We may not "initially" be authentic, but authenticity is still the (Romantic) goal of Heidegger's ethics. Rousseau's ghost has not disappeared.

Thus, paradoxically, by his own writing Heidegger shows how difficult it is to leave modern and romantic thinking. But what would it mean to think in a non-modern way? In the next sections, I will discuss three (rather failed) attempts to move into non-modern thinking. For now, we

Beyond *"Nature" and Modernity* 87

can suffice with negating the assumptions mentioned in the beginning of this introduction. This will lead us to thinking about a different conception of "environment".

6.2. FROM NATURE TO (A RELATIONAL CONCEPTION OF) ENVIRONMENT

In order to move towards a non-modern view, we must first question the disenchantment thesis as put forward by Weber and others (Weber 1919), and its related dualistic assumptions. The world was never disenchanted in the first place (see, for example, Szerszinsky 2005a, 2005b). What matters is that we discover its meaning and value (see, for example, Dreyfus & Kelly 2011). The world is not (entirely) of our own making. Ascribing meaning presupposes that the world was "first" a blank slate, whereas it was always related to us (Ingold 2000). We should reject the human-world dualism, the human-nature dualism, and the human-technology dualism implied in modern thinking. The knife we used to describe alienation is itself a tool of alienation. There is no separate world, no distinct "nature", no technology independent from the way we perceive our environment and act in it.

This does not mean that there is no value in contemplating what has not been touched by humans, in contemplating the "inhuman." McKibben may be right in saying that 'the comfort we need is inhuman' (p. 237) if that means that there is indeed value and meaning in contemplating, for example, the night sky, meaning that perhaps can give us comfort—or not. However, our perception when looking at the stars is not "neutral" but shaped by romantic and (as McKibben acknowledges) scientific ways of looking. We project our meaning on the heavens and see patterns. And even if we were to look at the night sky in a non-modern and non-ancient way (thus not even seeing spoons, swords, etc.), it is highly doubtful whether we can really experience the "inhuman"; we always relate to our environment, render it meaningful, and receive meaning from it—we receive, but then *we* 'let it speak'. We discover meaning and observe that what we see is not of our own making, but this is already a way of actively relating to our environment. There is no nature-in-itself, no wilderness-in-itself, no animal-in-itself, and indeed no human-in-itself. In perception and action we are already related to it.

In his environmental aesthetics, Berleant (2005) also prefers the notion of "environment" rather than "nature" since it is more inclusive of both the natural and artificial, built (urban) environment. He thinks that there is no "outside." Let me explain this view and say more about what I take to be his more *relational* view of humans and their environment.

In his phenomenological aesthetics of the environment, Berleant distinguishes between three models of aesthetic experience. The first model is the

88 *Beyond Nature, Beyond Modernity, Beyond Thinking*

contemplative model, which, in line with modern philosophy (e.g. Kant), focuses on the intrinsic qualities of (art) objects and requires an attitude of disinterestedness and epistemic operations of objectification. Berleant writes:

> The objectification of art is the predictable product of an intellectual tradition, one that grasps the world by knowing it through objectifying it, and that controls the world by subduing it to the order of thought.
>
> (Berleant 2005, p. 5)

The antithesis of this model of experience is one that puts more emphasis on the human perceiver. First the Romantics stressed the feeling of the spectator, and then in the 20th century philosophers such as Merleau-Ponty (1945) developed the notion of a lived body, which actively relates to things, people, and places. This means that the environment (and its spaces and landscapes) is no longer seen as a "standing reserve" or (as the Romantics viewed it) as a state of feeling or a state of mind, but as 'an intentional object in association with the perceiving body', as something that is infused by the 'meanings, force, and feelings' of that body (p. 8). This "active" model renders the environment dependent on a perceiving subject. However, Berleant also criticizes *that* model of aesthetic experience and attempts to go beyond it with a *participatory* model. The danger of the focus on the perceiver (and the body) is that we do not sufficiently recognize how the environment shapes us (and the body). He writes: 'Not only is it misleading to objectify the environment; it cannot be taken as a mere reflection of the perceiver, either' (p. 8). Instead, he proposes a model in which there is 'a reciprocal action of organism on environment and environment on organism, and in which there is no sharp demarcation between them' (p. 9). More, the active model recognizes 'the way in which environmental features reach out to affect and respond to the perceiver' (p. 9). The environment invites us to participate, acts upon us. According to Berleant, recognizing this requires us to re-think the notion of "environment." Attempting to cast off dualism, he says that the environment is not 'an alien territory surrounding the self' or—we may add—a kind of mirror that reflects our feelings, but rather 'the medium in which we live, of which our being partakes and comes to identity' (p. 13). This is his description of his non-dualistic view:

> There is no inside and outside, human being and external world, even, in the final reckoning, self and other. The conscious body moving within and as part of a spatio-temporal environmental medium becomes the domain of human experience, the human world, the ground of human reality within which discriminations and distinctions are made. We live, then, in a dynamic nexus of interpenetrating forces to which we contribute and respond.
>
> (Berleant 2005, p. 13)

Beyond "Nature" and Modernity 89

This model enables us to escape objectification: If the environment is 'a field of forces that engages both perceiver and perceived in a dynamic unity', then the environment can no longer be objectified; it is 'continuous with the participant' (p. 14). This is a very different notion of the environment than the idea of a "nature" separate from us.

Moreover, this approach to "environment" also leaves room for including the social. Berleant talks about the aesthetics of the social situation, since 'it is both needless and false to restrict environment to its physical aspects. No environment that we can know and speak about is without a human presence' and in aesthetic experience of the environment 'participants, physical setting, social conditions, along with time, history, and the powerful influence of culture and tradition' are all joined (p. 154).

Note that the existence of human-environment continuity does not mean that the environment cannot be hostile or oppressive; it obviously can be experienced in this way, whether it is the built environment, the social environment, or the natural environment (if we must make such distinctions at all—Berleant's aesthetics tries to avoid this dualistic thinking). But then we have to think of how it can be shaped in a way that renders it more inviting. More: We have the responsibility to shape the environment in such a way that it produces more flourishing—for us and for other beings. If, 'as participants embedded in an experiential field, we cannot stand aloof from our world' (p. 23), then "environmental responsibility" means that we have a responsibility both to ourselves, to others, and to our world. Berleant's environmental aesthetics as an aesthetics of the social situation and an aesthetics of engagement should be coupled with an environmental ethics as a social ethics and an *ethics of engagement*. The notion of "environmental skill" I will develop in this book is meant to contribute to articulating such an ethics.

Note also that acknowledging that there is no separate "nature" and that we are responsible to the environment does not imply that humans should always intervene, that one should never "leave nature alone". But it is good to be aware of the language used here: "Leaving nature alone" presupposes that "nature" is something entirely separate, something that has nothing to do with the human. We have always acted in and upon our environment, and even if we do not intervene in a particular part of the environment, we can only perceive and know it as beings that are already related to it. We are environmental by nature. If we decide to "leave nature alone", this is already a particular way of relating to our environment, a particular way of configuring the human-environment continuity. Moreover, the precise way of relating will depend on what this "leaving alone" implies (e.g. the creation of a reserve, having regulations that forbid humans to go in a particular area, etc.) but this will always imply a particular human-environment relation (and indeed human-human) relation and particular human meanings, which today are usually still colored by romantic or scientific ways of thinking. Important for environmental ethics is to avoid "leaving alone"

90 *Beyond Nature, Beyond Modernity, Beyond Thinking*

if this means that we remain disinterested or if we engage again in some kind of management and control (techno-scientific approach) or that we (ab)use "nature" or the "wild" as a mere resource for self-constitution, and to think about other ways of relating to our environment. Non-intervention in particular environmental situations may be part of this, but not under the description of "leaving nature alone". We cannot leave "nature" alone and "nature" cannot leave us alone. In a sense, we *are* the environment. As Berleant puts it:

> Marcel urged us to say not that I have a body but rather that I am my body. So we can say, similarly, not that I live in my environment but that I am my environment.
>
> (Berleant 2005, p. 13)

In addition, I think it is, in part, in becoming an environmentally better person—and a better person *tout court*—that we are confronted with, and engage with, reality. But the real should not be confused with the natural. To call the real the natural and vice versa is one particular construction and interpretation of the real, and has the scientific and/or romantic connotations discussed earlier. Reality has to do with our social and physical environment, is about the relation between a person and her environment, and to talk about the natural as the real (or the real as the natural) is already one way of perceiving and shaping that relation. Thus, it may be bad to slip out of touch with reality, or better with specific realities, but this is not necessarily the same as getting out of touch with "nature". Note also that the real has nothing to do with physical versus computer-generated: What we call "virtual reality" may well be (very) real in some respects. Virtual environments can be part of the real, just as any other environment can. The real can come in various shapes. A particular virtual environment is one kind of way we might encounter the real. This connects back to Berleant's thinking:

> This computer-generated 'virtual' world is not entirely new, for we also encounter so-called virtuality outside the computer. Consider the distinctive spatio-temporal-dynamic environments of memory, of history, of imagination, of letter-writing, of the telephone, and of each of the different arts, especially fiction and film. Each of these perceptual environments constructs its own mode of actuality or reality, and the electronic environment of cyberspace is different only in kind and not ontologically. [. . .] To paraphrase Hegel, the real is the virtual and the virtual is the real. [. . .] 'Reality', then, is multiple—'realities'. Following Spinoza, we can affirm that there is one world but that it can assume many different modes. The electronic world is neither more real nor less real that the world of dreams or the world of daily activities.
>
> (Berleant 2005, p. 73)

Furthermore, we can add to Berleant's view that there is not *one* "virtual world" or "electronic world" but many electronic worlds. I propose that we subscribe to a radical ontological and epistemological pluralism when it comes to understanding both "environment" and "the real."

Moreover, today we do not live *either* in electronic environments *or* in physical environments; electronic technologies have re-shaped experience and environment in such a way that both kind of environments merge. Again, an inclusive, radically pluralist definition of "environment" can cope with this: Our environment is at the same time physical, electronic, social, natural, and so on.

That said, it may be the case that many current computer-mediated interactions and many current electronic environments do not sufficiently confront us with what we call "the real"—for example, in the sense that they are not sufficiently inviting, do not give enough opportunities for engagement, and tend to mirror our (imagined) self rather than enriching our experience and identity—and that actively relating to our natural and social environment in other ways (but not necessarily excluding the use of electronic devices) provides us with more opportunities to face and engage with the real. But if we make claims like this we should specify what we mean by "the real" in these cases or, even better, avoid ontological talk and better define what it is, exactly, that is problematic in particular human-environmental situations and interactions.

Second, a relational view does not only mean that the world is intrinsically related to us, but also that we are intrinsically related to the world and that there is no "authentic" self separated from the physical-social-environments we live in. This means that our rationalist and romantic ideals of individuality and authenticity can no longer be upheld: Neither absolute individual autonomy nor original individual authenticity is possible. What we become is shaped by our "being environmental" and is based on the dynamic human-environment continuity described above. Neither are absolute individual autonomy or authenticity desirable. Ethically speaking, we should not aim to separate ourselves from others and from the world, but rather to connect with them. We are authors and creators, for sure, but at the same time we are also being "written" and shaped.

Third, the social is not a separate and artificial construct, but is something "given" that grows with and in relation to us. It is neither entirely makeable (designable), as the modern rationalist wishes it to be, nor should it be rejected as "inauthentic", as the romantic does. If we must use the term "nature" at all, the social is also "natural", and we can only grow as social beings, as beings in relation to others. There is no authenticity in absence of the social. We are always environmental, and, as I have argued above, "environment" always includes the social. As Rousseau's late works show, even if we write in physical isolation from others, we always write as social beings, who care about what others say ('Jean-Jacques' is solitary

92 *Beyond Nature, Beyond Modernity, Beyond Thinking*

but writes as if he is judged by others and justifies himself to others), and what others say is not the source of evil but, as the Humean and Deweyan philosophical traditions teach, (a necessary) part of our moral development and an inescapable part of coping with our environment—that is, of coping with ourselves.

In the next chapter(s), I hope to further elaborate this non-modern, relational view of environment and environmental ethics by using the concept of "skill". I will also explain how such a view can better deal with the problem of motivation. But in order to prepare the ground for that work, let me first briefly discuss some views that may present themselves as alternatives to modern thinking about the environment but that are not truly non-modern or are problematic in other ways. This will also enable me to further develop the analysis of modernity offered in the previous chapters.

6.3. (DEEP) ECOLOGICAL THINKING

Can ecology help us to reach a less modern, more relational view? Ecology provides a more relational view but fails to solve the problem of alienation if it comes in the form of (1) ecology as *science* or in the form of (2) ecology as a *romantic* view. Both forms of ecology assume that there is a "nature" out there (an ecological system or Mother Earth). This is still an alienating way of thinking, which leads to alienating ways of doing. The same is true for ecological thinking as a *metaphysics*, which comes as a system of propositions about the world. Although "standing back" or "taking distance" is always part of human existence (we *ek-sist*, to say it in a Heideggerian way—see also (other) thinkers in the tradition of German philosophical anthropology) and hence a kind of *existential* alienation cannot be avoided, (1) the very business of philosophy conceived of as a metaphysics is itself alienating and (2) particular kinds of metaphysics are more alienating than others. Can environmental ethics escape from alienating metaphysics and from a scientific or romantic approach—that is, can it really escape from a *modern* approach? Let us take a look at the 'deep ecology' tradition, in particular Næss and Leopold, and at literature on environmental philosophy and modernity.

First, 'deep ecology' might seem to be a non-modern alternative. Articulated by Næss in the 1970s, the 'deep ecology' movement was a reaction against the "shallow" ecology movement which focused on the fight against pollution and resource depletion, and was therefore mainly concerned with 'the health and affluence of people in the developed countries' (Næss 1973, p. 95). The deep ecology movement instead holds a deeper, *relational* view, which promotes an altogether different metaphysics than the one that is common in the West. Rejecting atomism and individualism, it sees organisms as knots in fields of 'intrinsic relations', by which Næss means that

Beyond "Nature" and Modernity 93

the relation constitutes the things. Without the relation, the things 'are no longer the same things' (p. 95).

This conception of relationality is very non-modern indeed. However, in Næss' view there are at least two aspects that remain highly modern. First, as remarked before (Chapter 3), the principle of 'biospheric egalitarianism' he endorses is very *modern* since it (1) stands in the tradition of Enlightenment principles (the revolutionary principle of equality) and (2) as a (modern) rationalist ethical principle it presupposes that we need (rational) principles in order to (be motivated to) act. Leopold's land ethic, which endorses the principle that 'a thing is right when it tends to preserve the integrity, stability, and beauty of the biotic community. It is wrong when it tends otherwise' (Leopold 1949, p. 225) is vulnerable to the same objections.

Second, in so far as Næss' 'deep ecology' view requires that we identify with nature, that we enlarge the boundaries of our self, it still stands in the modern—in particular, *Romantic*—tradition. As Brennan and Lo correctly observe:

> One clear historical antecedent to this kind of nature spiritualism is the romanticism of Jean-Jacques Rousseau as expressed in his last work, the *Reveries of the Solitary Walker*.
>
> (Brennan & Lo 2008)

Brennan and Lo do not explain why they think this is so, but in light of the previous chapter we can say why: The nature lover is supposed to reconnect to nature by enlarging her self, that is, the self is the starting point and is inflated to contain the whole of nature. This is the mechanism of Rousseauistic, romantic reverie, which has a strong idealist dimension to it.[1] Thus, while the philosophy of 'deep ecology' is non-modern since it promotes relational thinking, it is not "deep" enough and not non-modern enough in so far as it is committed to (a) modern principles and modern principle-oriented ethics and (b) a romantic conception of self-expansion.

Second, as Callicott has shown, the 'land ethic' involves a particular kind of metaphysics. For instance, the very notion of 'intrinsic value' is 'frankly metaphysical' (Callicott 1989, p. 136). But is this only a 'virtue', as Callicott thinks? In so far as the land ethic remains a metaphysics, and perhaps partly *because* it mainly comes in the form of a metaphysics, this version of deep ecology does not sufficiently motivate us. This does not mean that I object to articulating and discussing the world views that underlie our attitudes to the environment; in fact, this is also part of what I do in this book and I think Callicott and others have done an excellent job. For example, Callicott discusses the 'Judeo-Christian religious belief system', which sets 'man apart from the rest of creation' (p. 137); 'holistic rationalism', the views of traditional American Indian peoples; and other views. But given the problem identified in the beginning of this book, we must pay more attention to the moral-psychological problem of motivation.[2]

94 *Beyond Nature, Beyond Modernity, Beyond Thinking*

6.4. NEW NATURES

In response to the previous criticisms, one could present a "truly" non-modern view. However, in order to do that we first have to better understand the modern view. So far, I have treated modernity as a condition. But it is also interesting to look at it as a process. Let me present the following interpretation of the history of modernity as a process of self-alienation.

The problem with modernity is that we always want to gain more control over our environment. This leads to the following "dialectic" process. In order to gain more control (science and technology), we create a new nature[3]. But then we become nostalgic about the old nature (Romanticism), from which we feel alienated. If we want to break this vicious circle, the only way forward is to try to make ourselves at home in the new nature. Once this is achieved, however, we create yet another nature since as long as we think in a modern way, we are not content: We are still after more control and the new. This creates a new romantic reaction. For example, whereas before in the mechanical age people were nostalgic about agrarian times, in the information age they are becoming nostalgic about the mechanical age.[4] The only way to stop this regress, it seems, is to restrain our meta-desire to gain more control. But this is another kind of meta-control; therefore, it cannot be a remedy for our desire for control.

This analysis—which is not meant as a (neo-)Hegelian theory but as a hermeneutic tool to better understand modernity—helps us to better understand how modern alienation works and indeed how modern *environmentalism* works. It seems that present-day environmentalism, in so far as it is caught up in modern thinking about technology and the environment, does only superficially deal with problems and fails to re-think our more fundamental relation to the environment and to technology as shaped by modern culture. Modern environmentalism remains obsessed with control. For example, in climate ethics discussions it is usually assumed that we should re-gain control over spaceship earth by controlling human activities (regulation) and by controlling and transforming nature (new technologies). The narrative is that Nature, partly because our own doings, has gone out of control, and now control has to be restored: control over nature and control over human activities.[5] In the next section I start to explore an alternative, non-modern attitude and approach.

6.5. MYSTICISM AND *GELASSENHEIT*

If we want to construe a non-modern view, there are at least the following two traps that should carefully be avoided. First, a non-dualistic theory could lead to contemplation at the expense of real involvement with the world. We can have the "insight" or "vision" that subject and object merge; we can "see" or "feel" the ultimate unity of the world. But (this kind of) mysticism does not necessarily lead to environmental action. It takes too much distance; it promotes an attitude of disinterestedness and non-involvement. Second, to stop control (see the previous section), we could follow Heidegger's advice to let-go (*Gelassenheit*). However, at first sight this seems to amount to non-activity. It seems that the alternative to control is doing nothing, apathy. The same can be said of the Taoist concept of *wuwei*, usually translated as "non-doing" or "non-action". But these are inadequate interpretations of Heidegger and Taoism—even if is true that some Taoists have withdrawn from society.

A better interpretation of Heidegger's term *Gelassenheit* is that we should act, but without becoming trapped in the modern obsession with control. We are environmental beings and we actively transform our environment as much as we are transformed by it. But this does not necessarily imply that we should aim for total control of the environment (and indeed for total social control and total self-control), that we should act in a way that treats "environment" as something that is external to us and that can and must be managed, and that we should always think in an objectifying way.

A better interpretation of *wuwei* is effortless action or going with the flow, without a sense of self and without the need for rules. Interpreted in this way, it is a non-alienating and non-dualist concept and takes us to the next chapter, where I will explore and articulate a way of thinking that moves beyond an exclusive focus on *logos*, but is at the same time also very practical and material—indeed, not only a way of thinking and talking but also and especially a way of *doing*. This way of doing might be *gelassen* but not in a Stoic, apathetic sense. It might be a form of *wuwei* but then very active indeed.

NOTES

1. See also the feminist critique of deep ecology.
2. In this respect, Callicott's discussion of the sentimentalist tradition (Hume and others), which *also* can be found in *In Defense of the Land Ethic*, is more interesting. I already referred to Callicott's discussion of the moral psychology of Hume in Chapter 4. However, I will not further discuss this here and continue to explore (other) non-modern alternatives.
3. Note that this idea of "new natures" goes further than Bookchin's social ecology (see, for instance, Bookchin 1980) and philosophical discourse about culture as "second nature": In contrast to Bookchin, it questions the very distinction between a 'first', physical nature and a 'second' cultural nature. The 'first' nature is already seen through our modern glasses—for example, romantic ones. We have no access to a 'nature' independent from human perception and involvement.
4. See also shifting points of reference when we talk about the landscape: Most of us do not want to return to a pre-agrarian landscape but to an agrarian one. In the future we might start to miss industrial landscapes.
5. Note that in modernity we tell a similar narrative about technology.

7 Beyond Environmental *Thinking* (1)
Skilled Engagement

INTRODUCTION

In the previous chapter I have discussed several routes towards a non-modern, relational environmental ethics that is less alienating than its rationalist and romantic alternatives. It turned out that it is difficult to leave behind modern thinking, since attempts to construct such an approach easily slide back into detached and dualistic modes of thinking, usually either (1) Socratic or Stoic self-control and Enlightenment reason and science or (2) Romanticism. For example, ecological and mystical forms of environmental thinking turned out to be rather "unstable" in this way. And according to the brief history of self-alienation I sketched, we can take contemplative distance from the regress described (we continue to create new "natures"), yet it seems that within the modern view we have no way of thinking available that can really stop the regress, since we continue to crave for (meta-)control, and maybe also for metaphysics.

But perhaps these efforts to move towards a different way of *thinking* are themselves part of the problem. They seem to presuppose that to change our relation to our environment we have to change our *thinking* about the environment, and that once our thinking changes, our practices will also change. In this chapter I will question this presupposition and try to articulate the notion of a less contemplative, less detached, and more engaging way of relating to our environment, one that moves beyond environmental *thinking*—at least if thinking is conceived of as a "mental" activity removed from concrete embodied practice. In particular, I will use the notion of "environmental skill" to sketch a non-Stoic and non-romantic route to a non-modern environmental ethics, which sees skilled activity rather than detached thinking as the way environmental change can happen. In the next chapters, I will then explore what this means for our practices.

Let me start with revisiting Socrates' argument about knowledge and the good.

7.1. SOCRATES' ARGUMENT REVISITED: FROM THEORY TO PRACTICE AND SKILL

In Chapter 2 I first considered Socrates' view that knowledge of the good is sufficient for a good life, but then soon dismissed it and turned to modern moral psychology. But maybe this dismissal came too soon. Socrates' view that moral knowledge is sufficient for moral action must be rejected only if we understand "knowledge" as theoretical knowledge. This was Socrates' and Plato's assumption, but it need not be ours. There is also a different kind of knowledge, which Dewey indicated with the term "know-how" and which Dreyfus has articulated as *skilled* knowledge[1]. Let me explain this alternative moral epistemology and explore what it teaches us about environmental good and what it implies for the problem of environmental motivation.

In *Human Nature and Conduct*, Dewey makes a distinction between knowing how and knowing that, and argues that we '*know how* by means of our habits' (Dewey 1922, p. 177; Dewey's emphasis). In the latter case, knowledge is not theoretical but a matter of practical skill and habit. If we have *that* kind of knowledge, the claim that knowing good equals good makes sense: If we know how to do good, this means that we live the kind of life in which we acquire that kind of know-how, that we live a good life, and this is all that is required, ethically speaking.

If we adopt this view, then the problem of motivation identified at the beginning of this book is indeed due to a lack of knowledge, albeit not a lack of theoretical knowledge, but a lack of *know-how*. Theoretical knowledge alone does not motivate; paradoxically, we have to *move* in order to become more motivated. Becoming more "environmentally good" is possible by active and skillful relating to, and engaging with, our environment. Our task is not so much to gain more theoretical knowledge but rather to develop better habits.

In this way we directly tackle the underlying problem that emerged in the previous chapters: alienation. By skillful engagement with our environment, we can move beyond modern thinking (Enlightenment reason or romantic feeling) and beyond interpretations of non-duality that also detach us from our environment. Rather than reasoning *about* the environment or having feelings *about* the environment, we act and think in a relational, environmental way. We form and develop environmental habits that need no abstract "objective" thinking or "inner" feelings. If it is a way of thinking, it is a practical one that is directly related to the problems reality gives us. If it is a feeling and an imagination, it is a feeling and an imagination that is literally *in touch* with the environment, with its physicality and its materiality.

Indeed, this conception of habit also implies that technology and materiality are not separate from, but part of, and presupposed by, habit and

98 *Beyond Nature, Beyond Modernity, Beyond Thinking*

skilled activity. Dewey writes that habits 'involve skill of sensory and motor organs, cunning or craft, and objective materials', requiring 'manifest technique'. Habits and skilled engagement are relational by nature. He writes:

> We should laugh at any one who said that he was master of stone working, but that the art was cooped up within himself and in no wise dependent upon support from objects and assistance from tools.
>
> (Dewey 1922, p. 15)

Thus, this conception of environmental skill is not technology-averse, but rather recognizes that our engagement with the world is always already technological. (I will return to this issue in Chapter 10.)

In Dreyfus' work on skill, we find a similar moral epistemology, which can help us to further articulate this environmental ethics as an ethics of skill. Hubert and Stuart Dreyfus have argued that expertise is a matter of skill acquisition rather than knowing-that (Dreyfus & Dreyfus 1991), and this can also be applied to moral expertise. Moral knowledge must be conceptualized in terms of skill and habit. We are always already embodied and engaged in practices when we encounter a moral problem. Increasing moral knowledge is a matter of building practical know-how, of learning good ways of doing and developing good habits. For environmental ethics, this means that doing environmental good is a matter of knowing how to act in particular situations, in concrete contexts where moral problems arise. This requires moral experience, which crystallizes not so much in the form of moral principles but in the form of skills and habits, which give us the required moral perception, the right kind of comportment, and ability to improvise in new situations.

A similar argument has been made in (relation to) cognitive science. For example, based on earlier work in cognitive science (Varela et al. 1991) but also on Dewey and on Eastern thought (Confucianism, Taoism, and Buddhism), Varela has argued that ethical expertise is a matter of know-how: To do what is ethical is not a matter of following abstract rules, but about 'savoir faire', a practical coping and development of habits, the execution of which is the result of unconscious processes (Varela 1999). Again this implies that becoming "environmentally" better is a matter of finding a better way of doing, of training better habits, of developing the right kind of know-how, of good bodily engagement with materiality and physicality. It is not sufficient to know environmental ethics *theory* and ethical *principles*; what is needed is training the right kinds of habits and the right kinds of experiences: We need practical wisdom[2]. We know-that we should change our lives, but we don't know how, and we will continue to lack this know-how if we do not develop the right kind of skills and habits.

This focus on know-how and its ethical significance goes against old and strong currents in Western thinking that either place more value on contemplation than on action (see also the previous chapter), or that prefer activities having to do with the "head" and with *logos* (words, arguments, discourse)

Beyond Environmental Thinking *(1)*   99

over activities that have to do with the "hands", the "body", and with material things. Examples of the latter, dualist view can be found in ancient Greek philosophy—for example, in Socrates/Plato and Aristotle—but also in 20th century philosophy—for example, in Hannah Arendt's *The Human Condition* (1958).

Arendt makes a sharp distinction between three kinds of activities: political action, work, and labour. The first kind of activity concerns action (*praxis*) and speech (*lexis*), and she takes care to sharply distinguish this domain from work and labour, which are concerned with materiality (work) and with the metabolism of nature (labour). The political realm is the realm of freedom; the other activities, the domain of necessity. The latter are activities concerned with 'the maintenance of life' (p. 28). In the sphere of the household (*oikos*) happens the 'prepolitical': 'mastering the necessities of life in the household was the condition for freedom of the *polis*' (p. 31), for attaining the good life. It seems that in this view, skilled engagement belongs to the "lower" activities. Skilled activity is seen as "work", which in Arendt is curiously divorced from *praxis*.

Against this view, we can invoke Arendt's own more positive view of (material) things: they can also gather us and therefore play an important role in the polis. She writes:

> To live together in the world means essentially that a world of things is between those who have it in common, as a table is located between those who sit around it; (. . .) What makes mass society so difficult to bear is not the number of people involved (. . .) but the fact that the world between them has lost its power to gather them together, to relate and separate them.
>
> (Arendt 1958, pp. 52–53)

Thus, even in Arendt's view, things can also have a more positive, social function. Things help to make the social happen and sustain it. In this sense, they can help to reduce social alienation. But Arendt neglects a second role things can have: By skillfully relating to things, we can also reduce alienation from our environment—"natural" or "material". Thus, we could say that things and humans do not only relate in a "passive" way; by actively relating to things we may overcome environmental alienation. Political praxis as speech may "liberate" us from our environment, but how "liberating" can it be if it is also at the same time an alienation, an alienation from our daily dealings with the bodily and the earthly? By transcending the sphere of "necessity" and moving to the sphere of more abstract "political action", we also remove a crucial condition of possibility for flourishing: skilled activity and lived experience. To re-enforce Dreyfus' view again: It is only through true skilled engagement that we can really attain knowledge and wisdom—including knowledge of the good life and knowledge of the environment and of environmental good.

100 *Beyond Nature, Beyond Modernity, Beyond Thinking*

To conclude, if this is what true knowledge and expertise is, then the idea that knowledge of good equates (being and doing) good makes sense. If we knew *how* to do environmental good, then this knowledge would imply that we would be *doing* environmental good (and, especially, we would *have been* doing environmental good), since knowledge of the former could not be acquired without the practice and the experience of the latter. Moreover, as I will show in the next section, skilled activity and lived experience are not only (necessary conditions of) being ethically good, they also seem intrinsically motivating and meaningful. If this is true, it supports the conclusion that now we have found a way to solve the problem of environmental motivation: We do not need to be moved from the "outside"—for instance, by ethical principles or by a theory of environmental ethics[3]—instead, we have to move ourselves, grasp our environment, and learn to skillfully engage with it.

This seems to provide a good alternative to the alienating, disengaging ways of relating to the environment we discussed in the previous chapters. The turn to an epistemology and psychology of practical know-how and skill serves to literally "revive" environmental ethics. It turns from abstract knowledge of environment problems "out there" to the lived experience and engagement with the environment. (And as we will see in Chapter 10, this turn to skill avoids at least two types of alienation mentioned by Marx in the Paris manuscripts: alienation from the product of one's work and alienation from others.)

Let me further unpack and develop this view by relating it to recent philosophical literature on the value of skill and manual work.

7.2. FIREPLACES, WHEELS, MOTORCYCLES, MEALS, AND PATIENTS: COPING WITH THINGS

In *All Things Shining* (2011), Dreyfus and Kelly explore the roots of (what we experience as) our loss of meaning. They mention 'the Greek discovery of detached, embodied access to timeless, universal truth', which influenced Augustine, who uses bodily metaphors but 'cannot resist the Platonic pull to the abstract' and treats 'sensuous, bodily experiences entirely in terms of the inner states they bring about' (p. 116). After an interesting interpretation of Dante, they continue their history of ideas with usual suspects such as Descartes and Kant. Since Descartes we have come to understand ourselves as self-contained, 'almost infinitely free assigners of meaning who can give whatever meaning we choose to the meaningless objects around us' (p. 139) and since Kant we think that we should give the law to ourselves (p. 140). The result, according to the authors, is that we have been put on a direct road to nihilism.

In response to this nihilism, Dreyfus and Kelly—in a truly romantic spirit—propose to re-enchant the world, and their particular vision is a

Beyond Environmental Thinking *(1)* 101

(poly)theistic one: 'The ultimate story of the universe is not that it is indifferent to us (. . .). A whole pantheon of gods is really there' (p. 185). Rejecting 'a self-conception that destroys the possibility of a meaningful and worthwhile existence' (p. 204), they point to moments when 'the sacred shines' (p. 194), to contemporary versions of 'the whooshing up of a shining Achilles in the midst of battle' (p. 201)—for example, at a sports event.

However, they also point to another antidote to nihilism, which I think can help us to move not only beyond cold Enlightenment reason and its nihilistic tendencies, but—as I will further argue below—*also beyond the romantic response to it*. Dreyfus and Kelly show that *skilled activity* can counter alienation by giving meaning to what we do. Rejecting Nietzsche's solution to nihilism—'to become gods ourselves' (p. 46), they argue that by engaging in skilled activities, we can come to discern the meanings that are already there in the world (p. 209) and we can learn to care for things rather than treating them as 'a mere resource' (p. 217)—something Heidegger warned in his later work and something Marx warned (see Chapter 10). The authors write about the craftsman who sees how the wood 'will respond to an axe' (p. 208) and claim that the craftsman does not generate meaning but discerns 'meanings that are *already* there' (p. 209).

Dreyfus and Kelly make some suggestions that might help us to see what this would mean for our contemporary lives: They give not only the example of the historical craftsman (the wheelwright) who achieves 'intimacy' with the material and feels respect for it (p. 210), but they also criticize a contemporary technology: GPS navigation, which they argue makes us lose our sensitivities (see also Chapter 8). (I think a much more nuanced view of contemporary technology is needed here; I will say more about technology below.)

But skilled activity is not only important to give meaning to our lives; it is also important for moral *motivation*. Let me explain this.

As Dreyfus and Kelly say, 'it is hard to imagine how reason alone can motivate a person to act' (p. 96). But what *can* motivate a person? Although the authors make an argument about meaning rather than motivation, we might turn to the kind of Humean-romantic vision they propose as an answer to nihilism: a romantization of Greek wonder and religious culture, and a celebration of contemporary ways of being 'swept up into public and shareable moods' (p. 60). Such a collective feeling could indeed motivate. But we are not ancient Greeks; we have to live with the heritage of the Enlightenment and cannot easily turn to polytheism as an answer to nihilism. We cannot simply leave the modern order, which—in contrast to what the authors suggest—already gives meaning to our lives and gives us the distinctions "in" which we think. How *can* we develop a 'vibrant' polytheism (p. 223) after the Enlightenment and, more generally, in modernity?

Moreover, the mood Dreyfus and Kelly recommend could hardly motivate us into being more (actively) connected to the environment. Even if and when it is not dangerous in the way the authors describe, it remains

102 *Beyond Nature, Beyond Modernity, Beyond Thinking*

a kind of collective reverie, a collective fantasy. In the arena, no-one cares about what is really going on outside of the mood. Even on the playing field, someone could be torn apart. Such is Greek rapture, especially in its Dionysian form, and such is romantic rapture—for example, in its nationalist or "hooliganist" form. When we are in the mood, there is no longer an environment; there are no others. There is only our inflated, individual or collective neo-romantic self. This epistemic hooliganism is the real danger of the 'shining' Dreyfus and Kelly describe and has the effect of making the environment disappear.

However, if we consider again Dreyfus' view of knowledge, there is another, better solution to the problem of motivation. Skilled activity can do what feeling is not always able to do: It can connect us with our environment in an active, responsive way. As I already argued, skilled engagement cannot only create meaning; it can also *motivate* us. I will further develop this idea in the next pages, where I will also elaborate my criticism of Romanticism (see the next section). But in order to articulate an "ethics of skill", let me first continue my overview of authors who question contemporary processes of de-skilling.

In *Shop Class as Soulcraft* (2009) Crawford complains that our daily devices resist skillful engagement: By being 'unintelligible to direct inspection' they discourage repair. In response to the alienating experience of doing an office job, he advises us to develop manual competence and offers the example of his experience as a motorcycle mechanic. He argues that skilled activity involves 'a handling, using, and taking care of things which has its own kind of knowledge' (Crawford 2009, p. 69), which makes us more involved, attentive, and caring. Contemporary technology disburdened us of 'mental and bodily involvement' but 'this disburdening gives us few occasions for the experience of direct responsibility' (p. 56), and for the education of the will, instead according to Crawford the will needs to be educated 'so that it no longer resembles that of a raging baby who knows only that he wants' (p. 60). Yet in spite of defending some kind of idea of self-reliance and self-mastery, Crawford rejects a particular idea of autonomy: One that 'denies that we are born into a world that existed prior to us. (. . .) For in fact we are basically dependent beings: one upon another, and each on a world that is not of our own making' (p. 208).

Thus the answer to contemporary alienation and to the "raging baby" consumerism, which we know (at least theoretically; this is *knowing-that*) to be detrimental to our environment *and* to the quality of our human lives, is not necessarily motorcycle repair but, more generally, skillful engagement with things and with our environment.

In *The Craftsman* (2008) Sennett gives many examples of craftsmanship in a wider sense, including examples from cooking, medicine, and music. What matters is that we make and use things we understand, and which require 'making connections between head and hand' (p. 9): as Dreyfus would agree, skill is grounded in physical, bodily practice (p. 10).

Beyond Environmental Thinking *(1)*   103

This connection is lost in "design", when things are made in conception before they are constructed (p. 42), since tactile experience and relational understanding are lost. Like Dreyfus, he notes that the higher stages of skill involve 'tacit knowledge' (p. 50).

This kind of work is also good in an ethical sense. Sennett argues that skilled work produces excellence (*arête*) since it is 'quality-driven' (p. 24). And importantly for the purpose of this book: Sennett suggests that such work is intrinsically *motivating* since 'the satisfactions of working are their own reward' (Mills quoted in Sennett 2008, p. 27). He quotes Dewey's *Democracy and Education* to support his view that work and play are 'intrinsically motivating' but only become 'labor when the consequences are outside of the activity' (pp. 287–88). Command, extreme division of labour, and competition, by contrast, are demoralizing. He also refers to Adam Smith's observation that people who perform only simple operations become 'stupid' and 'ignorant' (see also the Marxist de-skilling thesis). Skilled work instead helps us to better understand the world, to experience wonder (p. 211), to develop our personality—for example, to become more patient (p. 220); to learn from resistance, as Dewey already advised us (p. 226); and to improvise.

Moreover, the workshop is a social space (p. 73). Like Crawford, Sennett stresses that skilled work also involves and promotes a form of working together, a particular kind of social relation. Thus, we may conclude from Sennett, skilled manual work does not only avoid alienation from things, but also alienation from others. Even if we may not want to return to the model of the medieval guilds, described by Sennett in detail, we are encouraged to think about novel forms of sociality that might emerge from (or that perhaps *already* have emerged from) cooperative skilled work broadly conceived.

Finally, it is worth noting that skilled work leads to absorption, a kind of 'focal awareness' (Polanyi) that renders us 'no longer self-aware' (p. 174). In concentration, we work on something and we forget our selves. A similar phenomenon has been described in psychology by Csikszentmihalyi: We can experience a kind of 'flow', a state of consciousness in which people experience total involvement, which occurs typically in high-challenge, high-skill situations (Csikszentmihalyi 1990). For Western people burdened by (post) Christian and romantic demands to think about themselves, this amounts to a kind of liberation. The self is no longer a barrier; there is better interaction with the environment.

But although Sennett presents an attractive and compelling view of skilled work, he risks returning to the *logos*-centred views from which these reflections on skill could liberate us when he says that 'the dialogue with material objects begins' (p. 269) and that 'material reality talks back' (p. 272). Thus he makes it seem as if the only way we can reflect on our experiences with skilled work is by framing them in the language of discourse: 'dialogue', 'talk'. In this way, he draws the experience back into the realm of *logos*.

104   *Beyond Nature, Beyond Modernity, Beyond Thinking*

Moreover, Sennett draws upon Arendt's distinction between political action and "labor" (see, for example, p. 7), but, remarkably, "making" is left out of view, whereas Arendt"s category of "making" seems much closer to the skilled activity Sennett recommends. This awkward use of Arendt renders his analysis less sensitive to the highly important difference here between, on the one hand, skilled work (*techne*, which I argue should not be removed from praxis) and, on the other hand, de-skilled labour (the negative consequences of which Marx and others rightly objected to).

In any case, what emerges here in Dreyfus, Dreyfus & Kelly, Crawford, and Sennett is a coherent argument about the value of skilled manual work as a direct engagement with materiality and as illustrating a different kind of knowledge. After a critical interpretation of their writings and after expanding their thesis to direct engagement with our *environment*, we arrive at a route towards a solution of the problem of environmental motivation. The emphasis on moral knowledge that emerges from concrete engagement with things, with materiality, and with others enables us to take distance from approaches to environmental ethics that focus theoretical reason. But does it also enable us to take distance from Romanticism, and how?

7.3. BEYOND ROMANTICISM

7.3.1. Borgmann

In my discussion of Dreyfus and Kelly I already criticized the romantic aspect of their views. In order to take more distance from Romanticism, let us now compare Dreyfus and Kelly to Borgmann's 'device paradigm'.

Dreyfus and Kelly seem to agree with Borgmann that devices make life easy for us, but that in doing so they also tend to remove the possibility for meaningful, skilled engagement. In the 1980s Borgmann already recommended skilled activity in response to technologies that seem to disengage us. By using the term 'device paradigm' (Borgmann 1984), he argued that our technologies have become 'devices' that are hidden in the background. They are available. This is too bad for us, since although they give us more comfort, they also withhold opportunities for skilled engagement with the technology, with our environment, and with others who share the same practice (note again both the environmental and social aspect). (And, in addition, we might say with Rousseau that the availability of goods and devices makes us into spoiled children.) Borgmann advised us to instead engage in 'focal practices' that are more "natural" and require a practice. He gave the example of a wood-burning stove (from the past), the warmth of which was 'not instantaneous'. Instead, it required work: 'work, some skills, and attention were constantly required to build and sustain' the fire (p. 41). In addition, 'it was a *focus*, a hearth, a place that gathered the work and leisure of a family and gave the house a center', providing for the family 'a regular and bodily engagement with the rhythm of the seasons' (pp. 41–2).

Beyond Environmental Thinking *(1)*   105

Like Dreyfus, Borgmann highlights the value of skill and engagement in this "things' world", but also points to the social and character dimension. He continues:

> Physical engagement is not simply physical contact, but the experience of the world through the manifold sensibility of the body. Skill is intensive and refined world engagement. Skill, in turn, is bound up with social engagement. It molds the person and gives the person character.
>
> (Borgmann 1984, p. 42)

Thus, here world engagement, social engagement, and virtue are entangled: More skilled engagement with things means also (1) more and better engagement with people and (2) becoming a better person (I will return to the latter point at the end of this chapter and in the next chapter). But what kind of things should we engage with then? What kinds of practices are better than others? Borgmann distinguishes between, on the one hand, focal practices such as gathering around a stove or drinking wine together and, on the other hand, (use of) modern technology that is captive of what he calls the 'device paradigm' (Borgmann 1984). He claims that the latter lets us engage less with the world and involves a kind of de-skilling: 'The machinery makes no demands on our skill, strength, or attention, and it is less demanding the less it makes its presence felt' (Borgmann 1984, p. 42).

This view makes sense given what has been said about the epistemic and ethical role of skilled engagement so far. However, both Dreyfus and Borgmann remain somewhat romantic in their vision of engaging, skilled activities and technologies. They seem to presuppose that there are "authentic" ways of doing and living, and in articulating these ways of living they are rather *nostalgic*. The examples of the wheelwright (Dreyfus & Kelly) and the stove (Borgmann), as well as their corresponding rejection of contemporary information technology, are very telling. Their examples all too easily suggest that we recreate a world similar to the world William Morris imagined in the 19th century (that is, *pre*-industrial society as imagined by people of the Arts and Crafts movement living in the industrial age) or the "Greek" world Heidegger imagined in the 20th century (Heidegger's ancient Greece, full of myth and wonder, imagined in the time of the atomic bomb).[4]

But is all modern, industrial technology necessarily bad? And is all contemporary *information technology* necessarily disengaging? Neither Borgmann nor Dreyfus enable us to ask these questions since they start from Heidegger's generalizing of "technology"—as if all things are necessarily part of a modern way of thinking and doing. Furthermore, examples of "good" and "bad" technology often appear to be chosen arbitrarily. Crawford criticises the Arts and Crafts movement for promoting 'spiritualized, symbolic modes of craft practice' that paved the way for 'therapeutic self-absorption' (p. 29), but tends to romanticize the *mechanical* age when he a priori rejects the idea that the internet may be a place for skilled activity

106 *Beyond Nature, Beyond Modernity, Beyond Thinking*

and human flourishing. But why is this a crazy idea by definition? Should we not evaluate particular (internet) technologies and particular uses of those technologies, and then judge which are alienating?

Sennett better manages to avoid romantic thinking. Although his response to this kind of thinking is largely inexplicit and certainly unsystematic, he makes some interesting claims—usually influenced by pragmatism. He says that we should not 'seek escape in idealized Nature' but confront 'the self-destructive territory we have actually made' (Sennett 2008, p. 13) and 'understand our own labors as part of [Nature's] being' (p. 15). Interestingly, he also writes that since both the ancient potter and the modern programmer are experiencing 'the experimental rhythm of problem solving and problem finding' they are 'members of the same tribe' (p. 26). This suggests that contemporary information technology *can* require skill and 'focal' practice, that this is not excluded in principle.

Furthermore, Sennett describes how the modern artist—in the Renaissance and, I would add, especially in romantic times—became less "outward" turned to his community and more 'inward turned upon himself' (p. 65). The maker becomes more important. By contrast, the non-romantic view I am articulating here by means of Sennett and other literature stresses that skilled activity makes one *lose* one's sense of self and personality, and that this is a good thing. By being absorbed in the work, by being in the "flow", I become *less* important. We can back up this view by Eastern thinking (Buddhism, Taoism), but there are also traces of this view in Western thinking. To take a recent example: The Swedish poet Tomas Tranströmer, who won the 2011 Nobel Prize in Literature, writes the following lines at the end of his poem 'Morning Birds':

> Fantastic to feel how my poem grows
> while I myself shrink.
> It grows, it takes my place.
> It pushes me aside.
>
> From Morning Birds, (Tranströmer 2006, p. 79)

This is how quality-driven, skilled work can be a remedy against self-absorption and the romantic celebration of individual personality. Indeed, the problem with much contemporary *work* (in contrast to work in the industrial age) is not that we cannot express our individuality. On the contrary, we are supposed to be "creative" as individuals, little gods who are supposed to "design" things (including, in the case of philosophers, concepts) and to display our "personality" on the internet and elsewhere (indeed, design ourselves). And the problem with contemporary *leisure* activities is not that they are forms of "play", but that they are *not playful enough*. According to Sennett, skilled work is a kind of play, but not if "play" means something that allows us to escape from reality; real play teaches children and adults how to be sociable (p. 269). I would add: It also

Beyond Environmental Thinking *(1)* 107

teaches us something about our environment. Skillful play and experience turns us outward: to our environment and to others; to reality.

7.3.2. Pirsig

In order to further construct the ethics of skill in response to Romanticism, let us consider a work that takes a more explicit non-romantic turn: Pirsig's well-known *Zen and the Art of Motorcycle Maintenance*. Here, too, skillful engagement is recommended as the solution to nihilistic and alienating modern existence (and already then motorcycle maintenance is chosen as an example), but the view expressed in this narrative is perhaps philosophically richer than that described by Pirsig's contemporary heirs (e.g. Crawford) since it is explicitly developed in response to two highly relevant competing epistemological positions, which Pirsig calls the 'classical' and the 'romantic' understanding.

> A classical understanding sees the world primarily as underlying form itself. A romantic understanding sees it primarily in terms of immediate appearance. (. . .) The romantic mode is primarily inspirational, imaginative, creative, intuitive. (. . .) The classic mode, by contrast, proceeds by reason and by laws.
>
> (Pirsig 1974, p. 85)

For romantics, technology appears as dull and ugly (if not dangerous), whereas for the scientist it has no relationship to humans; being "objective", she sees only underlying form—for example, the '*a priori* motorcycle' (p. 165). In the first case, the observer and her feelings are all-important; in the second case, the observer is missing from the picture. The narrator in Pirsig's novel sees both ways of looking at the world as 'valid' yet 'irreconcilable' (p. 98), although at first, in his over-reaction to Romanticism and as a lover of motorcycles, he appears a little more sympathetic to underlying form and especially regrets the romantic a priori rejection of technology. However, Pirsig also presents a way to go beyond the two positions: I take this "third" position to be (a) *not* the metaphysics of Quality that is developed during the book—which turned out to make its conceiver crazy and indeed *alienated*, removed from the world and from others, which is the very opposite we want to achieve—but (b) the position I have been articulating throughout this chapter: The view that craftsmanship is a good way of coping with, and understanding, the world. Let me explain what I take to be Pirsig's view and what I think it implies for environmental motivation and environmental ethics.

Metaphysics may well find a "solution" in theory, but this does not bring the metaphysician any closer to the world or to others. Neither environmental good nor human good is created. The craftsman, by contrast, engages with his environment. He neither follows instructions nor studies theories, but is

108   *Beyond Nature, Beyond Modernity, Beyond Thinking*

'absorbed and attentive to what he's doing'; his 'motions and the machine are in a kind of harmony' in what can only be described as an 'art' (Pirsig 1974, p. 209). Pirsig suggests that such a person will deliver quality, since he *cares*. There is a relation with the technology, involvement with reality. Moreover, the good and the beautiful merge in this activity. If there is ugliness at all, it is in 'the relationship between the people who produce the technology and the things they produce' (p. 372). The challenge is to do it in a beautiful way (p. 374). This avoids having to try to make things beautiful *afterwards*: If there is no quality, then the thing 'must be overlaid with a veneer of "style" to make it acceptable', but this only makes it worse (p. 375); 'classic understanding should not be *overlaid* with romantic pettiness' (pp. 375–6). Rather, Pirsig's narrator argues that understanding should be united 'at a basic level', amounting to a 'real unification of art and technology'. This happens in the craftsman involved in his work, attaining a 'harmony with the work' (p. 380). Leaving behind 'objectivity and disinterestedness' (p. 444), but also the loneliness often associated with new technological devices (p. 460), we have to be like the craftsman, who makes 'an art of what he is doing' (p. 460). In this way we can move beyond romanticism, but also beyond 'the pursuit of the ghost of reason' (p. 462) we inherited from the Greeks—especially from Plato's search for the Truth as something that is imperishable and removed from the affairs of men (p. 477–8) and from the idea of virtue as an ethical absolute (p. 482)—and reach excellence (*arête*).

For coping with our environment, Pirsig's insight means that, on the one hand, we should avoid "objective" and disinterested understandings of, and treatments of, our environment. "Nature" is not something outside us that we should attempt to model, shape, and control. But neither should it be only the projection screen of our feelings or the décor of our lives. We can only achieve environmental good (and therefore: human good) if we actively, skillfully, and beautifully relate to our environment; this is the art of being environmental.

This view resonates with the "skill" view of Dreyfus and others, and it sharply contrasts with the romantic view. Instead of seeking good in the "natural" somewhere "out there", separated from us, we can find it in the active, skilled relation to our environment. And instead of seeking "authenticity" in our "inner" self, and expressing our self (thereby imposing form on the world), we are called upon to open up to our environment, to actively respond to it. In that active relating to the environment and to others, we come to experience meaning. There is distinction, significance. We cannot produce or express meaning starting from an isolated self. We rather drink it in and respond to it. The art of being environmental is not the art of authenticity, of trying to be "authoritative" and of moulding and shaping everything according to our concept, our identity, our "true nature" or "essence". Instead, it is the art of responding appropriately to our environment, which invites us and challenges us to respond. In this way worlds emerge. Perhaps we get lost in our environment (human and non-human),

Beyond Environmental Thinking *(1)* 109

but the getting lost is not a form of romantic reverie, it is a flow that is actively brought forth. And sometimes a new world emerges. Not because we have a new concept, a new Idea, a Form or Concept that is then applied to matter, but because the new happens as a result of our appropriate and excellent response to our environment, including our response to *others*. If this happens, the relation between humans and environment changes. A new world is born. It is "made" but it also happens. *Poiesis* is linked to *physis*. It is similar to change and transformation in the natural environment. To use Heidegger's metaphors: It is an unfolding; it is a coming-out of a butterfly. It is a kind of growth. Indeed, the bringing-forth of environmental good is an art and requires training (acquiring skills), but it is not entirely a matter of human agency. In lived and skillful activity, activity and passivity merge. It is a *poiesis*, but the bringing-forth (Heidegger) means that we are not the single author of the making; the good that emerges is compelling, but not authoritative. The craftsman is not an author with a concept. We need to tune in and play, but when it is good, the music is not coming from the depths of our romantic "genius". It happens and it *fits*, although without skill and habit it could not happen and it could not fit. The art of being environmental is the art of doing fitting things. It has to do with "comportment": with gesture, form, manner, attitude, posture, habit, form, and practice. It is an art in which "big ethics" and "little ethics" (etiquette) merge: Doing good is about ways of doing, about how to do things. Doing environmental good means to do fitting things, to make and do things in a way that "brings together" and "agrees" (etymology of "comports") with the environment. This environment is both physical and social. The art of being environmental brings together humans with other humans, humans with non-humans, humans with environment.

Such an art does not require us to reject technology. As Pirsig writes: 'the real evil isn't the objects of technology' (p. 460). Instead, it is in the precise ways we relate to nature and to technology: Both the pursuit of 'the ghost of reason' (p. 462) and the romantic response to the environment produce the alienation; that is, we self-produce it. Instead, we should acknowledge a relational epistemology and live in a more relational way. In Pirsig's words:

> The Quality which creates the world emerges as a *relationship* between man and his experience. He is a *participant* in the creation of all things.
> (Pirsig 1974, p. 482)

If we are creators at all, the questions are: *How* should we participate and create? How should we relate to our environment? These also mean: What world should we experience and create (with emphasis on the former)? In what world should we live? And the answer Pirsig and others offer us seems to be that skillfully relating to our environment is a good way of experiencing and creating a world that is beautiful, meaningful, and good—indeed, of good 'quality'.

110 *Beyond Nature, Beyond Modernity, Beyond Thinking*

Having arrived at this preliminary conclusion, let us now re-read Rousseau and Thoreau, and see if we can discern something of this "craft" ethic or "ethics of skill" in their work in order to further articulate what would be good for our environment and (hence) for us. As we have seen in Chapter 5, in the writings of these "significant" moderns of the 18th and 19th century, which since then have directly or indirectly inspired environmentalists, we can find a lot of (1) romantic and (2) Socratic, Stoic, and Enlightenment elements. However, we can also find traces of the view articulated in this chapter: the ideas that the good life depends on skill and (direct) experience and that skilled engagement and direct experience with our environment are at the same time productive of "environmental" good. This will help to further elaborate this view, and offer the additional benefit of looking with new eyes at the texts, showing some more of their rich texture.

7.4. RE-READING ROUSSEAU AND THOREAU: THE VIRTUE OF SKILLED ACTIVITY

As we have seen in Chapter 5, Rousseau is not only representative of 18th-century Romanticism, of which he is often regarded as the founder; he also offers an interesting attempt to cope with the Enlightenment tension between reason (Stoicism, classical reason) and feeling (Romanticism)—for example, in the *Emile*, which interweaves both Stoic and romantic elements. But sometimes Rousseau also points to a route *beyond* reason and feeling, and at these moments he is closer to Pirsig and Sennett than to many of his contemporaries.

Consider Book II of the *Emile*, in which Rousseau argues against instruction and urges us to let children learn by their own experience. Rather than teaching them 'words, more words, always words', Rousseau says, we should teach children the 'sciences of things' (Rousseau 1762a, p. 108); that is, we should let them learn on the basis of what they experience as embodied beings. Exercising both body and mind, they will develop their judgment and enrich their memory. Rousseau writes: 'Our first masters of philosophy are our feet, our hands, our eyes' (p. 125). He praises engineers, surveyors, architects, masons, and painters for having that kind of experience (p. 140), indeed for learning in *practice*. He gives the example of a child who knows where the kite is by looking at its shadow (p. 163): what matters is learning by direct, lived experience; in this way, the child surpasses even young peasants 'in skill' (p. 161). In Book III the teacher (Jean-Jacques) takes Emile to the woods and lets him "get lost" (but the teacher knows where they are) in order to teach him geography and astronomy. The child is tired, hungry, and thirsty. Jean-Jacques lets the child orient himself by having him look at the position of the sun (via the position of the shadow). Rousseau argues that in this way the child will really learn and remember (pp. 181–182).

Beyond Environmental Thinking *(1)*   111

Although this may be called a "natural" way of learning and although the very idea of a direct, pure kind of sense-experience might well be called romantic (this is the romantic dimension in some pragmatist and phenomenology thinking), it is clear that Rousseau's "science of things" is neither romantic nor scientific in the following senses. First, in these descriptions of Emile's education we see no explicit longing for a "state of nature" or for remaining "primitive" but the advice to *learn*. Second, although the child's know-how does not "contradict" scientific knowledge (strictly speaking it cannot *contradict* because the know-how is "silent", not explicit), it is not framed by the child and by others involved in the terms of objective science. The experience and learning take place literally "in touch" with the environment. In contrast to the 'words, more words, always words' (Rousseau 1762a, p. 108) offered by metaphysics and philosophy, *this* kind of knowledge does not alienate but allows human beings to meaningfully and successfully relate to their environment and cope with the problems they encounter.

At times, Rousseau's view is close to the contemporary view that thinking and learning is *embodied*. He writes:

> To learn to think (. . .) it is necessary to exercise our limbs, our senses, our organs, which are the instruments of our intelligence. (. . .) Thus, far from man's true reason being formed independently of the body, it is the body's good constitution which makes the mind's operations easy and sure.
>
> (Rousseau 1762a, p. 125)

With regard to the issue of alienation, it is also interesting to mention Rousseau's adaptation of Plutarch's *On the Eating of Flesh*: Arguing against meat eating, Rousseau writes that meat eaters 'combat instinct without necessity in order to abandon [them]selves to [their] cruel delights' (p. 155), and that if they insist on eating meat, they should kill the animals themselves, with their bare hands:

> Kill the animals yourself—I mean with your own hands, without iron tools, without knives. (. . .) You shudder? You do not dare to feel living flesh palpitating in your teeth? Pitiful man! (. . .) You have to have butchers, cooks, and roasters, people to take away the horror of the murder and dress up dead bodies.
>
> (Rousseau 1762a, p. 155)

This passage is remarkably similar to a passage in Thoreau's *Walden*:

> True, [man] can and does live, in a great measure, by preying on other animals; but this is a miserable way,—as any one who will go to snaring rabbits, or slaughtering lambs, may learn.
>
> (Thoreau 1854, p. 216)

112 *Beyond Nature, Beyond Modernity, Beyond Thinking*

Whether or not this is a valid argument against eating animals, it presents in any case an interesting objection against a particular way of eating animals and indeed against a particular way of life. In both passages, it is suggested that our alienation from practical experience leads to miserable, hypocritical, and cruel lives. We are out of touch, lack direct experience; in this sense, we no longer know what we are doing.

There are more similarities between Thoreau and Rousseau, and, more generally, between Thoreau and the view I am articulating here. On the one hand, as I have argued in the chapter on Romanticism, like Rousseau's *Emile*, *Walden* emphasizes Stoic self-reliance (independence and abstinence) and is full of romantic sentiment, including the desire to live in a "natural way", the advice to engage in self-exploration, Rousseau-like reveries, and romantic individualism (like Rousseau's writings, it is about what *I am* and what *I* did). *Walden* also contains scientific observations and classifications—for example, when a microscope is held to a red ant (p. 230), or when a thermometer is used (p. 299). And as I noted, due to the influence from Emerson, it is even mystic and transcendentalist in its conception of Nature. In sum, *Walden* displays the Janus head of modern thinking.

Yet at the same time *Walden* is *also* a praise of practical experience and the development of skill, which opens up a different path—not only a path of thinking but especially a path of doing. It is a path that is not necessarily *anti*-science, but one that takes distance from the conception of science as "objective" and disinterested. Thoreau argues that students should not merely study life but '*live* it from beginning to end', try 'the experiment of living', 'the art of life' (Thoreau 1854, p. 51). He suggests that this does not necessarily mean that they should work with their hands, but nevertheless it would be 'a good deal like that' (p. 51). The same person who recommends reverie—he says that his seasons full of reverie were 'better than any work of the hands' (p. 111)—also argues that it is better to do things yourself, with your own hands. Thoreau builds his own house and maintains himself 'solely by the labor of [his] hands' (p. 69). He uses his senses and praises the *skillful* Canadian wood-chopper, who would never take a 'spiritual view of things' (p. 150), but—or so it is suggested—was more spiritual, *lived* in a more spiritual way, than any modern man. Thoreau also recommends plucking huckleberries, fishing, hunting, and other activities in the woods. In passages that now sound to us as rather 'Zen', his advice is to 'live in the present always', in a blessed spring morning (p. 314). Against restlessness, he says: 'Drive a nail home and clinch it' (p. 330).

Moreover, in *Walking* (1862) Thoreau also values being in the present and indeed being where his body is. Consider what happens when he does not manage to 'shake off the village':

> The thought of some work will run in my head and I am not where my body is—I am out of my senses. In my walks I would fain return

Beyond Environmental Thinking *(1)*   113

to my senses. What business I have in the woods, if I am thinking of something out of the woods?

(Thoreau 1862, p. 6)

Both walking and working in "nature" may help one to return to the feeling of embodied presence, and, finally, to acquire true knowledge of the world rather than accumulating 'a myriad of facts' (Thoreau 1862, p. 29). Thoreau's 'repeated examples of (. . .) practical know-how' in *Walden*, therefore, do not only make us trust the narrator, as Updike writes (Updike in Thoreau 1854, p. xix)—thereby revealing a romantic longing for authenticity—but also suggest that we re-shape our relation to the natural environment. Rather than getting absorbed in romantic *reverie*, we should develop practical skills and skillfully engage with the environment.

Following this advice may cure an attitude to our environment and to ourselves which Cafaro calls 'apathy'. He rightly calls apathy a key environmental vice (Cafaro 2005) since what prevents environmental good, it seems, is our disengagement. But in the light of what has been said before, apathy is not a mere "attitude". Thinking of apathy as an attitude would suggest we can just switch to a different "attitude" by *changing our mind*. This would amount to a "mental" change. But I have been arguing that this is not the right way of looking at the problem; we have to move beyond a dualistic approach altogether and (hence) from a view of motivation that seeks motivation in something external to a view that seeks that motivation in what we do and experience. Interestingly, Cafaro suggests that what motivates us to engage, rather than remain apathetic, is not something external to the activity itself, but joy in the activity. This implies that motivation for exercising environmental virtue lies in the practice of virtue itself. In this sense Cafaro is right when he concludes: 'In the end, action is the only answer to apathy' (p. 153).

Indeed, the 'third' route beyond Stoic or Enlightenment rationalism and Romanticism articulated in the previous pages can be reformulated in the language of virtue. I will say more about environmental virtue in the next chapter, but let me introduce the theme here. I already referred to White's point that environmentalists fail to examine their own lives:

It is convenient to imagine a power beyond us because that means we don't have to examine our own lives. And it is convenient to hand the work of resistance over to scientists, our designated national problem solvers.

(White 2007, p. 16)

In other words, we have to do some work ourselves and examine our own lives. Virtue ethics provides a language for engaging in this examination and for thinking about the good life. This includes (re-)thinking our relationship to the environment.

114   *Beyond Nature, Beyond Modernity, Beyond Thinking*

Recently, we have seen the emergence of a field called 'environmental virtue ethics' (Cafaro 2004; Hursthouse 2007; Sandler 2005, 2007; Sandler & Cafaro 2005; van Wensveen 2000). As a virtue approach to environmental ethics, it asks what character dispositions we ought to have regarding the environment (Sandler 2005, p. 2), rather than prescribing rules or principles of moral action (as, for example, deontology and consequentialism do). It asks the question about the (environmentally) good life. Since this approach allows us to attend to, and evaluate, our practical, daily ways of living, rather than focusing on "special" moments with "high" moral stakes, it must be regarded as a significant improvement to earlier approaches. (I will mention more advantages in the next chapter.)

Inspired by the virtue approach, we might therefore frame our position in terms of virtue: It is virtuous to engage in skilled activity, and—as Sennett also hints at—this also helps to develop other virtues (for example, patience). However, learning from the pragmatist tradition and from "ethics of skill" that I am developing here, we want to avoid that virtues are made as abstract as the rules and principles they were supposed to replace. If skilled, practical engagement with our environment is the key to environmental and human good, then this environmental "virtue" should not be externalized: It can only "live" within the concrete activities. Otherwise we introduce another kind of alienation. (In the next chapter, I will further develop my position and my main argument in terms of virtue, and say more about moral emotions.)

This "non-modern" approach does not imply that rationality, emotionality, or imagination are rejected. Only their grotesque and problematic forms are avoided: the detached, alienating kind of rationality, emotionality, and imagination that can be found in rationalist and romantic thinking. Rather than promoting the irrational, the unemotional, or the unimaginative (such a "negation" of the romantic would amount to a re-affirmation of the wrong kind of modernity, of over-rationalist Enlightenment), the approach defended here (a) acknowledges a place for rational, emotional, and imaginative thinking in ethics—on grounds not discussed in this book, it seems that these might even be *necessary* for moral thinking and moral action[5]—but (b) demands that reasons, emotions, and imaginations are "epistemically anchored", so to speak, in practical and active engagement with one's environment. It thus tries to avoid Pirsig's ghost of reason[6] as well as romantic anti-social and anti-scientific sentiment. The approach is not against reason, emotion, or imagination, but against reason, emotion, or imagination of a particular kind: the reasoning, the emotions, and the imaginations that alienate us from our environment.

Note that this skill-oriented and social-oriented approach provides an interesting, "mixed" answer to the Socratic question in the *Protagoras* whether virtue can be taught. On the one hand, it cannot be taught, at least if "teaching" means instruction and the transfer of knowing-that. Becoming (more) virtuous is not a matter of acquiring intellectual knowledge or

Beyond Environmental Thinking *(1)*   115

"intellectual" skill, but is a matter of developing our practical and skilled engagement with the environment—physical/natural and social, human and non-human. It is not a matter of rational calculation or vision, but of moral know-how. On the other hand, this means virtue *can* be taught, at least if "teaching" means the kind of learning that is involved in the learning of a craft. A moral craftsman[7] may teach the moral apprentice by means of example, by means of showing-*how*. Moral beginners need some instruction—children, for instance, need rules—but developing into "morally adult" humans demands that we grow into moral experts, whose response to a complex moral problem cannot be reduced to rule following, and who are only able to respond in this way from within their active, committed, and engaged relating to their environment—from within their lives.

To the extent that Socrates defined virtue in intellectual and theoretical terms, the non-modern approach to environmental ethics proposed here is not only non-modern but also non-Socratic or even anti-Socratic. Consider another Socratic dialogue: the *Alcibiades* (Plato 1997a). Again virtue is the topic of discussion. Socrates argues that Alcibiades should acquire intellectual skills in order to be able to rule over other people but also over his own body. In their discussion about which skills are needed, Socrates makes a strict distinction between 'cultivating yourself and cultivating what belongs to you' (128d), between the one who uses tools and tools—the shoemaker is different from the tools he cuts with and the lyre-player is different from the lyre (129c)—and between 'a man' and 'his own body' (129e). Indeed, he writes that man is 'what uses the body' and that 'man is that which rules the body' (130a). What uses and rules the body is 'man', and "man" is the same as the soul: 'soul is the man' (130c). Thus, long before Cartesian modernity we already meet a dualistic view of the human and the human-environment relation in this dialogue and in other Socratic dialogues such as the *Phaedrus*: the human is identified with the soul, the intellect, which must be distinguished and kept separate from the bodily, the material, and the technological. The former has to use and rule the latter. The body, the tools, and indeed the whole environment are merely instrumental to the human.

One of the implications of this non-relational, non-environmental anthropology is also a dualistic view of skill, which is already articulated in the *Alcibiades*. Socrates makes a strict distinction between self-knowledge and knowledge of (other) things. Socratic self-knowledge should not be confused with romantic self-knowledge. It is rather the skill to rule: to master one's body, to master other people, and to master the environment. Knowing yourself, Socrates argues, means knowing your soul (130e) and this means having the skill to be self-controlled: 'being self-controlled is knowing yourself' (131b). Socrates distinguishes this skill from the skills of a doctor, a trainer, a farmer, and 'other tradesman', who know only 'what belongs to them' (the body) or have skills that are 'about what's even further away than what belongs to them' (131a–b). Thus, care of the body (131b) and care of things is regarded as requiring entirely different skills than cultivating the

116 *Beyond Nature, Beyond Modernity, Beyond Thinking*

soul. Socrates then goes on to argue that a good statesman must have all these skills of control and mastery: If he cannot even manage a household estate, he cannot become a statesman (133a). Moreover, he cannot rule others 'unless he is self-controlled and good' himself (134a–b). This view presupposes the underlying dichotomy between "soul" skills and "body" skills, between what a "man" is and the things and people he rules and uses.

By contrast, the non-modern view proposed here rejects Socrates' dualist view of the human and its relation to the environment as well as Socrates' dualist view of skill. It holds that "the soul" should not be alienated from "the body" and from things, not in theory and not in practice, and that cultivation of the human and the cultivation of "the soul" is inextricably linked to the care of "the body" and the care of things. If we take care of things, of the body, and of the environment in particular ways, then this influences "the soul," and thus with regard to human good it matters how we related to others, to things, and to the environment. There is a continuity between "body" and "soul," "human" and "environment." Moreover, influenced by (Dreyfusian) Heideggerian thinking and by contemporary cognitive science, it holds that one cannot make such a strict distinction between (a) intellectual skills and skills of the "soul" and (b) the skills of the craftsman (including the craftsman-doctor), that so-called "intellectual" skills are rather parasitic on the so-called "lower" skills, and that separating them in practice is itself alienating and does not contribute to human or other flourishing. It holds that virtue does not so much consist in self-control, in the rule over other people, and in the use of things (assumed to be separate from the self-ruler), as Socrates, the Stoics, and Enlightenment thinkers taught, but rather in developing a more caring, non-instrumental relation to one's body, to other people, and to things. It holds that moral-environmental development is a matter of developing the skill to actively and intensely engage with one's environment—human and non-human—and that this skill is at once an "intellectual" and a "practical" skill, very much like Pirsig describes good motorcycle maintenance and Sennett describes good cooking. If we engage in such a non-alienating mode of relating to our environment, we are neither Socratic/Platonic rulers of bodies, things and people, nor romantic geniuses who try to make "authentic" things which have their source in our own unique individual "inner" selves; rather, in our active and skilled engagement with others, with things, with our environment, our "self"—if there is such a thing at all—is no longer standing in the way. It is no longer standing in the way of human/non-human good, of environmental flourishing. In the flow of good skilled engagement, thinking and doing, self and other, human and environment merge.

If the "aim" of this kind of environmental ethics as self-less skilled engagement, which bears resemblance to Buddhist and Taoist thinking, can be compared to love in any sense at all, it is not the 'Platonic' love of the *Alcibiades* or the detached love of "Nature" of the romantic *reverie*, but the love that risks itself by actively, bodily, and materially relating to its earthly

Beyond Environmental Thinking *(1)*   117

object, the love that renders itself vulnerable by engaging with reality, the love that is simultaneously love of the soul and love of the body, love of the human and love of the environment. It is the love that goes beyond thinking, beyond control and self-control, beyond rule and self-rule. It is the love that liberates us from "self" but also from "other". It is mystical, perhaps, but not contemplative or fuzzy and vague. It is in the concrete touch, in the act, in the skillful engagement, in the care, in the breathing, and in the flow. It is the love that lifts us up to the summit of our ultimate *environmentalization*.

7.5. CHANGING RELATIONS TO OUR ENVIRONMENT: THE ARCHER'S CHALLENGE

If we want to change, if we want to turn towards habits, practices and societies that are less environmentally alienating (and thus less romantic and less objectivist, and perhaps also less Socratic), how should we proceed? Although I will mainly discuss this question later, let me start with remarking that this cannot be a matter of will. To say that it is a matter of will, would be to re-introduce the ancient Greek and modern moral psychology and ethics according to which control and self-control is the primary virtue. But the change that is required here involves different virtues (e.g. the opposite of apathy) and cannot be enforced. Rather than being a matter of mere choice, will, decision, and agency, it is also and mainly a matter of growth.

The reason why this is so, has to do with the kind of learning (and meta-learning) that is involved here. Learning a skill cannot be forced; gaining experience requires time. In order to express what we have to "do", then, we can draw on Heidegger's view of *Gelassenheit* and more generally his later work on technology (in particular, Heidegger 1954), or we can refer to what Dreyfus and Kelly describe as 'to be drawn by a force outside oneself but not enslaved to it', to be 'neither wilful agent nor unwilling slave' (Dreyfus & Kelly 2011, p. 8). Another (perhaps less abstract but no less paradoxical) way of saying this is that in skilled activity, we cannot force ourselves to get into a kind of "flow". We can only try it, do it, and then hope that flow and learning happens. Of course we have our ideas, our principles, and our aims, also with regard to the environment. But to take up a famous Zen example also mentioned by Sennett: If the archer focuses too much on the aim, it goes wrong. And things will go wrong anyway. We learn skills by trial and error. Environmental ethics understood as an ethics of skill sees learning experiences not as problematic but as steps towards moral and environmental *excellence*. More generally, we can grow out of apathy only if we let certain activities and experiences "happen" to some extent; if we let a new form of life "grow" as much as it is created. This requires the (meta-) virtue of patience and perhaps also some courage: the courage to try, the courage to jump—even if we might fail and fall, *because* we will fail and fall before we learn. We need the courage to fail.

118 *Beyond Nature, Beyond Modernity, Beyond Thinking*

However, this turn to "life" and "activity" does not mean that we should stop reflection altogether or that (e.g. as teachers) we can no longer encourage by using words or evaluate particular kinds of activities as more or less environmentally good. Although ultimately we can only *experience* such good *in* the activity, as philosophers we can still (1) describe and reflect on the phenomenology of daily experience to show what might be bad and what might be better, exploring possibilities for different, better practices; (2) think about the social and political institutions that hinder or promote these activities; and (3) start to examine and evaluate the role of technology in how we relate to our environment. This is what I will do in the next chapters. But to further complete my articulation of a conception of environmental ethics as involving "environmental skill", let me first say more about environmental virtue and moral sentiment.

NOTES

1. Here I mainly rely on Dewey and—this time through Dreyfus—Heidegger for articulating the epistemology of know-how and skill on which I base the 'ethics of skill' I will propose later in this chapter, but one could also use different sources. For example, other philosophers may use Ryle's philosophy (see, for example, Bengson & Moffett 2012), which is also influenced by Heidegger (among others). See, for instance, Ryle's remarks on a fool who has a lot of knowledge-that but does not know how to perform (Ryle 1945, p. 8): Here Ryle is close to Dreyfus, including of course Dreyfus' criticism of (classical) AI.
2. Note that 'wis' in the word 'wisdom' derives from the same source as 'wise' and refers in Old English (*wise*), Dutch (*wijs*), and German (*Weise*) to a way of proceeding, a manner, a habit. To be 'wise', in moral and other matters, then means, originally, to know the way, to know-how, to know how to proceed, to have the habit.
3. See also Dewey's criticism of the standard view of moral motivation.
4. Note in this respect that Dreyfus (and Kelly?) share with Heidegger not only his problem definition (rejection of modern technology as alienating), but also his solution: He writes that 'we have closed ourselves off to the calling of the gods' (p. 221) but that 'the calling is there' and that 'those who are sensitive enough to the culture and to its rich heritage will hear it' (p. 221). Similarly, Heidegger talked about the 'calling' of the gods and turned to the Greeks—for example, via Hölderlin's poetry—in order to recover a sense of the Greek way of experiencing the world.
5. See, for example, my book on moral imagination (Coeckelbergh 2007).
6. I also might have referred to Ryle's ghost here.
7. Recently I have used the term 'moral craftsmanship' (Coeckelbergh 2014).

8 Beyond Environmental *Thinking* (2)
Exercising Virtue and Moral Sentiment

INTRODUCTION

In Chapter 2 I wrote about the ancient Greek understanding of virtue. In the previous chapter I developed the notion of "environmental skill" and argued that skilled engagement with the environment is a way to overcome the problem of motivation as formulated in the beginning of this book. I also mentioned that there is an approach called 'environmental virtue ethics' that seems to fit the requirement that environmental ethics should ask us to examine our own lives. However, I also warned that "virtue" may yet again be understood in very abstract or principled terms and that if this happens, it is not compatible with the demand of environmental engagement as practical, skilled engagement. So can we conceptualize "environmental virtue" in a way that is compatible with, and supportive of, the conception of environmental ethics and "environmental skill" developed in the previous chapters? Moreover, what is the place of (moral) *emotions* in such an account? And what role do luck and circumstances play in this kind of ethics?

In this chapter I further develop my discussion of the relation between "environmental skill" and virtue ethics by engaging with what modern and contemporary philosophers have said about virtue and moral sentiment—in particular, Hume and contemporary Aristotelians and Humeans.

First I will say more about the advantages of an (Aristotelian) virtue ethics. Then I will make room for a Humean interpretation of virtue, which does not pre-define a list of objective virtues but rather enables us to connect virtue to social and natural abilities and skills, and gives emotions a more important role in environmental ethics. This will lead to the conclusions that (1) being environmentally virtuous and having environmental skills also involves "environmental emotions" and that (2) whether or not one becomes environmentally virtuous and develops environmental skill is a matter of training but *also* of luck and circumstances.

120 *Beyond Nature, Beyond Modernity, Beyond Thinking*

8.1. ENVIRONMENTAL VIRTUE ETHICS

The standard ethical recommendation in response to environmental problems can be summarized as follows: (1) "Look at the facts!" and (2) "It is your duty to do something about it!" The philosophical background of these imperatives are deontological and consequentialist moral theory. In constructing justifications for why acting in an "environmental" way is good, consequentialist and deontological arguments focus on the bad consequences of our actions, on the harms we do to the environment, and (therefore) on our duty to protect the environment. We ought to stop pollution, to produce renewable energy, to eat differently, etc. Animals, humans, and perhaps the environment have rights; we have to respect those rights. Moreover, both kinds of approaches also have to refer to the scientific facts: "it is the case that" there are these and these signs of global warming; "it is a fact that" so many people lack access to safe drinking water, etc. Science tells us which harm is being done.

Furthermore, science may also help us to find solutions for environmental problems. Better technologies are proposed, for example. Better management is proposed. The whole planet is seen as something that needs better management. And *people* need to better manage themselves. They consume too much and they consume the wrong things. They need self-restraint, and if (literally) they do not manage, if they lack self-discipline, perhaps they need to be restrained by laws and discipline. We need limits, and it is our duty to impose those limits to ourselves. The philosophical theories appeal to us as beings that possess reason and can see that setting limits is necessary. People can see the facts and they can accept the arguments. And if they fail to do what is right, what they ought to do, then they feel guilty. They feel the appropriate moral emotions. They feel bad. They know the gap between theory and practice is too wide. The deontological moralist says: "Shame on you, humanity, you are not following the law you should, as beings with reason, give to yourself. Shame on you, because you know about the harm you are causing to the environment, to animals, and to other people, and you do too little about it." And the consequentialist may add to this: "What people need is fear. Let them see the consequences! Let them observe the pain! Let them feel the suffering, not only of others, but also of themselves, since in the end, with our bad behaviour we are harming ourselves."

However true and well-meaning this may be, this standard approach to environmental ethics, which appeals to reason and to facts does not seem to work. Very little change happens. People do not make the right kind of laws. And if there are rules, many people do not follow them. Most people do not show self-restraint and self-discipline. Why? I have argued that one reason why the gap between knowledge and action persists is the kind of knowledge that is assumed to do the work here to motivate people. The kind of knowledge presented to us by scientists and philosophers is theoretical knowledge. We are given facts and arguments. We are given laws, principles, and rules—in the best case, we can even make up such principles and rules

Beyond Environmental Thinking *(2)* 121

ourselves. Maybe we are even presented with a vision of a better, more sustainable, and environmentally friendly world. Maybe we have our own vision of a better world. Maybe we feel emotions like guilt and fear. But in the end, none of this really touches us. We experience the facts and the arguments as detached minds. And after the presentation or the film (e.g. Al Gore's film) the feelings are gone. We know, theoretically, that what needs to be done has to do with the way we live our own lives. But it remains knowing-that. Inspired by the pragmatist and Heideggerian tradition, I have drawn attention to a different kind of knowledge, a kind of knowledge that I think can motivate us: know-how. My claim was that true knowledge in environmental ethics (and, for that matter, any ethics) can never be only a matter of know-that, but instead needs to be rooted in experience, needs to have the form of know-how. According to this view, being environmentally good is not a matter of making or following laws or drawing the right conclusions from facts and arguments. Instead, it is a cultural and personal matter, a matter of becoming a better person.

In order to further articulate this view, the tradition of virtue ethics is helpful—in particular, interpretations of Aristotle that emphasize virtue as something that has to be trained, exercised. According to Aristotle, we acquire the virtues (excellences) by engaging in the relevant activities and by acquiring the right kind of habits. In Book II of the *Nicomachean Ethics* (NE) he writes that 'moral excellence comes about as a result of habit' (II.1, 1103a16–17, p. 1742) and that we have to exercise to acquire it. He compares learning virtues (excellences) with learning an art—for example, architecture or music:

> excellences we get by first exercising them, as also happens in the case of the arts as well. For the things we have to learn before we can do, we learn by doing, e.g. men become builders by building and lyre-players by playing the lyre; so too we become just by doing just acts, temperate by doing temperate acts, brave by doing brave acts.
> (NE II.1., 1103a31–1103b2, p. 1743)

This view implies that moral education becomes very important, and that this moral education does not so much consist in learning rules but rather in acquiring the right kind of skills and *habits*: 'It makes no small difference, then, whether we form habits of one kind or another from our very youth; it makes a very great difference, or rather *all* the difference' (II.1., 1103b24–26, p. 1743). It suggests that environmental virtue is a matter of acquiring environmental skills and habits 'from our very youth'. If we learn to live in a more environmentally friendly way early on in life, if we acquire the right kind of habits when we are young, there is no big problem of "motivation" later on. There is no gap between knowing-that and doing because there is a knowing-how that has been written into our minds and bodies when we were children.

Of course there are interpretations of Aristotle that rather focus on the theoretical, intellectual dimensions of virtue, but here I follow the current

122 *Beyond Nature, Beyond Modernity, Beyond Thinking*

of interpretation that emphasizes the training and practice of virtue (see also below). Instead of seeing virtue as a kind of remote concept, an idea, virtue is then understood in line with what Aristotle called *phronesis*, practical wisdom. A particularly useful way of clarifying this—also for the Humean interpretation of virtue as presented in the next section—is Aristotle's comparison between becoming virtuous and changing your lifestyle for health[1] reasons:

> It is well said, then, that it is by doing just acts that the just man is produced, and by doing temperate acts the temperate man; without doing these no one would have even a prospect of becoming good. But most people do not do these, but take refuge in theory and think they are being philosophers and will become good in this way, behaving somewhat like patients who listen attentively to their doctors, but do none of the things they are ordered to do. As the latter will not be made well in body by such a course of treatment, the former will not be made well in soul by such a course of philosophy.
>
> (NE II.4, 1105b7–17, p. 1746)

The approach to environmental ethics I try to articulate in this book attempts to replace the model of "the disobedient patient" with the model of the artist or sports person who exercises, trains skills and movements. Most of us are like the disobedient patient when it comes to environmental matters: the green "doctor" tells us that the planet is "sick", that we are "sick". We listen attentively to all the facts scientists, green politicians, and activist environmentalists tell us. We listen to their advice and recommendations. But we do none of it—or at least very little. As philosophers, we seek refuge in theory and think that we are on the right track. But Aristotle teaches us that this is not the way to become better people—including, we should add: becoming better "environmental" people. Unless we start the training, we are not made well—neither in body nor in soul. The point is, in Aristotle's words, 'how we ought to [act]' (NE II.1., 1103b30, p. 1743), and this we can only find out by doing.

However, this interpretation does not necessarily make Aristotle the main or only source of inspiration for the approach I am articulating, since in his work there is still much emphasis on knowing-that. Although he disagrees with Plato in that he thinks that ethical knowledge cannot be so precise as what we now call scientific knowledge (NE I.3.; see also Kamtekar 2013, p. 38) and although his distinction between theoretical and practical wisdom suggests indeed that 'nonphilosophers may have full virtue and lead happy lives so long as they possess practical wisdom' (p. 39), Aristotle still agrees with Plato that contemplation 'motivates rational activity throughout the world' (Kamtekar 2013, p. 38). Moreover, it seems that his moral "skill" is still a *deliberative*, judgmental skill. It is about *thinking* about what to choose.

In contrast, the approach I try to articulate here diverts from Aristotle since (1) it includes skills that are literally, not merely metaphorically, of a

Beyond Environmental Thinking *(2)* 123

very physical and bodily nature—and since (2) Aristotle seems to restrict the role of social environments to *learning* a virtue, whereas below I will outline the (more Humean) view that social environments are also needed in order to *sustain* virtue. This view will also include a non-Aristotelian understanding of the *stability* of virtue and character.

Nevertheless, the "skill" interpretation of Aristotelian virtue (say the conception of virtue as skill) supports the environmental ethics I am developing here: Training and exercise of environmental virtue requires engaging in practical activities and developing practical skills—"environmental skills". Environmental virtue is not only a matter of detached knowledge (e.g. in the form of "information") but also and perhaps most importantly of practical know-how and direct experience.

The "theoretical," detached attitude is then not the solution to environmental problems, but is itself part of the problem. Not only is "seeking refuge in theory" not the main route to environmental good; from the previous chapters we can also conclude that the particular *kind of thinking* about the environment many theorists and scientists seem to practice is also misguided. The idea of seeing the earth as an ecosystem and as something that needs to be managed and something that can provide services is also part of the problem. We first create distance, with our management and our science, with our facts and our arguments, and then we are surprised to find that there is gap between theory and practice. Great environmentalists of the past, by contrast, have shown that what matters is concrete, practical engagement with the environment. Think about Thoreau, for example. The lives of people like Thoreau—in the past and in the present—are much closer to "environmental virtue", with "virtue" understood in terms of skills and habits, practical engagement and exercise.

Furthermore, this understanding of environmental virtue offers a different picture of the moral emotions that are involved in trying to become more virtuous. Emotions of guilt or fear, which prevail in deontological and consequentialist theories, are no longer at the centre of moral experience. Of course we might experience negative emotions when we exercise virtue, especially when our moral exercise becomes an exercise in self-management rather than virtue (I will say more about this later—see Chapter 9), but generally speaking the emotion that accompanies environmental virtue training is joy. The joy we experience here is not in an external goal (defined by duties, principles, some utilitarian overall outcome or balance) but is in the activity, in the training, in the exercise itself. Other, positive emotions are relevant too. Flourishing, which in my view is always human and non-human flourishing at the same time, no longer needs external laws, facts, or arguments. It is and feels good in itself. When this happens, we have no need of external authorities telling us what to do (a human authority or Reason with capital "R"). Rather, we learn by example and by experience.

This does not mean that rules, laws, theories, and principles are entirely obsolete or that we can dispense with "environmental teachers" and with

124 *Beyond Nature, Beyond Modernity, Beyond Thinking*

environmental science. Following Dreyfus' view of expertise, maybe it is true that we first need some instruction. Maybe at an early stage in our moral-environmental development we cannot do without laws, rules, information, theory, reason, arguments, facts, etc.—without some knowing-that. But maturity in environmental ethics means having learned environmental skills and having the intuition to do environmental good. At that point, we do good because we have learned *how*. Thus, in order to really advance to a higher stage of moral-environmental development, we have to learn environmental skills and environmental habits. We have to change our comportment by training and exercise. We have to work on our *habitus* if we want a better *habitat*. And for this change to happen an "ought" is not enough. Words are not enough. Someone has to *show how* rather than say or show that. We know a lot *about* the environment and, as philosophers, *about* environmental ethics. But true environmental knowledge and expertise, like all real ethical knowledge and expertise, is in the "how".

Compare the moral change involved in moral and environmental learning with the problem how best to teach a child to cross a street carefully. As a teacher, I can say "Don't do this" when I see the child is running to the street without looking out for traffic. I might also say "If you do this, then bad things happen. You may have to go to the hospital. You may die." But I can also take the child by the hand and show it *how* to carefully cross. In environmental matters, many of us have to be taken by the hand. We have to be shown the "hows" and the joys of environmental virtue. Again a comparison with health problems and health expertise is useful: If you are a health expert, you can say to someone "Don't smoke" or you can inform someone about the consequences. But you can also focus on training different habits, different ways of doing things. You can say "This food is bad, you ought not to eat this", you can tell about what happens if you eat it every day, but you can also show someone how to choose healthy foods, how to prepare a different kind of food, where to get ingredients, etc.

Here is an overview of the different approach offered by virtue ethics:

knowledge	ethical theory	main concept(s)	action	examples of emotions
know that	deontological (categorical imperative)	duty	argue, protest, say THAT	guilt
	consequentialist (hypothetical imperative)	consequences causes	argue, observe, show THAT	fear
know how	virtue ethics, Aristotle	virtue, habit, skill, the good life, flourishing	example train exercise show HOW	joy, gratitude, . . .

Beyond Environmental Thinking *(2)*   125

This emphasis on the positive emotion of joy does not mean that someone who tries to be virtuous never feels any negative emotions. If one fails to become a better person, for example, one can feel bad, weak, and so on. But the main way the moral psychology of virtue works, the main way the *motivation* works, is not by means of obedience or fear but by seeing and experiencing good. This happens when one encounters an exemplary person and when one is engaged in pro-environmental action. More generally, the virtue approach is not so much focused on what we ought (not) to do (this is right and this is wrong), but on the open question of how we can change our lives in a way that makes us and our environment *flourish*. Virtue ethics (as well as Deweyan pragmatism) is not so much focused on restriction but on opening up new possibilities for acting and living. Again this is a more positive orientation and one that requires us to imagine and explore better ways of living.

Exploring how to live environmentally better lives, then, is not about "big" principles and "big" words, but about "little" virtue and vice, concerning "ordinary" things. In his introduction to environmental ethics, Jamieson objects to environmental virtue ethics that much environmentally destructive behaviour is not vicious but 'humdrum and ordinary'. It involves

> many people making small contributions to very large problems. They do not intend to cause these problems, and in many cases feel quite powerless to prevent them. The "soccer mom" driving her kids to school, sporting events, and music lessons does not intend to change the climate. Yet, in a small way, that is exactly what she is doing.
> (Jamieson 2008, p. 92)

I agree with Jamieson that much of our environmentally destructive behaviour is of this "ordinary" kind, and in Chapter 2 I have used the term "banal". But contrary to Jamieson, I do not think this is a problem for virtue ethics; instead, if we have an adequate understanding of virtue, virtue ethics has an *advantage* over other theories on this point. Virtue and vice come also in the "small" ways described by Jamieson. Virtue ethics asks us to examine our own lives—*my* life. To frame the problem as a "collective action" problem, as Jamieson does, denies our own responsibility to examine our lives, including the *details*. It leaves the problem in the hands of "them", of the "they": "they" (politicians, scientists, engineers, business people, etc.) are supposed to solve it and *I* can just continue to live my life in the way I do. But if virtue or vice were *not* in our ordinary, banal doing and habits, where else would they be? In the environmental ethics books written by philosophers who seek refuge in theory, avoiding the "ordinary"? No, environmental ethics is and should be about what we do in daily life, in the patterns in these doings (habits) and in the skills we have. There are people, for example, who have the skill to live without a car or at least to organize their lives in a way that minimizes car use. There are people who

126 *Beyond Nature, Beyond Modernity, Beyond Thinking*

choose to live near a school because they want to avoid car use. There are people who do not buy an SUV to drive their kids to school. And so on. Moreover, if ethicists or environmentalists want to change the behaviour of the "soccer mom" it is neither desirable nor effective to forbid her to live in this way; instead, it is more effective and more *motivating* if "soccer moms" and indeed all of us "ordinary" people see the example of people who are like ourselves in many ways, but who live in a more environmentally virtuous way: the example of people who have the skill to do things in a different way and who might show others *how* to do it and let them experience the joy of it.

The "soccer mom" example also shows that good intentions are not enough. What matters is what we do and *how* we do it. Similarly, a person who cooks and eats meat does not usually intend to kill animals (or rather have animals killed for her). Yet in agreement with Rousseau we can say that this is exactly what she is doing. "Ordinary", "small" habits are part of environmental problems, and making changes to them is much harder than putting the problem in scientific or technocratic terms. The truly virtuous person does not externalize the problem; she has the courage to examine her own life and trains in order to change it.

8.2. HUME: VIRTUE AND MORAL SENTIMENT

The close link between virtues and skills made in the previous section is compatible with Hume's broad interpretation of the term *virtue*, but this interpretation is controversial (it has been criticized by Foot 2002, for example). Let me explain this.

In the mainstream virtue ethics tradition, from Aristotle to MacIntyre, Foot, and Annas, a sharp distinction is made between virtue and skill. But this can, has, and must be criticized. It may well be that ancient philosophers such as Aristotle or Plato were interested in extracting principles and in intellectual justification, as Annas (1995) argues, and that today many philosophers are still mainly interested in that, but as I have shown such a view of virtue neglects a different type of moral knowledge that is at least as important: know-how. Virtue is not only and not mainly a matter of intellectual reflection but of learning the appropriate skills and habits. Virtue is not only *like* exercising a practical skill, as Annas (2011) has argued; it is not only about practical reasoning but actually involves and *is* partly and perhaps mainly a practical skill. There is *more* than an analogy between virtue and skill. Virtue concerns ways of *doing*, which cannot be reduced to knowledge of principles or justifications. Let me say more about how this interpretation of virtue ties in with Hume's ethics—in particular, with his interpretation of virtue and with his view on the role of 'moral sentiment'. This will enable me to elaborate on the moral emotions dimension of "environmental skill".

Beyond Environmental Thinking *(2)*   127

In Hume's sentimentalist virtue ethics, a character trait is a tendency to feel sentiments, and Hume thinks it is sentiments (rather than reason) that move us into action. In his *A Treatise of Human Nature* (1739–1740)—in particular, in the part 'Of Morals'—he argues that reason can distinguish between true and false, but not between right and wrong. He writes:

> If morality had naturally no influence on human passions and actions, it were in vain to take such pains to inculcate it; and nothing would be more fruitless than that multitude of rules and precepts, with which all moralists abound. [. . .] Since morals, therefore, have an influence on the actions and affections, it follows, that they cannot be derived from reason; and that because reason alone, as we have already proved, can never have any such influence. Morals excite passions, and produce or prevent actions. Reason of itself is utterly impotent in this particular. The rules of morality therefore, are not conclusions of our reason.
>
> (Hume 1739–1740, p. 294)

The role of reason in influencing our conduct is limited. This was also my observation with regard to what we may call "environmental reason": There are plenty of principles, theories, scientific findings, etc., but they do not move us into action. Environmental reason itself is 'utterly impotent'. So what *can* motivate us? Hume thinks sentiments can. Let me explain his conception of virtue.

Hume thinks that what we call 'virtuous' is what pleases:

> An action, or sentiment, or character is virtuous or vicious; why? because its view causes a pleasure or uneasiness of a particular kind.
>
> (Hume 1739–1740, p. 303)

Thus, according to Hume, sentiments and impressions can be agreeable or not, and if a character trait makes an agreeable impression, it is a virtue. Now I think there is more to virtue (and to environmental virtue) than pleasure or uneasiness. While the practice of environmental virtue and skill often feels pleasurable and agreeable to oneself and to others (but sometimes not, see Chapter 3), acknowledging that there is some relation between virtue and pleasure is not the same as equating them.[2] Nevertheless, with a view to further elaborating the "environmental skill" interpretation of virtue, it is interesting to further explore Hume's idea that we have a kind of 'moral sense' that is partly learned. Hume thinks that rules of justice are artificial; they are a matter of education and convention. Furthermore, at least some virtues arise from what Hume calls 'the circumstances and necessities of mankind' (p. 307). If this is true, then (1) if we understand virtue in terms of skill we should also include *social* skill, and (2) we should reflect on the role of circumstances in relation to environmental virtue.

128 *Beyond Nature, Beyond Modernity, Beyond Thinking*

Hume holds that we acquire a full 'moral sense' in society. In contrast to Rousseau, who thinks that society corrupts our 'natural' goodness, Hume comes close here to many neo-Aristotelians who teach that we learn virtue in social environments. For environmental virtue ethics, this means again that virtue is at least partly something that must be learned and trained in an appropriate social environment, which gives us the 'moral sense' that enables us to distinguish between good and bad. We feel good when we see virtue in others, and we imagine that others find it agreeable if we display virtue. We may conclude that "environmental skill" includes a kind of "environmental sense" that responds to virtue and vice in ourselves and in others. We are not only motivated by skilled engagement, but also by our moral sentiments, by our emotions that "know" and "feel" if the action is environmentally virtuous or not. We know that our action is good because we feel and imagine that others (would) approve of it and because we ourselves approve of it and feel good about it. Thus, it seems that in Hume's writings we meet another kind of 'tacit' knowledge: not the know-how of skilled activity, but the knowledge that originates in our socially conditioned sense of what is good. We can learn from Hume that for environmental motivation and action it is extremely important to be in an appropriate social environment, with "appropriate" social environment meaning: an environment that helps us to develop an "environmental sense". Once we have such a sense, we have a kind of 'tacit' moral knowledge that we do not need to make explicit; we simply *feel* that a particular action (or habit) is good or bad, virtuous or vicious.

Hume's broader understanding of virtue—virtue is not only a matter of reason and we do not only need the skill of deliberation but also a 'moral sense'—helps us to understand why we are often *not* motivated to act in pro-environmental ways. His account gives us the insight that it is highly problematic if we live in social environments that do *not* enable and stimulate us to develop an "environmental sense" and environmental virtue, that do *not* give us the capacity to feel whether our actions and habits are environmentally good.

However, in a Humean interpretation of virtue, even skills that one "naturally" has may be counted among the virtues and thus qualify as "moral". Indeed, Paul Russell has drawn attention to the fact that Hume included 'natural abilities and talents' in his account of virtue:

> Hume maintains that our natural abilities and talents (e.g. intelligence, imagination etc.) constitute important qualities of mind and that they are also liable to arouse our moral sentiments of approval and disapproval.
> (Russell 2013, p. 95)

It is unclear here why Hume limits 'natural abilities' (or acquired abilities, for that matter) to qualities of the *mind*, but his view makes us wonder if environmental virtue and environmental skill might also depend on abilities

Beyond Environmental Thinking *(2)* 129

and skills that are innate. Perhaps some people are more inclined to skilled engagement with their environment than others. It might well be easier to achieve environmental virtue for some people than for others, even if they are situated and raised in the same social environment.

In addition, as Russell shows, Hume accounts for (1) degrees and combinations of virtues in persons, (2) 'complexities and subtleties in the way the individual virtues and vices may manifest themselves in a given person and in particular circumstances' (Russell 2013, p. 100), and (3) variance in the virtues we approve of 'depending on the particular social and historical circumstances we are placed in' and hence their 'fragility and vulnerability to fortune and contingent circumstances' (p. 101). Indeed, Hume writes a lot about fortune in the *Treatise*. In contrast to Aristotle, he seems more aware of the important roles luck and contingency play in our lives—and indeed in ethics. Let me say more about this.

Hume thinks that there is a sense in which, to some extent, we cannot help being virtuous or vicious, depending on our talents and on luck. Hume 'denies that voluntary or intentional action is the sole basis on which we may assess a person's virtues and vices' and 'maintains that moral character is, for the most part, involuntarily acquired' (p. 105). I am not sure if I fully agree with Hume's claim, but his acknowledgment of the role of talents and luck is an interesting addition to the account of environmental virtue and environmental skill (and more generally, moral skill) I am developing. Against possible voluntarist interpretations of environmental virtue as "environmental skill", it is helpful to note that environmental virtue is not *all* about acquisition of skills by means of *willing* and *intending* to do so; with Hume we can say that it *also* depends on natural talents and skills (determined before birth), and on circumstances (during one's life). For example, if one has the luck of having parents who show and teach their children environmental virtue, then the environmental virtue of these children in later life is at least also related to that circumstance and luck. (This seems to be at least one reason why a Humean account of virtue may be better in line with what the natural and social sciences tell us. See also the next section.) And if we live in a time when modern thinking is still dominant, then this is a cultural-historical circumstance that helps to explain why environmental virtue defined as skillful engagement with the environment is more difficult to attain.

Furthermore, a Humean understanding of environmental virtue and skill also helps us to understand that being an environmentally virtuous person and having environmental skill can take different forms, depending on context and circumstance. Even if we are trained and have exercised under circumstances A, there may be circumstances B under which we fail to act as virtuous persons since it is much harder to act under these new circumstances or rather different skills are needed. What "environmental virtue" consists in also depends partly on context and circumstances. Adopting this Humean qualification renders our view of environmental virtue not only

130   *Beyond Nature, Beyond Modernity, Beyond Thinking*

(more) morally pluralist (there can be different forms of environmental good, being environmentally virtuous in one country, culture, or time may mean something else than being environmentally virtuous in another country, culture, and time), but also sensitive to the fact that even if one *tries* hard to become environmentally skilled and environmentally good and is *willing* to change, this may be harder or easier depending on talent and on the circumstances, on luck.

Like Callicott, Russell does not think that accounting for moral variation and contingency leads Hume to relativism and skepticism: Hume holds that we all have a capacity for sympathy, that we can take a general point of view, and that while morals vary in different times and among different nations, 'the basic principles which animate and govern them remain fixed and constant' (p. 102). Indeed, there are various ways in which this view can avoid (a strong form of) relativism. Even if environmental virtue means something else in two different cultures or places, in *both* cultures or places it is not the case that "anything goes"; instead, in both cultures or places the person must develop a moral sense of what is environmentally good and will meet (or imagine) approval and disapproval from her community. In both cultures, what one does (or not) and *how* one does it *matters*. In addition, the moral capacities one needs to do good are the same, and in both cultures there will be variations between people when it comes to their environmental skills and abilities to learn environmental skills. Furthermore, in both cultures, whether or not one actually can do environmental good and meet with approval depends partly on circumstances and luck. Training and education do not guarantee that the relevant environmental virtues and skills can and will be exercised under specific circumstances and in particular situations, let alone that they will be met with approval.

To conclude, Hume attends us not only to learned, acquired virtue and its "moral skills" (that is, to the social dimension of virtue) but also to the role of natural talents, contingency, and luck. Moreover, Hume's account gives us a pluralist understanding of virtue. Both insights are important when we try to define "environmental skill". We need to take into account that environmental virtue and "environmental skill" cannot be defined *a priori* as an objective list of virtues and skills; what environmental virtue and environmental skill mean depends on the social-cultural context in which we develop our "environmental sense." Furthermore, whether we can actually acquire and maintain environmental virtue and skill depends also on natural talents (and skills) and luck. (Below I will say more about the maintenance of virtue as distinguished from the training and acquisition of virtue.)

Note, finally, that next to Hume, Dewey, and Heidegger one can also draw on Eastern thinking to make the connection between virtue and skill. I already mentioned Varela's view of ethical expertise, which also connects virtue with skill. Another interesting contribution to this line of thinking has been offered by Stalnaker's interpretation of Confucian ethics. He argues that virtues are not just exercised in practical contexts, but are in fact

Beyond Environmental Thinking *(2)* 131

partially constituted by the mastery of certain skills (Stalnaker 2010). I will not further discuss this "Eastern" route here, but it deserves more travellers.

8.3. HUME AND THE SITUATIONALIST CHALLENGE FOR (ENVIRONMENTAL) ETHICS

An additional advantage of learning from the Humean interpretation of virtue is that, as Merritt has argued (2000), its emphasis on the social dimension of virtue better enables it to deal with the challenge of 'situationalist' social psychology. Let me draw on Merritt's article in order to explain this, and then draw conclusions for environmental ethics.

In the Aristotelian view, virtue motivates independent of social relationships and social settings. Once we have a virtuous character, we can expect that we will act virtuously in all kinds of situations. Once we have had a good upbringing, we will display our virtues in all situations. Social psychology, however, has challenged this view and has shown that personality traits are not as robust as we think they are and how we act will depend on situational factors. Some philosophers have argued that this poses a problem for virtue ethics (Doris 1998; Harman 1999). If, according to science, there is no such thing as "character"—that is, if character is understood as a set of very robust and stable personality traits—then why focus on ethical character, as virtue ethics does? And if few persons display the robust personality traits that conform to the Aristotelian ideal of virtuous character, then it seems that the Aristotelian ideal of virtue can never be realized in practice (Merritt 2000, p. 367). Assuming that situationalist psychology and its philosophical defenders get it right, and assuming that this is an adequate interpretation of Aristotle, it seems indeed that an Aristotelian virtue is problematic. However, Merritt argues that a Humean interpretation of virtue can remedy this problem. According to her, Hume's position in the *Treatise of Human Nature* has less strong requirements concerning the stability of virtue and includes a recognition of the importance of the social settings in which we (try to) exercise virtue:

> What is important for Hume's purpose is that one's possession of the virtues, which he characterizes as socially or personally beneficial qualities of mind, should be relatively stable over time somehow or other, not that it should be stable through taking a special, self-sufficiently sustained psychological form.
>
> (Merritt 2000, p. 378)

Thus, for a Humean virtue ethicist it is no problem that virtues need to be socially supported; on the contrary, it is argued that the social contributes to character, that character is shaped in social settings. Whereas in the (supposedly) Aristotelian view the motivational structure of virtue is independent of social relationships and settings, in the Humean view such relationships

132 *Beyond Nature, Beyond Modernity, Beyond Thinking*

and settings can help a person to become *and* to remain virtuous. It can contribute to the stability of virtue we want. Social psychology, according to this view, is not a threat to virtue ethics, but can help us to become aware of how the social contributes to virtue. Merritt writes:

> We must come to grips with psychological reality in understanding and explaining what kinds of things can possibly bring about stability in the possession of virtuous qualities.
>
> (Merritt 2000, p. 381)

This is also partly what I did in my chapter on contemporary psychology: We should not ignore this "reality". However, science is not the only way one can 'come to grips with psychological reality' and ethics should not be reduced to the science of self-management. Keeping in mind criticisms of modernity, it is good to remind ourselves of the insight that rationalist and empiricist Enlightenment thinking and Enlightenment practices may contribute to alienation from one's environment and indeed alienation from one's self. If we come to see ourselves as objects that can be, and need to be, manipulated and controlled, and if we think that scientific knowledge about the human is the *only* knowledge that is relevant to ethics, then we already take distance from the environment and from ourselves and neglect other forms of knowledge, including personal tacit knowledge: the know-how that results from one's own experience with relating to one's environment (natural and social, natural and artificial).

Moreover, a significant difference with Merritt's account (and with Hume and with Aristotle) is that I do not think that virtues are only a quality of the "mind"; they are qualities of mind *and* body. The concept of skill is meant to go beyond a dualistic understanding of the human and of virtue. In line with views about "embodiment" in cognitive science and in line with the philosophical and sociological accounts of expertise and craftsmanship reviewed previously, I believe that the stability we should talk about here is at the same time a stability of mind and of body; if we must seek stability of virtue then that stability must be understood as being constituted by the stability of *skill*. This non-dualist orientation is also one reason I use the term *skill*: in skilled activity, there is as much "mind" as there is "body". The stability of skill means stability not of "mind" or of "body" but stability of person-environment relations, which involves both body and mind (if such a distinction is helpful at all). What Hume and the social sciences get right is that this stability can and must be built and sustained in social relationships and settings. In this sense, any virtue ethics properly understood must not only be an ethics of skill but also a *social* ethics. We learn the appropriate environmental skills in groups, in communities, in societies, and in cultures. In this sense environmental skills are not "individual" skills but social skills, even if there will be always individual differences in the training and performance of virtue.

Beyond Environmental Thinking *(2)* 133

This social nature of environmental skill does not mean that we should always conform to social opinion and social example; sometimes it may be ethically required to divert from this opinion and act in socially unaccepted ways. But—to use one of the routes Merritt offers in response to this problem—these are rather rare instances and occasions. Let me express the optimistic view that the social should not be seen as an enemy of virtue or as necessarily corrupting—as Rousseau's Romanticism led him to believe—but as a ground that carries us and supports us in our efforts to become better persons, including *environmentally* better persons. Moreover, environmental good is both "social" good and "natural" good; making a sharp distinction between the two is itself a source of alienation. We relate to both human and non-human entities and environments, and skills are at the same time biological and social. The way we interact with our environment is at the same time a bodily and a cultural comportment, and the environment is experienced in a way that is at the same time physical-biological and cultural. Any "environmental ethics" as an ethics of skill must therefore transcend dualistic thinking in terms of minds versus bodies or nature versus culture. Environmental good understood in terms of environmental skill cannot be fully understood by using modern distinctions.

Let me further explore "non-modern" thinking about environment and environmental ethics, and especially what it means for our practices.

NOTES

1. Note that in Chapter 3 on contemporary, empirical psychology I already observed a link between health problems and environmental problems. This link does not only seem to be metaphorical, as in Aristotle, but has also to do with the way human psychology works.
2. This is also why I think Kate Soper's "alternative hedonism" (e.g. Soper 2004) is problematic. While I sympathize with Soper's objections to proposals to return to a "natural" mode of existence, her search for non-consumerist, intrinsically beneficial ways of living, and her argument that environmental deprivation and absence of pleasure go hand in hand, I take issue with the hedonist core of her view. It is one thing to acknowledge that pleasure is an important value, ethically speaking, and that alternative ways of doing and the exercise of what I call "environmental skill" should preferably be pleasurable and agreeable to others; it is quite another thing to put pleasure at the centre of our environmental-ethical concern. Perhaps contemporary hedonism, including Soper's, is an over-reaction to the puritanism in protestant Western culture. Both are two sides of the same coin. I believe that the environmental ethics I articulate in this book, understood as a virtue ethics and as an ethics of skill, can be a joyful ethics and will inspire a pleasurable way of life, but I also hope it can leave behind the pleasure-versus-restraint moral psychology that has roots in Plato and Aristotle and which continues to trouble the Western mind. (The relation between virtue and pleasure deserves more discussion, but on the next pages I will focus on making a point about the social dimension of environmental virtue.)

Part IV

Implications for Environmental Ethics and Philosophy of Technology

9 Implications for Environmental Ethics (1)

Beyond Walking in "Nature"

INTRODUCTION

> *We walked in so pure and bright a light, gilding the withered grass and leaves, so softly and serenely bright—I thought I had never bathed in such a golden flood, without a ripple or a murmur to it.*
>
> (Henry David Thoreau in *Walking*, 1862)

In the previous chapters I have articulated an approach to environmental ethics that focuses on skilled engagement with the environment and that goes beyond modern thinking about environment and about environmental ethics. But the form of my inquiry was still rather theoretical; that is, it started from a *conception* of environmental ethics. But what does this "environmental ethics of skill" or this notion of environmental virtue as "environmental skill" imply for our practices? In this (final) part of the book I will further spell out the implications of the previous chapters and give more concrete examples of what is problematic about our current practices, and how they might be changed in a way that constitutes what I have called "environmental skill". This work cannot be done by means of taking distance from practice, but requires us to attend to the phenomenology of those practices.

In this chapter, I start with discussing walking practices. In the next chapter I will also say something about other practices.

9.1. HOW WE (SHOULD) WALK TODAY: THE PHENOMENOLOGY AND ETHICS OF WALKING

An environmental ethics understood as an ethics of skill needs to carefully analyze the phenomenology of specific practices in order to (a) identify ways of doing and thinking that alienate us from our environment and (b) explore possibilities for better, skillful engagement with our environment.

Consider "walking in nature" and related practices. As we have seen in the chapter on Romanticism (Chapter 5), walking is a romantic activity *par*

138 *Implications for Environmental Ethics*

excellence, and given the influence of Romanticism on our contemporary practices, to talk about walking today is to talk about a particular romantic experience and practice. When we walk through the hills and woods, we are always in the company of Rousseau and Thoreau. Can we move beyond this romantic walking?

Let me start with a more elaborate analysis of contemporary walking. Why do we walk in nature today? And, more importantly for the purpose of this inquiry, *how* do we walk in nature? First, to talk about "nature" already pre-constructs our relation to the environment in a way that promotes disengagement. We set up our environment as entirely separate from ourselves. It seems that we are first outside nature and then enter nature, as a separate sphere. Second, we walk for a specific purpose, which is different from "work". When we talk about "walking in nature" we have in mind a "leisure" activity, done "for its own sake" rather than in order to survive, to make money, "to get something done", etc. Third, our desire for walking in nature suggests that we value the "natural" environment as opposed to the "artificial" environment. We want to walk in "nature", not in the city or in the supermarket. As Romantics, we want to leave the busy city, an "artificial", "polluted" environment that is perceived as ugly and stressful. We escape to "nature", to the "wilderness" where purity and calmness can be found. "Indoor" is the artificial, the sphere of lies and pretending; "outdoor" is the natural, where we can become authentic persons.

Aimed at harmony with, and closeness to, nature, others, and oneself, walking is a technique and exercise of the soul as much as it is a technique and exercise of the body. For those who work "with their hands" it allows time for (self-)reflection; for those who work "with their head", it allows getting in touch again with their own body and with their (natural) surroundings. The romantic aim is to find again the nature outside and within yourself. Walking is supposed to be "wholesome" in the sense that it heals you from modern alienation and unites you with nature. In romantic modernity since Rousseau, the natural is seen in opposition to the social and cultural. Liberation means: walking out of the city into the wilderness. To quote again Thoreau's words in the beginning of *Walking* (see also Chapter 5):

> I wish to speak a word for nature, for absolute Freedom and Wilderness, as contrasted with a freedom and Culture merely civil,—to regard man as an inhabitant, or a part and parcel of Nature, rather than a member of society.

> (Thoreau 1862, p. 1)

Furthermore, walking can also be done with a *scientific* purpose. As I noted in Chapter 5, Rousseau was not only a romantic dreamer, but also a botanist. The romantic and the scientific attitude can be combined in one person and one walk. The romantic subject observes objects in "nature" and at the same time makes itself—one's own self—into an object of study. Both natural objects and one's self are studied and can then (later) be exhibited in museums and books.

Hence the cultural significance of walking in nature can hardly be underestimated. It is not just a way of "spending your leisure time"; it is part of a culture—in this case a romantic modern culture and a scientific modern culture. Walking in nature is part of a form of life—in this case, our *modern* form of life. In this sense walking is a deeply cultural activity.

However, the very idea of seeing walking as "expression" of a particular (Romantic) culture is itself a very modern way of understanding things, since it presupposes a dichotomy between, on the one hand, a surface of practices which function as "symbols" or "representations" of culture and, on the other hand, the "deeper" culture these practices represent and express, a culture which is "prior" to these practices and is not itself a matter of praxis but rather a collection of ideas. To avoid such a dualistic view of culture, we had better explore whether we can construe different meanings of walking that are closer to the "skill" ideal articulated in Chapter 7. From a non-modern perspective, walking is not just an *expression* of "culture", as if culture is removed from the physical and can exist independent from it. Rather, with Ingold and Vergunst (who are influenced by Bourdieu) I propose to understand walking as constituting 'itself a way of thinking and of feeling', which has to do with 'the body's active engagement in its surroundings', and which itself generates cultural forms (Ingold & Vergunst 2008, p. 2). Thus, if anything is "prior" at all, it is not cultural form but praxis and experience, which are as much "natural" as they are "cultural". Ingold and Vergunst helpfully refer to Mauss' 'techniques of the body' and to what Bourdieu called a *habitus*: a way of doing and a kind of 'practical mastery' (p. 2)—in other words, a skill. The concepts of skill and habitus are not only "of the body" but are in the body and in the mind at the same time.[1]

Taking this approach, we can ask the following question in preparation of an ethics of walking as an ethics of skill: What kind of "habitus" or skill does walking in nature promote? What kind of active engagement do we (mind-body) have in our surroundings when we walk?

Lee and Ingold distinguish three specific modes of interaction involved in walking in nature (Lee & Ingold 2006, p. 69): (1) in contrast to other means of transportation such as driving or train travel, there is time to look around, (2) there is also time for thinking (which we modern Romantics conceptualize as "inward"-looking in contrast to the first, "outwardly" directed perception), and (3) walking allows us to become aware of our body, its movements, and its interactions with the environment. The latter mode of interaction seems to promote the kind of experience of, and engagement with, the environment that can be described as involving "environmental skill." Walking in "nature" is an embodied experience that is (and must be) experienced *as* embodied. It is a specific mode of mind/ body-environment interaction that allows us to sense the movements in of

140   *Implications for Environmental Ethics*

our body (e.g. movements of our legs and feet on the ground, our heartbeat when we climb a mountain) but also specific interactions with the environment, such as the impact of the weather on our body and mind.

In addition, walking increases sociability by promoting particular kinds of social interaction. For example, Lee and Ingold argue that walking replaces the mode of talking where one looks *at* each other (face-to-face conversation) with a more companionable mode of talking which they characterize as 'going along together' (Lee & Ingold 2006, p. 80): When people walk together, their conversation also seems to create similar conversational patterns. As one walks along, the conversation assumes a similar 'rhythm' (p. 81).

Thus, walking in nature seems to be what Borgmann calls a 'focal practice', which is meaningful in itself, requires skilled activity and bodily engagement, discloses the significance of things, and forms a person's character. What Borgmann writes about the family stove (or fireplace) seems also applicable to walking (see also the chapters on environmental skill):

> It provided for the entire family a regular and bodily engagement with the rhythm of the seasons (. . .). Physical engagement is not simply physical contact but the experience of the world through the manifold sensibility of the body. That sensibility is sharpened and strengthened in skill. Skill is intensive and refined world engagement. Skill, in turn, is bound up with social engagement. It molds the person and gives the person character. (. . .) And in these wider horizons of social engagement we can see how the cultural and natural dimensions of the world open up.
>
> (Borgmann 1984, p. 42)

Ethically speaking, these reflections suggest that walking is a good way of relating to one's environment since it promotes awareness of nature and of one's body, reflection, and sociability. However, we should be careful not to be lured too much into the romantic interpretation and practice of "walking in nature" and qualify this conclusion in at least the following ways.

First, we must question the strict distinction between "natural" (and "wild") and "artificial" assumed in this discussion of "walking in nature". Not only because the environments we consider as "natural" or "wild" are usually subject to management and maintenance by humans (e.g. most European woodlands may appear as "natural" but they can also appear as *tree farms*), but also because such descriptions assume a metaphysical distinction, the natural-artificial distinction, that is highly suspect. In so far as it *tries* to be anti-modern, Romanticism attempts to overcome dualism but in the end retains it: It still assumes distinctions such as the human versus the natural, the artificial versus the natural, the alienated versus the non-alienated, "hands" versus "head", etc. By using the term "nature", it pre-constructs the on-going relation between humans, environment, and technologies as dualities of humanity and nature, cultural and natural, artificial and natural. As such, it denies the very relational-transcendental

Implications for Environmental Ethics (1)   141

ground that makes walking possible. We are always already related to our environment and we are always already technological and artificial. The question is not "Should we be natural or artificial?" but: "*How* should we relate to our environment?" Walking might indeed promote a good way of relating to our environment, not because it allows us to connect with "nature", but because it makes us aware of, and shapes in a particular way, pre-existing relations that are already in place, also in "artificial" environments: relations to our body, to our self, to our environment, to others. At its best, walking makes us aware of, and allows us to flourish as, the relational beings we already are. But if it succeeds in doing that, it is not because it is a "natural" activity or because it makes us more "natural", but because it has specific characteristics that make us flourish by promoting a specific relation to the environment that involves the development and exercise of particular skills. The term "nature", then, is not an appropriate way to conceptualize what happens when we walk in this way. Even when we say we are "in nature", we are beings who relate to their environment in a particular way, which involves particular skills and *techne*. Using the term "nature" in this manner misleadingly suggests that our environment is entirely external to us, to our actions and to our thinking, whereas we are always already "environmental".

Second, I write "at best" since the romantic interpretation of walking—and hence romantic walking *practice*—may actually prevent us from the enjoying the benefits it attributes to walking in "nature". One reason why people walk in "nature" is to enjoy the scenery, to engage in the aesthetic contemplation of nature (and of themselves). If we perform this kind of walking, we are what Benjamin called a *flâneur*[2], albeit a nature wanderer instead of a city wanderer, paying close attention to the details of living nature. But such a disinterested aesthetic attitude promotes disengagement rather than engagement with the environment. It constructs our relation to our environment as the gaze of a detached observer, who is not herself part of his object of contemplation. It presupposes and reinforces a gap between observer and "nature". This betrays again the relational-transcendental ground that makes such walking and thinking possible in the first place. If we need an aesthetics at all to understand this, it is not the aesthetics of the *flâneur* we need but rather the participatory environmental aesthetics Berleant proposes, which is in line with Ingold's thinking about the environment. To quote Berleant again:

> There is no inside and outside, human being and external world, even, in the final reckoning, self and other. The conscious body moving within and as part of a spatio-temporal environmental medium becomes the domain of human experience, the human world, the ground of human reality within which discriminations and distinctions are made. We live, then, in a dynamic nexus of interpenetrating forces to which we contribute and respond.
>
> (Berleant 2005, p. 13)

142 *Implications for Environmental Ethics*

Thus, on the one hand I can never be totally alienated from my environment. I can only develop the technique of "detaching" myself from "nature" as a *flâneur* if I am safely with my feet on the relational ground. Even in "detached" contemplation, I remain an embodied, social, technological, and environmental being; my flight into the sky of disengaged reflection and god's-eye observation remains dependent upon this ground as a condition of possibility. The same is true for other kinds of detached reflection. On the other hand, my practice and experience of walking can be more or less engaged or detached, depending on the particular *how*: how I know, how I walk, how I experience my environment. My response to the "dynamic nexus" in which we live (our environment) can be more or less active, more or less participatory, more or less skillful.

In sum, walking in "nature" is a *particular type* of walking and a *particular way* of relating to the world that *seems* to be very beneficial, but risks destroying the environmental benefits it promises if it remains motivated by, shaped by, and dressed up in the terms of that paradoxical branch of thinking called Romanticism—or in the terms of objectivist science, the flip side of modern thinking and doing. Love of "nature" and its aesthetic qualities, but also the scientific or quasi-scientific study of "nature", may give shape to a kind of walking that disengages us from our environment. What must be promoted instead is the development and exercise of a range of ethical-environmental skills or competences that are valuable in various environments (not only in so-called "natural" ones) and which may or may not be easier to develop in the particular kinds of environments we call "nature". This range of skills includes at least (1) the skill of relating to one's environment in a way that allows one to attend to its features and reality rather than focusing (only) on getting to one's destination, (2) the skill of reflection while remaining aware that this reflection is rooted in one's relational and embodied being and cannot and should not be totally disengaged but must remain open to the environment, (3) the skill of being open to one's *senses* and to *sensations* of the environment and to remain aware of one's body-in-action, indeed of one's skillful engagement in and with one's environment, and (4) the skill of companionable conversation in the way of 'walking along together': *talking along together* rather than face-to-face dialogue (at least to the extent that this promotes more confrontational ways of talking and doing).

While these skills may also be promoted by other activities, walking seems to be a particularly apt way of realising their development and flourishing. But to bring this out, there is no need to focus on the "natural" aspect of walking. The main question for an environmental ethics in so far as it is understood as an ethics of skill and a "walking ethics", then, is not whether or not a particular environment is "natural" or "artificial", but whether or not it suits the development and flourishing of these skills of appropriate attention, rooted reflection, open sensation, and social talking, which discloses and creates worlds of meaning and significance *in interaction with the environment.* This list of skills gives us a normative framework to evaluate different ways of walking and seeing.

Thus, based on these criteria one may have a discussion about the suitability of particular environments, and particular walks in particular "natural" environments may turn out to be very good in developing these skills. But it is not clear that "natural" environments are always a priori better. For example, it is true that, as Ingold writes, city environments seem to prevent leaving traces (Ingold 2004, p. 329) and seem therefore less good than many non-built environments. Yet in "natural" environments traces might also disappear sooner or later. Moreover, mobile electronic equipment increasingly allows people to leave electronic traces of their city walking. (For example, people use smartphones to "draw lines" and publish them—online, of course.) The most important question for environmental ethics here is not if we should choose an "artificial", built and human-made environment or a "natural" environment, but rather how we should relate to and can shape and re-shape our environment *tout court*, which has both "artificial" and "natural" aspects. What forms of 'dwelling'—to use a Heideggerian term—are environmentally good?

This is not a proposal for rigidly categorizing activities as either "good" or "bad". The point is not to condemn certain activities, but to evaluate the "how," the ways we do them, and in particular the kind of relation to the environment they shape and constitute. Moreover, in the same activity several "hows" can be identified. As it turns out, our walking practices and other practices are often ambiguous with regard to skilled engagement and its ethical benefits. As we have seen, walking may promote embodied and disembodied experience, skilled engagement and alienation. And even within "modern" experience, there might be a mix of Enlightenment and Romanticism. Consider also two practices related to "walking in nature": bird watching and hunting.

The bird watcher may have either a romantic attitude and/or a scientific attitude: he may love the "nature" he is observing and/or he may study the "nature" he watches. But whichever attitude he has (or whichever mix of the two attitudes he has), as a *voyeur*—romantic or scientific—he is detached from his object of observation. He is a detached observer. He tries to hide for the bird. In a sense, he wants to bracket his presence. He wants to see the bird from a point of *nowhere*. He wants to be invisible. He wants and takes up the position of a god: the god's eye point of view.

This experience is even more clearly disengaged when we consider the use of webcams. By means of the webcam, the "nature" voyeur achieves nearly full invisibility. His presence *in* the environment is reduced to his eye (or to the artificial extension of his natural eye). This technological practice goes further than using binoculars, telescopes, and cameras, which already alienated the watcher from his environment. Whereas the use of (for example) binoculars still involves a form of embodied presence (although already then the body of the viewer is reduced to a *stand*), the webcam reduces the

144   *Implications for Environmental Ethics*

viewer's body to the eye (an artificial-natural, indeed hybrid eye) and blends out the body. Of course the webcam viewer is still embodied and experiences the world as an embodied being, but his relation to the environment of the animal(s) he is watching is an alienating one (though perhaps not as alienating as in the case of someone who never even looks at "nature").

Ironically, hunting turns out to be a far more *engaged* way of relating to one's environment than merely "walking in nature" or "watching nature". In particular, if we believe what Ingold says about hunter-gatherers, traditional hunting practices seem to promote respect and reverence for the animal rather than the instrumental attitude Heidegger thought was very problematic. An interesting aspect of hunting in contrast to, say, industrial-style farming, is that the hunter does *not* have full control over the animal. The animal may show itself or not, may "give" itself to the hunter or not. This lack of control and the *acceptance* of lack of control is rather un-modern. Furthermore, the skilled hunter who is engaged in the hunt is not generally busy with his own self and feelings. His gaze, his thinking and doing, his comportment, is directed to "reality": to the reality of the animal and to the environment. Body and mind are intensely related to the environment. In so far as the hunter *hunts*, there is no *rêverie*, no space for the disinterested *flâneur*. This is especially so in the case of hunters who hunt to feed their families, who are hungry, who depend on the hunt for food. Then there is no time for dreaming and there is no concern with the self; all care and concern is directed outward; there is only the flow of the concentrated, immersed conscious and active body-mind engaged in the hunt.

However, there are at least three remaining problems with hunting as we know it today. First, today it is usually done for pleasure, and ethically speaking killing for *pleasure* is itself a morally problematic thing to do, to say the least. Second, if one concludes from the phenomenology of hunting for food that "originally" it was better, since hunter-gatherers would at least do it to survive, one risks to fuel a Romantic, nostalgic motivation for hunting, which may lead to a re-enactment of "natural" hunting in order to put one again in tune with the "authentic", "natural" way of living. Third, contemporary hunters do not kill with their bare hands, as Rousseau and Thoreau would recommend. They use *guns*. But guns, like much hunting technologies and military technologies, allow killing at a distance: as tele-technologies, they bridge the distance, but at the same time, by rendering possible remote killing, they also *create* distance, including the psychological, emotional distance needed to be able to kill. Of course the hunter "knows" that the animal feels something (this is his *scientific* voice speaking, knowing-that), but he does not really feel it; like military training, hunting training even tries to reduce possibilities for the development of empathy. In these various senses, hunting turns out to be alienating as well. It seems better than buying stuff in the supermarket, but it is still a form of remote killing, and it may be motivated by romantic thinking and focus on the self.

Implications for Environmental Ethics (1) 145

That being said, the "authentic" hunter-gatherers of the past also used spears and other remote killing devices. Technology is and has always been part of human living and human existence. Moreover, supermarket behaviour could be interpreted as a kind of gathering, although promoting this *as a form of gathering* is then again a romantic way of thinking: we want to do something that is "natural" for us to do, something that is "authentic" because it was done in the pre-historic past. As often, such interpretations from evolutionary science (or those popular writers who use or abuse evolutionary science) then play the role not as the enemy of Romanticism but as its companion: The romantic draws on her interpretation of evolutionary science to retrieve "authentic" and "natural" ways of doing.

In sum, walking and related "nature" activities seem environmentally good, but at closer inspection they confront us with the problems of modern thinking. When we try to find a different way of doing and thinking, we continue to meet again our own Romantic-scientific selves. Can we get out of the modern mirror palace?

In order to further explore the relation between walking and technology, and more generally environmental practice and technology, let me discuss wayfinding technologies. Again this will raise the question how non-modern we can be.

9.2. WALKING AND WAYFINDING TECHNOLOGIES

What kind of walking is made possible by GPS technology? What kind of seeing is promoted by this technology? And are those ways of walking and seeing better or worse than others, evaluated by what the ethics of walking understood as an "ethics of skill" recommends?

Before I attempt to answer these questions, let me first observe that different ways of walking involve different kinds of wayfinding and associated skills (or competences), which may or may not enhance the ethical walking skills and competences identified. For example, the skill of navigating in a supermarket is very different from wayfinding in a mountainous "nature" area, and even within these activities-places there are different possible styles (e.g. depending on person, experience, persuasive techniques and strategies by the retailer or park manager, etc.) and different *modes* and *techniques* of wayfinding (e.g. using a map versus using visual marks or using an "app")[3]. In this section, I will focus on wayfinding while walking in "nature" by using handheld GPS navigation technology (i.e. as part of a smart phone or sold as a separate "navigation" device).

GPS technology allows the "nature" walker or "outdoor" enthusiast to find the way by enabling her to continuously update her position on a digital map. But like all technologies, its significance and influence goes further than simply being a new tool. It also has epistemological and normative-ethical consequences.

146 *Implications for Environmental Ethics*

First, as Willim remarks, to be able to use the device we are 'dependent on a complex array of technologies, including satellites and the whole industry that is required to run it' (Willim 2007a, p. 2). Using actor-network theory (see, for example, Latour 2005), we could draw attention to the whole network of people and things on which the workings of the device depend. This "network" approach to technology implies that technology is not just about devices but also about patterns of organization, economy, people. Moreover, as any user of GPS navigation technology knows, the use of this technology may make us dependent on the device when it comes to wayfinding. When we do not know the place, we are lost when the batteries are empty or when the device 'turns its back on us' in other ways (in scientific terms: different kinds of malfunctioning). However, there is the possibility of a deeper and arguably worse effect: we might actually lose the *skill* or *competence* to navigate without the technology (see also Willim 2007b, p. 675).

Second, the handheld device literally mobilizes the sitting people we have become (see also Ingold again, but also Urry 2006, p. 361), which certainly is a good effect, although not all handheld "mobile" devices are always used while walking (for example, a mobile phone can be used while sitting at a desk, in a train, etc.).

Third, as these suggested effects illustrate, an ethics of walking as an ethics of skill concerns not only the 'operation of the device' and its more direct consequences, but the way changes in skill generate a different kind of wayfinding altogether and perhaps even a different practice of walking. Let me further explain and develop the latter claim.

A device like this typically engenders normativity in at least two ways. Consider first how it is used. One can create or download a route beforehand, which one then follows, or one can point to a particular aim and the device will show the direction to follow. This is already a first, perhaps rather trivial kind of normativity of the technology: Although in one sense humans decide where they want to go, in another sense the device "says" where to go (sometimes literally, as in most car GPS systems). Although humans have their aims and decide to switch on the device, once the device is used, it creates its own normativity: 'You should now take this path and not this path'. Of course we are "free" to change our route (and can use the device to do so), but the point is that we are not encouraged to do so. We experience it as if *we are kept on track*.

However, there is also a second, "deeper" type of normativity. Not only does using this device promote particular kinds of wayfinding; it also promotes or discourages particular skills (ways of doing), ways of perceiving, ways of thinking, and (in sum) ways of relating to one's environment. In order to elaborate this point, let us further consider the phenomenology of GPS wayfinding. The following analysis is based on my own experience with using a GPS navigation device, which I will connect with Willim's and Ingold's ethnographical theorizing when appropriate.

Implications for Environmental Ethics (1)   147

GPS navigation makes possible and promotes what I call a "cursory" mode of experience. When I use the device, I learn to identify with the cursor on the screen. In a sense I *become* the cursor on the screen. There is a mixture of subjectivity (*I* walk) and objectivity (I experience myself as an object moving on the screen). In this particular mixture of subjectivity and (experienced) objectivity, it seems that I become disembodied: It seems that I practice what Willim calls 'disembodied screen walking', similar to what happens in a computer game (Willim 2007a, p. 3). However, I do not think 'disembodiment' is the appropriate term here. Rather, what happens in experience is that my physical body is replaced by the virtual "body". I become an arrow on a grid, a vector. I become a *cursor* (the one who follows a course) rather than a walker. This takes me out of my environment in the sense that the "natural" environment is replaced by the "virtual" environment: the environment "in" the device. Thus, there is a kind of re-embodiment, but my body is now the cursor, and there is a new environment or, to the extent that I am still connected to the physical environment, what we could call a "dual" or "mixed" environment.

This experience of becoming a cursor is not entirely unique to wayfinding by using GPS technology; it also happens already to some extent when I use a map and follow a route. As Willim appropriately remarks by referring to Bolter and Grusin's (2000) well-known work on re-mediation, GPS technology re-mediates the earlier technology of map reading. However, the map is not a mere representation of "reality", as Willim seems to suppose (Willim 2007a, p. 4); rather, in the experience of the walker the "real" environment becomes a 3D version of the map. The map environment becomes the "first" environment and her movements on it become her "first" life, whereas "nature" becomes the "second" environment and the "second" life. To the extent that it comes to be experienced as a secondary environment, there is a sense in which "nature" becomes less real and more virtual than the map. The only difference with map reading, it seems, is that in GPS navigation one's position on the map is given a pre-defined avatar by the device (e.g. an arrow), whereas when I read a map I have to imagine my avatar and its position. Since the "work" is already done by the electronic device, so to speak, the effect is increased. Phenomenologically speaking, then, *I walk the map* rather than the ("natural") environment.

Furthermore, the device is not only an extension of my body, as a "cyborg" phenomenology would have it; rather, I also become an element within the system as I experience myself as moving "in" the device or "on" the map. The device is then not an extension of the user; the user becomes an extension of the map. Using GPS, we are indeed 'walking through an advanced technological system', as Willim writes (Willim 2007a, p. 7). The system needs our bodily movement to work; then it can update the image and move the cursor (Willim 2007b, p. 672). I am both guided and "moved" (or even "used") by the device (see also the first type of normativity identified above: I am kept on track)[4].

148   *Implications for Environmental Ethics*

Walking a map—with or without the help of GPS—also means that 2D perception takes priority over 3D perception. The earth becomes a surface. What happens in the third dimension gets somehow lost. For example, trees, themselves 3D objects par excellence, connecting earth and sky and branching out into space, disappear on a map that will usually show only an *area* of woodland. Ironically, by means of GPS technology depending on satellites turning around the earth, the world becomes more *flat*. But, as Ingold puts it, 'human beings live in the world, not on it' (Ingold 2004, p. 333) and as such the technology gives us a problematic perception. (More generally, maps are always selective; they do not only simplify reality but also offer a selective outlook on it.)

Part of my phenomenological description of what GPS technology does to our navigation experience is strikingly similar to what Dreyfus and Kelly have recently written about it. Their interpretation is especially useful since it also focuses on the questions regarding skilled engagement. They argue that 'to the extent that technology strips away the need for skill, it strips away the possibility of meaning as well' since the art of skilled navigation reveals 'meaningful distinctions' (Dreyfus & Kelly 2011, p. 213). They also talk about a 'flattening' of the world, but then in the sense of a loss of meaning: The world becomes 'nondescript' and 'your understanding of the environment is about as minimal as it can possibly be' (p. 214). Using GPS, then, is

> to lose the sensitivities—to the landmarks, street signs, wind direction, the height of the sun, the stars—all the meaningful distinctions that navigation skill reveals. (. . .) Indeed, in an important sense this experience turns you into an automated device the GPS can use to arrive at its destination.
>
> (Dreyfus & Kelly 2011, p. 215)

This is similar to what I said about being moved by the device; it helps to bring out the ethically-epistemically problematic effects of de-skilling.

However, to say that GPS technology promotes this particular way of walking, wayfinding, and seeing does not imply the claim that when we walk we are in this mode of walking and mode of experience *necessarily* and *all the time* or that we are always *entirely* in this mode. The cursory, disengaged, and "flat" mode of experience is likely to alternate with other experiences of the environment. Perhaps it is more accurate to say that we travel between two or more "worlds". There may be a kind of Gestalt switch between them: At one moment the environment appears as a map, at another moment I engage with a particular feature of the environment and immerse myself in it. But it is also possible that the two worlds meet and merge, or even "clash" in my experience, as happens when I bump into a tree or stumble in a ditch while looking at my GPS device. And perhaps there are more complex relations between these two modes of experience (or two worlds) that I have left out of the analysis; this issue certainly deserves more attention.

Moreover, even if the GPS device were to keep us always in a "flat" experiential mode, I disagree with Dreyfus and Kelly that the "flattening" mode amounts to erasing *all* meaningful distinctions. Rather, as my descriptions show, *different* meanings and distinctions are created, different sensitivities emerge, and indeed different *skills* are needed. Even navigating in a "flat" world requires skill. And why not create new, different technologies, or adapt, "hack" existing technologies by using or changing them in unintended ways, in order to let new meaning arise? For example, even if we use the same device, a new "app" may add new meaning to the environment rather than (only) removing meaning. For example, we may be informed about particular landscapes, plants, or animals, or about the history of a place. Different technology, instead of alienating us from our environment, might help us to attend to it and engage with it. We can create new possibilities.

Thus, while it might be true that when walking and wayfinding with the help of a GPS device, one mode of experience tends to become (pre)*dominant*—either by occurring more frequently or by influencing my experience in other ways that, on the whole, make my experience more cursory, disengaged, and "flat"—this does not mean that the technology necessarily *excludes* other possibilities. (I will further discuss this below.) Yet to the extent that it *does* exclude other possibilities, wayfinding by using a GPS device supports romantic contemplation or scientific study of "nature", but does not promote an (inter)active, intense, engaged relation with the environment.

9.3. WALKING SKILLS AND ENVIRONMENTAL VIRTUES

With this phenomenological analysis, we are now in a better position to evaluate walking in nature by using GPS wayfinding technology. If we consider again what we could call the four "central" walking skills or walking virtues, we can conclude that wayfinding by using maps and, in particular, GPS technology has the following ethical-epistemological implications with regard to the environment *if and in so far as* it promotes (and renders dominant) a cursory, disengaged mode of experience.

First, by drawing attention to the route of the cursor on the digital map, using GPS technology discourages paying attention to the features of one's environment. As one is drawn into the world of the map and perhaps even becomes an extension of the system, the focus is on moving on the map and within the system—in particular, on getting from A to B. As Willim writes, 'navigation is a goal-oriented movement, it can be described as the process or activity of accurately ascertaining one's position and planning and following a route' (Willim 2007b, p. 668). This means that one gets *de-skilled*

150   *Implications for Environmental Ethics*

in attending to features of one's environment and that one is *trained* in what philosophers call "instrumental reason": thinking about the means of reaching an end. The end is the destination, the mean is oneself. The body becomes an instrument to "do" or "follow" the track or route. The environment appears as a background that is at best irrelevant and at worst standing in the way. There is a kind of "tunnel" effect, much in the same way as in a car race (in reality or as a digital game): What matters is the routing and the handling of the technology, everything outside the track is perceived as décor. Perceptually speaking, one is no longer "in touch" with one's environment. If a cyborg phenomenology is appropriate at all here, it is one in which human and machine merge to reach a goal. What matters is reaching the goal or destination; the environment is relatively unimportant. Thus, the point is not that there is a general de-skilling but that certain skills are un-learned and others are developed (e.g. we may become a better GPS-walker, a better cursor). There are processes of de-skilling and re-skilling.

GPS technology thus promotes a particular mode of experience; it helps to constitute and shape not only a particular way of walking, but also a way of moving and indeed living. Ingold makes a distinction between wayfaring and transport as two modalities of movement. Whereas the wayfarer 'in following a path of life, negotiates or improvises a passage as he goes *along*', transport 'carries the passenger *across* a pre-prepared, planar surface' (Ingold 2010, p. 126). Transport involves 'a series of *strategic* moves from location to location' (p. 127). This is what GPS technology does: it *transports* us; it makes us a passenger in the transport we have organized by using the technology. And being a passenger means being detached from one's environment and observing or contemplating it. As a romantic traveller, the passenger sees only his own expanded self. As a modern traveller, he sees a world that is external to him and a world that is *his*—a world that is his property, that is there for his use. This is made possible by the technology, which gives the passenger-walker a *window*.[5] In terms of knowledge, as a passenger-walker we take the 'superior and stationary vantage point' (p. 128), we 'fly with the birds' (p. 127). The digital map gives us an outline, which we then walk. The walk is an execution of the plan. We become Ingold's 'Kantian traveller', who reasons over a map (p. 135)—or rather, we delegate the reasoning to the GPS device. The GPS user's walking risks to 'be reduced to the mere mechanics of locomotion, getting from point to point' (p. 135). The wayfarer, by contrast, 'is not a walker of shapes or outlines, and his vision unfolds at ground level, as he goes along' (p. 128). She knows as she goes along (p. 134), 'draws a tale from impressions in the ground' (p. 135). This is a different way of knowing as much as it is a different way of life.

Second, in so far as the technology supports "instrumental rationality", the type of disinterested or contemplative reflection favoured by philosophers, artists, and others is unlikely to flourish, since one is too busy with

Implications for Environmental Ethics (1) 151

map-reading and routing. In the perceptual tunnel created by this kind of walking and wayfinding, both physical and philosophical vision is restricted. But more importantly, the type of reflection that tries to achieve a kind of "grounded" or "rooted" way of thinking (as described above) is even harder to achieve, since in experience one is already "uprooted" by using the device. A décor is not a soil or a living whole, just as a 3D projection of a map is not the real. Our surroundings then *stop being an environment*, they stop being a whole of which we are part and a reality in which there is something at stake. Using the device denies our relational nature. The plurality of relations is reduced to one kind of relation: our position on a surface. Other beings and natural surroundings become part of the background, to which the foreground figure (the self) cannot relate in other ways than framed by this foreground-background scheme. The route, the thick line, the arrow are the foreground; everything else fades away into non-significance. Modern use of GPS technology thus contributes to what we may call "the death of the environment", an event comparable to the famous "death of God"; it seems to amount to yet another kind of loss of meaning and, ultimately, to "the death of the human" since humans can only exist as environmental beings.

Third, sensing and sensation in relation to one's body and one's environment is not promoted in so far as the GPS device disembodies and de-engages. When and in so far as I am in the "GPS world", there is de-sensing and de-sensitizing. The virtual environment of the map does not smell and does not give haptic or other feedback. The ground becomes an area on the map. The weather mainly shows itself as annoying sun rays or rain drops on the screen. My virtual self, my avatar, cannot feel them. I cannot feel them in so far as I experience through my avatar. The cursor is not a real body, since bodies are by definition environmental. The arrow has no skin, no interface with the environment; the map itself is a skin that has been removed from the earth, an operation that always results in the skin being no longer a skin.[6] The cursor-self has no feet that touch and feel the ground, no breathing rhythm and sound that connects me with my environment, no body that experiences and co-creates a rhythm, a pattern, or that leaves a trace. There is a line and there is movement, but there is no lived rhythm. There are notes and sounds, but there is no music. In the background birds are singing, but their song is not part of the "soundscape" in which I roam and which I co-shape; it is rather part of the sound*track* that accompanies my locomotion across the map, my planned *movie*. My body has become as un-earthly as the satellites that allow me to use my GPS device; it does not touch the wet, damp, dirty, noisy, living earth but hovers over it in serene and strategic calculation (*walk*ulation so to speak).

Finally, sociability as "talking along together" is made more difficult when doing GPS-walking if the rhythm is regularly interrupted by the question *where we are*, which interrupts the continuous interaction with the environment and with others. When this mode of experience takes precedence over

152 *Implications for Environmental Ethics*

(or dominates) other modes of experience, the group moves as a "collective" avatar through the digital, 2D world of the map, which does not create true conversation (etymology: living together, a manner of conducting oneself in the world, to keep company with) since the social and natural world is temporarily suspended. When engagement ceases, (other) worlds come to an end.

One way to deal with this problem is to make one person the guide, which "liberates" others to converse. More generally, a comprehensive ethical-phenomenological analysis must take into account not only the "default" use of a device. Indeed, one may object that I have exaggerated the effects and that all this only happens with a particular kind of (intensive) use of maps and GPS. This is true; I have used a little exaggeration in order to bring out more clearly what happens in modernity and with modern technology to our ways of seeing and ways of doing. But (1) if the technology makes a particular mode of experience predominant this does not mean that other modes are excluded, as I said before, and (2) we can use the device in different ways, including ways not intended by the designers. Since use is not *determined* by the device, we have this possibility. We can conceive of "strategies of resistance", so to speak, and "outdoor" people use some of them. By using the term "resistance" I do not mean that designers of GPS devices have malicious intentions, of course, but that we can use the device in ways not necessarily foreseen by the designers and in a way that "resists" the dominance of the way of walking and seeing I described above. For example, I sometimes use the strategy of "getting lost"[7], which involves postponing navigation (by whatever means) in order to become more focused on the environment ("nature" or "city"). This strategy is compatible with the use of GPS navigation; one can save one's initial position, then turn off the device and "get lost", and only turn it on later in order to navigate back to the starting position. The point is to get the virtue-skill benefits of a different kind of walking and wayfinding and to relate to one's environment in a more responsible way—understood as "being *responsive* to". Moreover, as mentioned previously one could conceive of applications added to the device that draw attention to features in and of the environment. Consider educational apps that would allow you to spot and identify various animals and plants (e.g. birds and their songs, trees, etc.)—such devices may already exist as I write this. Thus, it turns out that the technology does not only have implications for "older" ways of walking but also makes possible new and different ways of walking.

Thus, the point is not that we need non-technological walking, as a romantic environmental ethics would have it. In a sense, all walking is technological—even without "navigation technology" in the strict sense. As Urry writes, 'walking is interdependent with many technologies, footwear, clothing, places of rest, paving and pathways, other means of movement, places to walk to, rules and regulations about movement and access, signage and so on' and these technologies 'intersect with the capacities of human

Implications for Environmental Ethics (1)   153

bodies' (Urry 2006, p. 362) to create not only ways of walking but also ways of seeing, ways of thinking, and ways of living together. The question is *which* technology we use and what corresponding mode of walking and wayfinding, and indeed mode of life, we want to engage in. (In Chapter 11 I will say more about technology.)

9.4. WORKING IN "NATURE"

Since walking—with or without GPS technology—so easily becomes a modern, detached way of relating to our environment, we might search for other ways of relating to our environment. When it comes to "nature" or the "outdoor" (if we use this word we define the environment as the negative of the "indoor"—e.g. the house or the office), perhaps *working* in nature is a better way of avoiding the Romantic-scientific pitfalls discussed in the previous sections. In order to become more "environmental," we may want to *work* rather than walk. But what kind of work? What *way of working* is environmentally best?

Working in "nature" seems to constitute an active, perhaps less contemplative, *habitus* that allows for intense engagement with one's environment. Unless it is hijacked by modern-industrial ways of thinking and doing (standardization, efficiency, automatization) and when it happens in close connection to the materiality and physicality of the environment, it appears to me that it might be a more whole-some physical, bodily activity that involves the whole body and better connects us with our environment as we transform it (and are, as persons, transformed by it). If one works in "nature", there is some time for contemplation during breaks, but most of the time the type of thinking at work here is involved and immersed thinking, rooted in concrete activity and lived skill. This is whole-some since one's sense of (non-relational) self evaporates. In concentration, there is what psychologists call "flow", which means that there is happiness. There is no detached contemplation and no ego. Such work also seems to connect us better to others, with whom we "have" to collaborate and can talk freely as we work along. In addition, non-humans in the environment benefit from the activities (the "primary" goal of "environmental" work anyway). Thus, ethically speaking, the "nature" worker might be a good alternative to the bourgeois *flâneur* and perhaps even to the "outdoor" walker or sports enthusiast, who may seldom achieve the former's degree of attentiveness to her environment, engaged-grounded reflection, sensing and sensation, and sociability. In "nature" work or, better, "environmental work", skill, purpose, practice, companionship, meaning, virtue, character formation, and environmental flourishing merge in a feast of what we can only call environmental good.

I prefer the term "environmental" work since using the term "nature" still implies a dualistic view: Work in "nature" is contrasted with work in the "artificial" office, the "outdoor" is contrasted with the "indoor".

154 *Implications for Environmental Ethics*

The suggestion is that only in nature we can authentically and naturally work and are free, whereas in the house we are "artificial" and enslaved by necessity (see also Arendt) and in the office we are part of the "system". But why exactly is the first kind of environment better *per se*? As we have seen, walking can be a very "artificial" experience, and some people might feel more "authentic" when they work in their office. What matters, it seems, is how we experience a particular environment and *how* we work in it, not the precise "nature" or "essence" of the environment as defined by science (organic or not), not the precise ontology as defined by philosophers. The environmental virtue or vice is in the way we relate to our environment, in the "how". Someone working in "nature" with "organic" materials and "authentic" tools may nevertheless relate to her environment in a way that uses it as a 'standing reserve'—for example, as a mere means for the worker to improve her health or to socialize with others, to express her "authentic" self and identity, or to improve "eco-diversity" as an abstract goal. The point is not, of course, that such things are all bad per se but that they can pursued in more or less "environmental" ways, and that this "how" matters, more than intellectual efforts at justification, since it matters to environmental *motivation*.

But even if Romanticism and industrialism are avoided here, if one works, for example, in a nature reserve then it will be hard to avoid the managerial, controlling attitude typical of modernity. The problem is not intervention in the environment as such, since from a relational-environmental point of view one cannot avoid "environmental being" in an active sense. Humans have always been "technological" in this sense: They have always intervened in their environment; they have always transformed it. Absence of intervention in our environment means death. The problem is rather that in modern thinking and doing we start treating the natural environment and natural beings as mere means to our ends, as resources or objects that are part of our "household". To the extent that working in nature becomes "wildlife management" or "ecosystem management", the environment as a whole becomes an *oikos* (Greek word for household) and our relation to the environment becomes ecological and economical. Then we study, administer, and control the environment. Even the planet as a whole becomes our household; we are managers of "spaceship earth." Etymologically, ecology means the "logos" of the household, the *oikos*. We *domesticate* our environment, we bring it into our house, and we do this in a *modern* way. The beings we encounter in our environment become our resources or our pets. The planet becomes our house. It is no longer an environment in a strict sense; it is a self in which we can no longer encounter an other, an inside without an outside (perhaps only outer space).

If this is what an ecological approach to environmental ethics implies, we should not want it. If our relation to the environment becomes the scientific study and transformation of "nature" as "household", we close off better, more wholesome, and more flourishing ways of relating to our environment

Implications for Environmental Ethics (1)   155

(for us and for other beings). Therefore, an environmental ethics understood as an ethics of skill, which aims to promote more environmental engagement, should oppose the "eco-logization" and the "eco-nomization" of the environment.

Again, this argument should not be interpreted in a romantic way: The problem is not that any human intervention in the environment is bad (not at all—it is even necessary for us to survive, to live, and to flourish) and the solution is not that we try to restore our environment to a "natural" state which is entirely "wild" and undomesticated. The problem is excess of control and intervention. The problem is a *modern* relation to the environment, which, by making *every* "*thing*" part of the household, and by organizing this household in a modern way, is an alienating mode of thinking and habit which makes us less rather than more environmental. The point is not about what we "do to nature" (good things, bad things). The point is that *before* we even do something in "nature", we have already pre-constructed it as our household. It is already our 'standing' reserve. This cultural-linguistic operation is the condition of possibility of the transformation of the environment into an ecological "system" (which can be studied and managed by means of scientific methods) and a resource used by the modern, romantic eco-tourism industry to give us "authentic" experiences.

Thus, let me stress again that a non-modern, non-dualistic, and especially *non-romantic* environmental thinking must avoid the term "nature", or must at least always remain aware of its romantic presuppositions. It must construe the environment in a way that goes beyond the natural/artificial distinction and act in ways that avoid a re-affirmation of the modern project.

NOTES

1. Note that Bourdieu still expressed this in a rather dualistic way. He wrote about practical belief and practical sense as being 'not a state of mind' but 'a state of body' (Bourdieu 1990, p. 68–69).
2. Ingold and Lee also refer to Benjamin's figure of the flâneur (Ingold & Lee 2008, p. 15), but evaluate this way of walking in far more positive way.
3. It is important to note that a particular environment or activity does not *determine* a particular kind of walking, wayfinding, or skill. My transcendental, post-Heideggerian argument is always about pre-structuring and promoting, but not about causing or determining. This also gives us the freedom to change and makes possible an *ethics* of walking. (See also below.)
4. One could even imagine a future GPS device that creates so-called 'augmented reality' by projecting the map, arrow, and lines onto reality (e.g. by means of special 'glasses'), which somehow 'solves' the split between the two 'worlds' by re-enforcing the mapping and digital way of wayfinding—including its disadvantages. 'Nature' becomes a computer game; we become our own avatar.
5. For an illustration of the phenomenology of passenger experience see, for example, the lyrics of Iggy Pop's song, 'The Passenger'.

156 *Implications for Environmental Ethics*

6. When animals are killed for food consumption, their subsequent de-skinning signifies ultimate symbolic death since it is the destruction not only of the living body but also of the interface with the environment. It is part of a process of de-contextualization of the animal, making it non-relational and non-environmental. This process makes possible disengaged 'meat consumption' in the first place by making the animal appear as meat rather than as a previously living being that lived-in-relation to its environment and to human and non-human others. It is only by denying the animal's relationality that it can be treated and eaten in this particular way.

7. Note that I use a different, more positive meaning of 'getting lost' than Ingold and Lee, who compare losing the way with falling asleep and even death (Ingold & Lee 2008, p. 18). Of course it is true that when you never find your way back, your journey ends. We need to have a sense of space, its structure, and our position in it. But if you get lost in the sense of losing your position on the map, you are not really lost in Ingold and Lee's sense; rather, you live as long as you remain engaged with your environment and finding your way without a map requires a particular kind of intense engagement. I propose that we strongly connect the meaning of 'life' with relationality and engagement: 'death' is then defined as the absence of relations to the social and physical environment, or more precisely, the absence of the possibility of having such relations.

10 Implications for Environmental Ethics (2)

Exploring the Possibility of Non-Modern and Non-Romantic Environmental Living

INTRODUCTION

In the previous chapters I have argued for shaping our relation to the environment in a less "modern" way, which means, among other things, thinking and living in a way that avoids problems related to scientific modernity and romantic modernity. Can we do this? In the previous chapter I have explored what it would mean to walk and navigate in a non-modern, or at least less modern, way. Defining what this means turned out to be rather difficult, since we are so used to navigating and experiencing walking in romantic or objectivist-scientific ways. More generally, these difficulties raise the question: How can we skillfully engage with our environment and at the same time avoid romantic or objectivist-scientific ways of doing and thinking that hinder such skillful engagement? In the next pages, I will not present a final answer to this question, but I will (1) identify some problems with our current practices related to modern thinking and doing, and (2) explore just a few ways in which we might change them. I selected some domains relevant to environmental issues: health, food, relations with animals, energy, and climate change. Together with the previous chapter, this renders my argument about "environmental skill" more relevant to practical, daily life issues. Finally, I will argue that an "ethics of skill" may well need new political arrangements, but that this requires a different, non-modern approach to politics.

10.1. NEW ENVIRONMENTAL SKILLS AND PRACTICES

10.1.1. Health Skills: Beyond Living "Natural" versus the Body Studied and Controlled by Science

The way we currently think about health is strongly shaped by modern thinking. On the one hand, medical science and biology have taught us to perceive our body as a thing or as a machine. To use Merleau-Ponty's famous distinction (1945), we now see it as something we "have" as opposed to a

158 *Implications for Environmental Ethics*

non-thing (I avoid the word "something") that is part of what we "are". This distance between "me" and "my body" is a precondition for a variety of practices, ranging from medical treatment to "enhancement," sports, and management of the body. If it is a kind of machine, the body can be repaired and improved. If it is a thing I "have", I can try to manage and control it. I can exercise it and improve its functioning. And in relation to the environment, my body becomes a tool that mediates my relation to the environment, and which can be extended with other tools. "My body" is my ownmost technology. If it is a thing, I can also own it, use it, and even sell it, including its parts. For example, I can own and sell my organs. Health care then means to take care of the thing called "body": to manage and use it in appropriate ways, to have it repaired when it is broken, perhaps to improve it in ways that go beyond treatment and "maintenance" (sports and "enhancement" of the body).[1]

What is missing here is the possibility that we can relate to our body (and mind) in a different way. What is also missing is the environment as something we actively relate to and engage with, and that co-constitutes us. The environment is seen as a collection of factors and can "cause" things to the body, something external. But as authors such as Ingold and Berleant rightly remind us, we should get rid of such overly modern and dualistic conceptions of the relation between humans and their environment. This is not easy. Notions such as "nature" or "the body" have a role in environmental thinking and in science that is similar to what Wittgenstein called 'a picture': embedded in our language, they frame our way of seeing and thinking and hold us 'captive'. He writes in the *Philosophical Investigations*:

> A picture held us captive. And we couldn't get outside it, for it lay in our language, and language seemed only to repeat it to us inexorably.
> (Wittgenstein 1953, PI §115, p. 53e)

Later in this book I will say more about the role of language in modern thinking about the environment. But it is clear that dualist modern thinking, which was already present in Descartes and has flourished in Enlightenment thinking, still influences the way we think about health and environment. Shaping "how we look at matters", modernity is still our *Weltanschauung* (§122, p. 55e) and our form of life; it pervades our ways of speaking and our ways of doing. It pervades our practices, including health care.

Moreover, our current health thinking and health practices are also very much influenced by *romantic* thinking. To be healthy comes to mean: to live in a "natural" way, to have a "natural" body, to eat "natural" food, to heal yourself or to get healed in a "natural" way (as opposed to the "artificial" sciences). This way of thinking attempts to close the distance between "the human" and "nature" by saying that we should live in a way that is "closer" to nature. But this presumes that there is a distance, that "nature" is something we are alienated from. Romantic thinking sets

Implications for Environmental Ethics (2) 159

up itself as the antithesis of scientific objectivism, but shares the assumption that we are not directly engaged with our environment. It sees the detached, scientific-objectivist way of thinking as a kind of "Fall" from which we need deliverance. We need to *re-ligare*, re-connect to nature, to *heal*, re-unite what has been separated. But this presumes that "the human" and "nature" *are* entirely distinct things, that there *is* a gap that needs to be bridged. This picture, this (use of) language which effectively constitutes a *denial of environment*, still bewitches us, even if—and because—we try to "reconnect."

As argued in Part II and III, detached science and romantic naturalism are two sides of the same (modern) coin, and this is also true for modern thinking about health and the environment. In the scientific view, the environment is seen as something that may cause all kinds of things to our body, making "it" healthier or sicker. There are, for instance, medical-ecological approaches, which see disease as being effected by interactions with the environment. In the romantic view, the environment is divided up between an "artificial" part and a "natural" part. In both views of health, humans are not seen as beings who actively make sense of our environment and who transform their environment in ways that also transform themselves. Both views presuppose that we can have unmediated access to an external reality called "nature" or "the body" (as part of "nature"), and that there is an ontological division between nature as object and human subjectivity, between the natural and the artificial, the natural and the social, between body and mind, between non-self and self. Health is then seen as something that has nothing to do with the way we interpret and re-shape our environment as mind-bodies, subjects-objects, individual-social beings, natural-artificial beings, *environmental* beings. In modern thinking the ethics of health becomes an ethics of self-management, an ethics of scientific medical treatment, or an ethics of "enhancement".

Starting from different (i.e. relational, environmental, and phenomenological) assumptions, the "health" of a person could be conceptualized as a person's *active relation to* her environment (which is always a response to things that happen to us) and as, at the same time, an *interpretation* (by that person and by others) of that relation. The health skills and ethical skills needed then are not so much "repair" skills, "management" skills, or "healing" and "re-ligious" skills (in the romantic sense), but specific environmental skills related to particular health-environmental practices and perhaps the meta-skill "environmental skill": the skill how to best relate to one's environment (which is at the same time natural and social, natural and artificial) and how to best interpret that relation. Indeed, this conception of health also includes the social question (how does this person relate to others, how to shape the collectivity) and the technological question (how to relate to tools and how to use them to transform the environment). Thus, questions of health are not separated from questions regarding environment, community, and technology.

160 *Implications for Environmental Ethics*

To get a clearer idea about what a non-modern way of thinking about health and those skills mean in in practice, we can read anthropological accounts of present and past non-modern cultures and communities—while being careful to avoid scientific-objectivist or romantic readings (which, again, is rather difficult). This may attend us to the influence of culture on what is considered "healthy" or "sick", "pathological" or "abnormal", give us examples of non-scientific ways of defining health issues (whether or not an issue is a matter of "health" or something else) and of coping with health issues (i.e. processes of healing) in other cultures, and promise an approach to health that is not entirely based on objectivist science.

The latter aim is not easy to attain by medical anthropologists themselves, since they are also influenced by modern assumptions. For instance, Scheper-Hughes and Lock have argued that anthropological research is influenced by Western assumptions about mind and body and have proposed different perspectives from which the body may be viewed (Scheper-Hughes 1987). According to them, the body can and must also be seen as a phenomenally experienced body self, a social body, and a body politic. Against 'the Cartesian legacy' and its 'rather mechanistic conception of the body and its functions' (p. 9), by which anthropologists and clinicians are often 'trapped', they propose a range of different ways of seeing the body, which also involve different ways of seeing "nature" that are not based on modern Western dichotomies. The body is then seen in relation to its (social and natural) environment; it is itself both natural and cultural. For example, the metaphors we use to describe the body depend on the technologies we use, or the world is seen as a macro-body.

The lesson to learn from medical anthropology here is not so much that health care is "influenced" by cultural practices or "socially constructed" according to cultural "context" but that health care practices *are* cultural practices as well as environmental practices. People in a particular culture, including ours, always experience illness in a way that deeply depends on cultural interpretations and co-shapes those interpretations and cultures. For example, in a modern culture health and illness are interpreted in a modern way (and then there are differences among people with different ethnic and cultural backgrounds), whereas people in non-modern or *less* modern cultures interpret and experience health and illness differently, for instance as being caused by spirits or witches. Moreover, in less modern societies, health is not necessarily a matter for professionals (modern doctors, Shamans, traditional healers), and health problems (e.g. mental health problems, but also others) are also related to community and society issues. If there is the "sick" body, there is also the "sick" society, and both are related. Questions regarding social and cultural meaning cannot be separated from health; the fact that we try to do this in modern society is itself a specific feature of modernity. Both in "the West" and elsewhere, the social is crucial with regard to health. To stay healthy, we need social skills 'to establish and maintain social contacts and relationships' and there are 'systemic

Implications for Environmental Ethics (2)   161

social conditions that produce alienation and anomie and place entire communities at risk' (Winkelman 2009, p. 310). We also need to be critical of socially accepted behaviours that are direct causes of mortality (e.g. smoking or firearms). It is also questionable if the "Western" modern lifestyle is healthy at all. But to change it, scientific or romantic responses are insufficient and off the mark. What we need is not more control of "our body" or a more "natural" way of living; what we need is to examine our lives, our society, and our culture, and improve them by re-shaping how we interact with the (social and natural) environment. The modern way of shaping this interaction is only one way to do this; anthropology shows that there are other possibilities. The ethics of health is part of ethics at large, including its social and political dimensions.

Health skills understood as environmental skills, then, include skills that have to do with how to interact with and interpret one's natural and social environment. They are embedded in, and part of, the range of skills we need in specific practices. We need these health skills for "the good life", for human flourishing *in a particular environment*. "Environmental skills" includes social skills, technological/work skills, etc.—although it does make little sense to make strict distinctions between them: Work is always already social and "the social" is meaningless apart from particular practices. Moreover, if we think beyond modern Cartesianism, there are no separate "bodily" skills, since all these skills by definition involve the body and the mind (if they must be distinguished at all). Finally, it seems that looking critically at one's own culture, including science and technology, is also a (meta-) skill we need to stay healthy: Without such criticism, "unhealthy" behaviour and practices will continue.

In practice, this means for example that we must think about how to change health care in such a way that both care givers and patients engage more with one another and their environment and contribute to human flourishing, rather than being made into care tools and care objects in care factories, while avoiding a romantic rejection of science and technology. There is no need for a more "natural" medicine and "natural" healing if this means non-technological and non-material medicine. We have always used tools, also for diagnosis and healing. But there is a need to view and treat patients in an "environmental" way, that is, they must be approached as beings that stand in relation to others and to their environment, and as beings whose illness is not only and not so much a "medical condition" but is crucially connected to these relations—"natural" and "social". Developing this approach requires re-thinking the role of technology and science, but the main criterion for such an evaluation is not "naturalness" but "environmentality" understood as skillful and responsive engagement.

We know that the present, modern approach does not work very well. Rather, as Illich has argued, it produces more illness rather than less (see also my discussion of Illich in the next chapter). The approach outlined here suggests that skillful engagement is not only more "environmental" in the

162 *Implications for Environmental Ethics*

broad sense described here but also better: It is more likely to make people better and to make better people. Whether or not this works in health practice and in life is not something which philosophical reflection can settle; what we need now is *experience* with new ways of dealing with health and illness, ways which recognize care givers and care receivers as environmental beings and which overcome alienation between people and between people and their environment by means of skillful engagement.

10.1.2. Food and Eating Skills: Beyond Eating "Natural" Food Versus Industrial Food Production

An "environmental", relational approach to (ethical issues concerning) food can also best be clarified by distinguishing it from scientific and romantic approaches. One the one hand, science provides descriptive and normative messages about food ("nutrition")—for example, about healthy diets and about the substances in our food (e.g. fat and cholesterol) or about sports nutrition. Science and technology also help to industrially produce food and food supplements (e.g. vitamins, omega-3). Thus, science provides "objective" definitions of what particular foods *are* and what *good* food is, and develops food technologies. Eating the right food is then part of good management and self-management, including management of one's body and one's health. On the other hand, today food is often viewed in a romantic way. Good food is defined as "natural" food. Good eating is eating "natural" and "authentic" products. If what you are is what you eat, and if you want to be an authentic person, then you need to eat authentic products. Food also needs to be "wholesome", making you whole again. "Natural" and "authentic" is often associated with "organic" farming and more "natural" ways of living. People also want to taste how a particular food "really" tastes when it is "natural", as opposed to the "artificial" mass product taste that is forced upon us. Indeed, food also means freedom and self-development: I, not others, decide what I eat, and I will develop *my own* taste. It also means self-expression: by eating this rather than that, I show what kind of person I am. I express my identity. Again: I am what I eat. We also travel to other countries to find "authentic" food. Moreover, eating is good but cooking is even better, since in that way we can make our own, authentic, real, and *unique* food, expressing and shaping our unique personality and selfhood.

Can we see food and eating in a different way? Is a non-modern food ethics possible? Again a focus on "environmental skill" can help here. Let us start with changing the object of our inquiry. Science focuses on food (and the body) as an object, from which we can and must take distance in order to study it or use it in the management of our health and our lives. romantic views see food as a sign of nature (or the artificial), of authenticity (or non-authenticity), etc.; that is, they relate it immediately to the subject. What matters, in the end, is *my* naturalness and authenticity. In both views,

Implications for Environmental Ethics (2) 163

the object of inquiry is food. What remains concealed in both views are the *practices* and *cultures* of eating and cooking and the relations between food and environment and between persons and their environment. This environment is also cultural. My descriptions show that food and eating are not only material, physical, and biological but also at the same time cultural. They are full of meaning and are deeply connected to culture—here: modern culture.

Again anthropology can help to open up a different conceptual space in which to build a different understanding of food and its relation to "environmental skill". Anthropological studies show how important the role of food is in human life and existence. In their literature overview, Mintz & Du Bois (2002) write: 'Next to breathing, eating is perhaps the most essential of all human activities, and one with which much of social life is entwined' (p. 102). This means that learning eating skills is also at the same time learning social skills and vice versa. Eating culture is a crucial part of any culture. The way we deal with food thus tells a lot about our culture—for instance, about its scientific-technological and romantic orientation. Can we think differently about food and have a different food ethics?

Ethnographers have studied how food is related to rituals, symbols, and belief systems. They have shown how ritual meals are important for religious purposes—for instance, for connecting people to invisible, supernatural beings. But rituals also perform social functions: 'Eating in ritual contexts can reaffirm or transform relationships with visible others' (Mintz & Du bois 2002, p. 107). Food is thus used to create and maintain social relationships. For example, it may confirm group membership or ethnicity. Moreover, food has also relations to the natural environment. For example, it may be connected to particular practices such as hunting, gathering, farming, slaughtering, etc., which each require a specific set of skills. Thus, "food skills", understood in a relational and environmental way, also means "eating skills", "hunting skills", "farming skills", etc. The modern-scientific way of thinking about food, however, has separated "food" and eating ("consumption") from these practices and their environments, and has produced both physical and moral distance between them. Consumers can buy "products", commodities, which generally show little connections with the other practices: the practice of eating and the practices that have to do with where the food comes from. Romantic thinking wishes to re-establish this unity and end the alienation, but with its emphasis on the "natural" and "authentic" it actually reconfirms the alienation, since all ethical-environmental attention goes to the "I", the consumer and to food as a tool used by the consumer to confirm her naturalness and authenticity. The (relation to the) environment remains absent. Assuming and constructing an unbridgeable gap between external nature and inner self, the romantic turns food, animals, and practices into tools for identity and self-expression. In this way, both modern views contribute to food alienation.

164   *Implications for Environmental Ethics*

In order to solve this problem, a non-modern approach is required, which promotes a way of engaging with food and with human and non-human others that does not reduce food to a collection of substances, to a tool in a nutritional strategy or diet, or to technologies of the self[2], and that does not turn food-related practices into production processes, identity politics, and (styles of) consumption. It implies a food ethics that is neither focused on norms for production and diets—say, quantities (grams, calories, etc.)—nor trapped in the romantic language of "nature" and "authenticity", but that encourages people to engage with their food and with the practices and environments that surround it.

The Slow Food movement seems to be an example of a more engaged, skillful relation to food and eating, although traces of Romanticism remain present. For example, its emphasis on the local, on taste education, and on small-scale production seem to promote a less alienated relation to food and its discourse stresses the pleasure of sharing good food ("conviviality"). However, as Germov et al. have shown there is also 'Romanticism' in the Slow Food discourse—for instance, the idyllic 'slow' rural life as an antidote to 'fast' urban life (Germov et al. 2011). In this respect, the movement is (still) all too modern. Conceiving of a non-modern food ethics seems to be very difficult. What we can do, however, is learn about how people in less modern cultures deal with food and how they eat, and try out new ways of eating and new foods *in practice*, and see what works best and what gives us a better relation to our environment.

10.1.3. Animal Relations Skills: Beyond "Friends" Versus "Standing Reserve"

Food ethics is always related to animal ethics. The usual way to approach animal ethics is by means of normative philosophical theories—for instance utilitarian (Singer) versus deontological theories (e.g. Regan). They try to establish clear principles that could guide our treatment of animals. My criticism of these theories does not engage with them at the level of normative theory, but at a meta-level, making explicit (modern) assumptions shared by these theories.

First, the idea that ethics is *mainly* a matter of conceptualizing, applying, and following principles and laws is a distinctive modern idea. Ancient and, more generally, non-modern ethics shows that it is possible to think about ethics in a different way. For example, the version of "virtue ethics" proposed earlier in this book focuses on flourishing, without a priori defining flourishing in terms of moral principles.

Second, these theories assume that there is only one (scientific) way of looking at animals. But there are many ways of perceiving animals and—connected with this—many ways of dealing with animals, many types of relations with animals, many ways of talking about animals, and many meanings that can be given to animals. For example, we talk differently about animals in the

Implications for Environmental Ethics (2) 165

context of a farm (e.g. "cattle") or in the context of eating ("meat") than in the context of the home ("pets"). These perceptions and meanings matter for ethics, since they have all normative implications. If I perceive an animal in terms of "meat" or encounter it in the context of a lab where it is used in experiments, I can and will do different things to it than if I perceive an animal as my pet and give it a personal name. More generally, there is not one "moral status" of an animal, there is not even "the animal". As I have argued in *Growing Moral Relations* (Coeckelbergh 2012), the moral and ontological status of an animal depends on relations: linguistic relations, social relations, technological relations, spiritual relations, historico-spatial relations, etc. The scientific and technological way of viewing animals is only one, very specific way of constructing animals and of shaping our relation to animals. Like health and food, a specific kind of animal is connected to particular practices (including sometimes eating practices and health practices), which each have their own normativity. Recognizing this does not mean giving up the project of ethics, but rather doing ethics in a way that remains sensitive to the phenomenology of animal relations and animal practices (which, again, can be revealed by anthropological inquiry) and which can and must be critical of particular practices. It also means understanding animals in an "environmental" way: How we view animals depends on the social, material, and physical environment and the meanings that are connected to them.

For example, within the context of modern industrial "meat production", animals do not appear as living beings, but as what Heidegger called a "standing reserve": a reservoir of things we can use for our purposes (here: meat production). Within the home environment, however, the same animal may appear as a "pet", a "fellow", a "friend", or even a "family member". The appearance and, hence, treatment of, and relation with, an animal thus depends on our moral language, which is in turn connected with specific social-material-physical environments and practices. It is important to better understand, interpret and evaluate these practices; attention to moral language contributes to this hermeneutic and normative project.

Animal ethics is also connected to specific cultures. For example, in some cultures dogs are eaten, in others this is a taboo. In our (modern) culture, too, particular ways of relating to particular animals are promoted rather than others. For example, universalism talks about "the animal". Modern scientific thinking lets animals appear as machines (as in Descartes), as member of a species (Darwinist biology), as an expression and manifestation of DNA code (contemporary genetics), as a collection of meats (industrial meat production), and so on. These modern ways of seeing animals disengage us; they create moral distance between us and "the animal": a particular animal is rendered abstract and remote, which enables us to kill it, eat it, study it, and so on. But the modern-romantic way of seeing animals in an idyllic way—for example, as friends or as belonging to an idealized picture of the past or as a tool to construct our identity (show me your dog and I'll tell you who you are)—is equally distancing: Particular animals

166 *Implications for Environmental Ethics*

then become instruments in the service of a person's romantic purpose, attempting to recreate an idyllic past or an ideal relationship.

Both ways of thinking and doing are connected to the use of a range of skills and technologies. Consider the skill of slaughtering a particular kind of animal with a particular technique, the skill of training and managing a dog, or skills that help you to construct your identity (e.g. making an animal part of your social media communications). But what would "environmental skill" mean with regard to animals? It means, perhaps, not regarding an animal as an isolated "thing," but recognizing that it has its own active relation to its environment (social and physical), including an active relation to us humans. It means: engaging with that particular animal without treating it as a tool (a technological tool or a self/identity tool). It means: not only being concerned with "the animal" but also with the relation between that animal and its human and non-human environment. How do animals skillfully transform their environment, how do we do this, and how can both environmental relations be connected in ways that promote human and non-human (animal) flourishing? Answers to this question will involve not only new concepts of flourishing in particular environments, but will also and mainly require that we learn new ways of doing and learning new skills. We will have to experiment in order to find out what works. No principles or laws can do this job for us.

There are already (groups of) people that try to reconfigure their relations to animals—for example, by raising their own animals and then slaughtering (or not) and eating them (or not). There are artists who go to farms and explore different relations to their animals—for instance, by taking pictures of them or by playing video games with them. Some of these attempts may still be too modern (e.g. too romantic) in order to qualify as fully opening up the possibility of, and contributing to, an "environmental" animal ethics and as involving "environmental skill". But even if change is slow and the development of new skills takes time, these attempts show *that* there are other, not necessarily modern, ways of relating to animals.

Moreover, learning new skills in the absence of principles or laws that can bring change is not itself an "imperative", a new "principle" for environmental ethics that people "have to follow", as standard normative ethical theories say (including virtue ethics as it is often interpreted). Instead, it is *experience* and observation which tells us that the present modern approach does neither motivate nor fundamentally change things, and it is *experience* that will tell us what works better, what brings more flourishing to humans and animals.

10.1.4. Energy Skills: Beyond Fireplaces Versus Centralized Mass Production

Modern-scientific energy production is a matter of large installations (e.g. installation for oil production and processing, nuclear plants, hydro-electricity power plants and dams, wind turbines, etc.), mass production,

Implications for Environmental Ethics (2) 167

centralization, and usually "mindless" consumption since the energy is *available* and all too easy to use. There is a distance between production and consumption. Think about electricity, oil, or gas: It is produced in a distant country or distant place (Not In My Backyard) and then distributed and made available to us in our homes and in petrol stations in a way we have no need to think about. The modern-romantic response to this consists of producing one's own energy and consuming it in a more "authentic" and "personal" way—for example, by chopping wood and then burning it in a wood stove or fireplace (indoor or outdoor).

Perhaps Heidegger's discussion of energy is part of this Romanticism, although he attempted to articulate a non-modern approach by drawing inspiration from ancient Greece and by outlining his concept of 'the four-fold' (Heidegger 1971). In 'The Question Concerning Technology' (1977) he talks about a hydroelectric plant that is set into the Rhine, which makes 'the Rhine itself appears as something at our command' (Heidegger 1977, p. 16); that is, it makes it appear as a 'standing reserve' of energy. Heidegger contrasts this 'monstrousness' with 'the old windmill', which, according to him, does not demand from nature 'that it supply energy that can be extracted and stored':

> Its sails do indeed turn in the wind; they are left entirely to the wind's blowing. But the windmill does not unlock energy from the air currents in order to store it.
>
> (Heidegger 1977, p. 14)

He also contrast the power plant to 'the old wooden bridge that joined bank with bank for hundreds of years', and refers to Hölderlin's hymn 'The Rhine' (p.16). In 'Building Dwelling Thinking' (1971), he says that the bridge lets the river run its course and 'gathers' earth and sky, divinities and mortals. This suggests the view, also present in present-day environmentalism, that nature should be left to itself, that we should not intervene in nature; we should let it 'run its course'.

What the modern-romantic response gets right, is that we should engage more directly with energy. Like food, we are often ignorant where it comes from; we are alienated from its production. Developing energy skills understood as "environmental" skills, then, means here developing skills that enable a person to engage with energy making and energy consumption; this makes that person is aware of what happens. As Borgmann has pointed out, this engagement is much better than what he calls the 'device paradigm': Modern energy technology makes it too easy for us, de-skills us, and we do not sufficiently attend to energy production and use. However, in contrast to what Borgmann's examples suggest, I think this does not mean that we should only use old technologies. Perhaps new ICTs can also play a role in this (see the next chapter on technology). Both Heidegger and Borgmann are very helpful in opening up the possibility of a different way

168 *Implications for Environmental Ethics*

of relating to energy and in convincing us of the value of craftsmanship and skill; however, their thinking does not entirely manage to take distance from a modern-romantic approach. They are nostalgic for pre-modern times (as Ihde and Verbeek have also pointed out, see, for example, Verbeek 2005), and I think this nostalgia must be understood as rooted in a form of Romanticism. Hölderlin was of course a major romantic poet, and the descriptions of historical technologies place these technologies in an idyllic, ideal world of the past. Heidegger and Borgmann and, indeed, contemporary people who try to "do their own thing" when it comes to energy are rightly trying to get away from the modern-scientific way of shaping one's relation to the environment. Heideggerian criticism is still very relevant in this respect. But in their nostalgic moments and dimensions, they do not manage to move beyond modernity; instead they submit themselves to romantic thinking.

Like re-thinking health, food, and relations with animals, re-thinking energy means re-thinking our lives and our culture. For example, "oil" is not just a "product"; it is an entire way of life: We have oil practices and oil lives. It influences our way of transportation and therefore influences where we live (e.g. not near work) and how we live (e.g. little bodily exercise needed to move from one place to another due to available transportation). And the discussion about windmills and power plants makes clear that the question of energy is directly related to the question regarding modernity and technology.

Conceptualizing a new, non-modern energy ethics is therefore very difficult. We are used to thinking about energy in a modern way, and *living* in a different way is even harder: We are used to living in a modern way, including when it comes to energy. We have modern *habits*. Even if we chop our own wood and burn it in our own stove, we have difficulties getting away from modernity—in particular, romantic modernity in this case. We interpret what we do in romantic terms. Romanticism, like modern-scientific thinking, has deeply shaped our understanding of our relation to the environment. If we want a new environmental ethics, involving new "environmental skills," then we have to experiment with different habits and ways of living.

For example, there are (small groups of) people who produce their own energy, not by relying on old technologies, but by using solar panels, small windmills, etc. and electronic technologies that help them to manage their energy production and consumption. Even if they may interpret their own activities in terms of "sustainability"—a concept that rather belongs to scientific-modern thinking, or is at least usually interpreted in this way—and even if these activities can also be interpreted in terms of management (energy management) and self-management, it is possible that some of these experiments exemplify how to do things better; that is, they are examples of how to find different ways of environmental flourishing.

However, even if one tries to use a different language and thinking one can always easily slip back into modern discourse. For example, the line

Implications for Environmental Ethics (2) 169

between (A) training the virtue of self-control and (B) psychological and technological techniques of (self-)manipulation is thin, and the line between (A) re-shaping one's relation to technology by using different technologies (e.g. non-oil based or related technologies) and by developing different habits and (B) becoming a consumer of pre-established marketing concepts and implementing national energy strategies, is also thin. Yet we must not be afraid of this "danger" when we try out different ways of living. In the end, the proof of the pudding is in the eating: The first approach will *motivate* us to change our lives and lead to more human and non-human flourishing; the latter will remain impotent.

10.1.5. Climate Change and Skills: Beyond Leaving Mother Earth Alone versus Planet Management

Today climate change is high on the agenda of environmentalists (even to the extent that many other environmental issues become neglected—the attention paid to carbon emissions to the neglect of other problems is almost perverse). Again modern approaches dominate. On the one hand, there is climate science with its observations, models, and predictions. Like energy scenarios, we are offered climate scenarios. Technological and regulatory means are then proposed to reach certain targets. The assumption made here is that there is a planetary "ecosystem" or "biosphere" that we can understand and control; we have the duty to act as *managers* of our planet. The planet, including the people living on it, is an estate that can and needs to be managed. With the right kind of technologies and laws, it is believed, we can regulate this immense greenhouse. We also need to better manage ourselves and our lives—for example, by reducing our "carbon footprint" (which, like other measures, can be calculated).

The modern-romantic approach, by contrast, proposes to leave Mother Nature alone or to re-establish the ecological "balance." It seeks more natural and more authentic ways of living, which do not involve the use of anything "artificial" such as pesticides, cars, and other things that are not only bad for the atmosphere (climate change) but also bad for us, humans, who should stay unpolluted and stop polluting. Nature is a virgin, a vulnerable woman, which should not be stained with our human footprint. Moreover, there is an original Balance, a Paradise before the Sin of carbon emission and other sins, to which we must try to return (again Romanticism shows its Judeo-Christian religious side; "pagan" influences are limited). We must return to a "state of nature" when there was little or no influence from humans.

It turns out that both approaches assume a distance between humans and "nature", between subject and object, between us and "*the* environment". A more "environmental" understanding of climate change and a non-modern climate ethics tries to overcome these assumptions by assuming an active relation between us and our environment, by starting from the

170 *Implications for Environmental Ethics*

human being as an "environmental" being. To talk about "the planet" and "the climate" then turns out to be only one particular way of relating to one's environment. We can also try to open up the possibility of a different environmental relation, which requires more engagement with our physical and social environment. To conceive of "the planet" and its problems such as "the climate" as things that can and need to be managed, an epistemic operation was necessary: We had to take distance from the earth; we had to literally and otherwise leave "the earth" in order to perceive it as such (something which Arendt also suggested, see Arendt 1958). But this means that our thinking and doing has also distanced itself from concrete human life and existence understood as being intrinsically environmental. Our thinking has also left the earth and looks upon it from space. This alienation also made it possible to "pollute", to use carbon fuels and carbon technologies. It is only if we regard ourselves as humans separate from "nature" or from "the planet" (be it by means of modern-scientific or modern-romantic thinking) and if we understand our lives as separate from "systems" and "ecologies," that we can come under the spell of what we may call "environmental forgetfulness" or, in German, *Umwelt-Vergessenheit*—a term which I coin in analogy with Heidegger's term *Seinsvergessenheit*. The distance we created with our language enabled us to forget about our environmental nature and constructed the environment as "this thing called nature"; this made possible that we did all the things that now turn out to be environmentally problematic, if not disastrous. Even if well-meaning environmentalists focus on problems regarding "the environment", they risk retaining their modern Environmental Forgetfulness. All of us are in danger of seeing "the environment", "the planet", "the climate", etc. as things external to us. Informed by science, we may recognize that we also *cause* climate change, but such "causes" and "causal relations" are still far away from us. They are very abstract. We may even try to manage our "footprint" (and there are computer programs and apps to assist us with that), but we do not realize that our managerial way of thinking and doing itself is problematic.

A truly "environmental" climate ethics, therefore, cannot be a planetary "climate ethics" at all. It must be an ethics that centres on bridging the distance with our environment (social, physical, etc.) at the level of concrete and personal engagement, a bridging which includes re-shaping our food practices, energy practices, and so on. This means leaving behind the exclusive focus on "the climate" of "the earth" or "the ecosystem" and instead paying attention to local "climate" problems in the sense of attending to concrete problems people, animals, plants, etc. face, and finding new configurations of common flourishing, new forms of human/non-human conviviality ('conviviality' is a term from Illich—see the next chapter).

My point is not so much that modern ways of thinking are "bad" in themselves and *necessarily* have bad consequences, but rather that they have *made possible* environmentally bad practices by not recognizing our environmental nature. In addition, modern ways of thinking and doing

Implications for Environmental Ethics (2)   171

are unsustainable from a moral-psychological point of view: Abstract climate models and policies cannot really *motivate*; skillful engagement *does*. Responding to climate change in a way that recognizes this is the only way to move forward, to move towards more environmental living.

10.2. IMPLICATIONS FOR ENVIRONMENTAL POLITICS: SOCIETAL GROWTH AND POLITICAL SKILL

In the previous section and chapters I have argued that many of our current skills, technologies, and practices are still very modern, and I have suggested that a focus on "environmental skill" can help us to explore non-modern, truly "environmental" ways of living. But what are the implications of a focus on "environmental skill" for politics and society? Is the acquisition of "environmental" skill a matter that should be left to individuals? Should our governments take action to support the development of "environmental skill" or should they leave that to people themselves? And if the government should play a role at all, what kind of action should be taken? Who should decide about this anyway? How democratic is modern environmentalism? How democratic can it be? And what might be the meaning of "political skill" in relation to the environment? What are the implications for environmental thinking?

New environmental skills and practices may well need new political arrangements and new political institutions. However, before thinking about specific arrangements and institutions (which I will not do in this book) we need to re-think our conception of politics, which is (still) very modern. In Chapter 4 I have said that the main political ideologies are *modern*—including what I have called "modern environmentalism"—and in the previous chapters I have explored what a non-modern approach to the environment might mean for the way we shape our practices. So what does a "non-modern" approach to politics mean?

10.2.1. A Substantial but Pluralist View of Good and a Non-Nationalist View of Politics

Philosophical (neo)liberals believe that politics should be neutral on substantial ethical issues, that they are a private matter and should be left to the discretion of the individual. If we endorsed this view, then we would have to say that whether or not people develop and exercise environmental skill is *up to them*. We would have to say that it is "up to you" and "up to the market". This privatization of ethics is very common today, but that does not make it good. To make ethics a *lifestyle* or a product one can buy on the market is itself a "modernization" of ethics: It treats normative orientations as commodities; it turns philosophical reflection into theory as a standing reserve or a product. It makes ethics appear as a matter of choice in the

172 Implications for Environmental Ethics

(on-line or off-line) supermarket: it asks "Should I buy deontology, utilitarianism, virtue ethics, or ethics of skill?" in the same way as it asks "Should I buy red toothpaste or blue toothpaste?" It is "up to you" what you choose, it seems. But ethics is neither a private matter nor a commodity. It is not "up to me"—and perhaps even not "up to us" (see Chapter 12).

The ethics of skill defended here opposes the (neo)liberal view, since its ethics involves a particular conception of the good life and—as I will argue—demands of politics to facilitate a particular conception of the good life—even if this conception is formulated at a general level and leaves plenty of room for interpretation and variation (see again Hume's pluralism). Indeed, an environmental politics conceived of as a politics of "skill" cannot be neutral vis-à-vis conceptions of the good life. The recommendation that we engage actively, skillfully, and care-fully with our environment is not "ethically neutral" but suggests a particular way of life. It asks us to live in such a way that we do not treat other beings (human and non-human) as a 'standing reserve', as a system we must control, as resources for our production and our well-being, as our service providers. It asks us to walk, work, and live in ways that do not alienate us from our environment (including other humans). It asks us to break the mirror that throws us back onto ourselves; it asks us to grasp with and handle reality—which is always *environmental* reality.

What this ethical demand means will vary in different social-cultural contexts, and whether or not persons and societies succeed will also depend on circumstances and luck. But this does not make the ethical demand less pressing or less authoritative. It does not render environmental ethics "subjective" or "relativist". The real danger of relativism is present in the idea that it is "up to you" what you do with regard to the environment and with regard to your life.

Furthermore, this ethical demand has political consequences. Its recommendation to de-alienate and (re-)skill ourselves can only be met under appropriate political conditions. And whatever these conditions are, it is highly doubtful that the present conditions are sufficient for an ethics of skills to flourish. For example, under a modern "politics of nature", which treats the environment as its household and thus becomes a "political economy of nature" (including the management of "nature reserves" and "ecosystem services"), you have basically two choices if you do not want to be part of the household: Either you become a rationalist *manager* in the system or you try to escape to "nature" where you seek "authenticity" and indulge in romantic reverie. Some of us do both: The former is usually seen as a public activity, which you do at *work*, the latter a private, *leisure* activity—it is "up to you". Moreover, the romantic activities are then "colonized" by the system (to borrow a Habermasian metaphor); they are turned into commodities themselves. We buy romantic, "authentic" food, holidays, art objects, etc. Under these conditions, the option of skillful engagement with the environment is hardly

Implications for Environmental Ethics (2)   173

available. We remain trapped in modern practices and their commodification and romantization.

Moreover, as the question "What should the *state* do?" or "What should the *government* do?" suggests, modern environmentalists—that is, environmentalists to the extent *that* they are modern—assume that politics should mainly take place at the level of the nation state. This thinking has roots in Romanticism. According to the romantic view, we should not only restore nature to its "original", "authentic" state, we should also respect the "nature" of the nation. The nation has a "natural" and essential identity. In the course of history, the land becomes *our* land, the country becomes *our* country. Some people think they have a "right" to their land—a "natural" right, I suppose. Here the environment, the people, their habits, and their artefacts are treated as resources in the production and consumption of national identity. To be authentic, then, means to be natural and national. This collectivist form of Romanticism is a threat to environmental good.

Another way of interpreting nationalism as a form of Romanticism is to say that nationalism is also a return to the self, but then a collective self. It then becomes a "true" self, in the name of which individuals can be oppressed. To use Berlin's description of positive liberty:

> the real self may be conceived as something wider than the individual (. . .), as a social 'whole' of which the individual is an element or aspect: a tribe, a race, a church, a state, the great society of the living and the dead and the yet unborn. This entity is then identified as being the 'true' self which, by imposing its collective, or 'organic', single will upon its recalcitrant 'members', achieves its own, and, therefore, their, 'higher' freedom.
>
> (Berlin 1958, pp. 161–162)

We may think here of Rousseau's notion of the 'general will', which is often interpreted as the tyranny of the people (although Rousseau may have intended a different meaning). In any case, in romantic political thinking, democracy becomes the expression of this collective self, this general will. Romantics want individuals to express themselves and often they also want the "Nation" or the "People" to express itself. In this way, romantic politics aims at individual *and* collective authenticity. Politics becomes a politics of identity. What matters to such a politics is not argument, participation, reconciliation of interests, etc., but creating conditions for individual self-expression and making sure that what is done by the state reflects, expresses, and unfolds the true nature of the "Nation" and its "People". In this way of thinking, a politics of nature, which protects the "natural" environment and individual authenticity, is coupled with a "natural" politics, which protects the "natural" nation and collective authenticity.

The environmental ethics developed here, by contrast, rejects the romantic focus on "the People" and "the Nation." Yet the alternative it proposes

174 *Implications for Environmental Ethics*

is not merely a re-affirmation of the rationalist Enlightenment conception of politics as deliberation by means of argument ('communicative reason' etc.), as rational and bureaucratic social engineering of people, or as management of the household (political economy). Instead, it recommends creating public spaces for the growth of environmental virtue defined as skilled engagement with the environment. It does neither reject the use of reason nor the value of organizing things, but demands that deliberative reason, reasoning about how to do things, and household matters should not be divorced from active and skilled engagement with the environment. They should not be understood as giving us norms that stand "above" praxis in order to discipline and regulate it. Disciplining and organization are not bad per se, but if they are necessary at all they should emerge from skilled activity rather than the other way around. The Platonic Idea must not be prior. Instead we better engage in a collective process of trial and error through which people become more environmentally skilled, through which a "community of skill" emerges that has its own bottom-up discipline and organization.

This is a participatory ideal of politics. Based on Dewey's view of politics, we may argue that an ethics of skill requires both personal and societal growth and therefore requires a participatory approach to politics. But the participatory and indeed "emancipatory" power of the politics of skill is not something that "has" to be imposed on people "top-down", because otherwise people are not "rational" enough to do what is right and good or because detached reasoning and contemplation shows that this is the best for people. Rather, this kind of political organization grows within particular practices and skilled activities. It is participatory because skilled activity is *already* social and participatory, before any rationalistic model or management vision can be applied to it. It is emancipatory because it is *already* humanizing and liberating—with "humanization" understood as "environmentalization" rather than setting humans apart from the environment, and with "liberation" understood not as an escape from the artificial into the natural, but as the development of skilled engagement and the opening up *of* the environment and the opening up of humans *to* the environment. Being (fully) human means being (fully) environmental. It means living as if one is an opening, ready to receive and handle what is given in relating to one's environment, ready to respond. Then one is not a closed "authentic" self that projects itself onto its environment without engaging with it. Then one is neither a passenger nor a driver, but a participant. Then freedom is not being free from society by retreating from it into the self, but rather the letting-go of self in environmental action, which is always already "social" since the skills and the habits are formed and re-formed in a social, dynamic context—in an environment which is as much "social" as it is "natural," physical, and material.

But how *democratic* is the politics of skill? And how democratic is modern environmentalism? Moreover, we must further explore the implications

Implications for Environmental Ethics (2) 175

of "environmental skill" for *environmental* thinking and environmental politics: What would it mean to move towards a non-modern, non-romantic environmental politics?

10.2.2. The Politics of Skill: Towards a Non-Modern Environmental Politics

Modern environmental politics faces at least the following fundamental problems (one might call them dilemmas), which have to do with its modern—Enlightenment and romantic—heritage and which are based on dualisms that need to be overcome.

First, within Enlightenment thinking there has always been a tension between a "technocratic", Baconian (perhaps also Platonic) current and a democratic current. This tension is inherited by modern environmentalism, which is torn between its desire to bring about environmental change in a top-down way based on scientific understanding (for instance, ecology as science) and its will to respect if not promote democracy (for example, in the form of a participatory democracy). Do we want to "save the world" by means of philosopher-kings or scientist-kings who can bring about a New Atlantis—a much *greener* Atlantis? Or do we want to leave environmental matters to slow, often "irrational" democratic politics, which might be blind to "the truth" and set us up for disaster and doom?

Second, universalist Enlightenment thinking often clashes with romantic particularism, which tries to foster local identity, culture, and authenticity (national or local). The scientist-environmentalist wants to study and manage "nature" in a rational way. The universalist environmental ethicist recommends universal principles and general rules. But the relation with our environment is shaped by "environmental cultures". Prior to the philosopher's words, there are already habits, skills, practices, and so on. There are ways of thinking about the environment and way of relating to the environment that are "given" to us as social-cultural-natural beings. In other words, there is a culture, including an "environmental" culture. Now romantic particularism interprets this culture as *our* local and national culture as opposed to the "environmental globalization" promoted by scientists and policy makers. Should we follow the "Enlightenment" side of modern environmentalism here, or should we embrace the romantic version and embrace identity? Should we restore ecosystems or should we protect our "natural heritage"? Should we call in the experts, or leave environmental matters to the "irrational" forces of habit and tradition, unresponsive to ethical, reasonable laws and principles? How "local" should we become if major "global" environmental troubles await us?

How can environmentalism cope with these problems? Can these dilemmas be resolved? I think we can resolve them if we use the insights from the "ethics of skill" that is under development in this book and from other attempts at less modern thinking. I will make suggestions for a non-modern

176 *Implications for Environmental Ethics*

approach to these issues, which challenge assumptions made about expertise, community, truth, and tradition.

Before I make explicit and question these assumptions, however, let me first observe that the dilemmas presented here presuppose that one can and must *choose* between these ways of thinking and doing, that one of the two options is "true" or "right" whereas the other is "false" or "wrong", and that there are no other options. But these presuppositions can already be questioned.

First, do we really have a choice? Changing ways of thinking and doing is not entirely a matter of choice. To think in terms of will and choice here is a very modern way of approaching the problem. As I will further argue in the last chapter, moral-environmental change—as all moral change—is bound to conditions of possibility we have to cope with as would-be environmental revolutionaries.

Second, even if we have more than one option, then this does not necessarily mean that one option is necessarily better than others. Both might be "true" or "right" (there are different *perspectives* on the same matter; there are many interpretations) or both might be "false" and "wrong".

Third, returning to the dilemmas, I think the latter is the case here. There is a third, non-modern option, which shows that in each case the horns of the dilemmas have something in common: Both options are modern ways of approaching environmental politics, which are often combined in practice, and which are misguided for the following reasons:

First, the technocracy-democracy dilemma assumes that "experts" know environmental problems. But in what sense do they "know" them? Even if we disregard "classical" skepticism offered by philosophy of science and traditional epistemology (say, the question concerning the foundation of our scientific knowledge claims), it may well be that the people we call "experts" *know-that* such and such is the case, but still lack a good *grasp* of the situation and cannot *handle* the situation because they have propositional knowledge, but lack the appropriate environmental know-how, skill, habit, and culture, because *as objectivist*[3] *scientists* they are alienated from the relevant contexts in which environmental problems arise. The "experts" that are called in are environmental scientists but they are not craftsmen, let alone master craftsmen. There is gap between the people who know-that (scientists, "experts") and the people who are told what to do (politicians, citizens, consumers, environmentalists working in nature reserves, etc.) but who do not necessarily have the right kind of know-how either. What we can learn from Dreyfus, Sennett, and others is that proper expertise, including ethical expertise and hence also expertise in the area of *environmental* ethics, requires not facts and rules, but *experience* and skilled engagement with the environment.

But if this is so, then the technocracy-democracy dilemma turns out to be false. If environmental expertise is a matter of know-how, then the problem is not so much the gap between what experts and lay people know about the

Implications for Environmental Ethics (2) 177

environment, but rather between those who lack know-how (the scientific "expert" and many lay people alike) and those who have know-how based on experience in skilled engagement with their environment. Moreover, if environmental expertise is a matter of know-how, then in principle[4] *everyone* can learn to become environmentally skilled and environmentally better persons. This is the "democratic", or at least *participatory* aspect of the politics of environmental skill. We do not have to choose between technocracy and democracy (in the usual sense of the word), since in their current modern form *both* are alienating and partly *ignorant* ways of doing politics. If we—that is, all of us—would engage in skilled activities in concrete practical contexts, then we would acquire adequate knowledge—understood as know-how—of the problems *by handling them* and *by working with others and within a practice and a tradition*. Then there is no need for top-down management by people who claim to represent us or to act in our best interest, since then the political is not conceived of as a household or a system, and citizens are not seen as voters or consumers. In such a *polis*, there are environmental masters and environmental apprentices. There are people who provide an example and help others to train and develop. But in communities of environmental virtue understood as communities of environmental skill, there are no "masters and slaves". There are people who are more skilled (masters) and people who are less skilled (apprentices), but none are slaves. The master has greater freedom, perhaps, but it is not the freedom to oppress others but a freedom in creativity, imagination, and inspiration, a freedom of achieving "flow" and quality in relation to the environment and to others.

This kind of politics does not come for free but requires effort. Personal and societal learning cannot be replaced by a system of laws or by automated control. Moreover, it is not enough to create, endorse, and follow an ideology. It is not enough to have a "concept". It is not enough to consume a system of thinking (and digest it at your leisure). Becoming an environmentally good citizen-politician is about learning environmental-political skills. Participation in this politics is not about finding out and communicating one's consumer preferences (in order to make the supermarket type of choices); instead, it is an active, practical process through which one learns the appropriate skills—skills appropriate to the specific practice. These political skills include knowing how to use words, but politics is not reduced to concepts, communicative reason, argument, and rhetoric. It also has to do with how to actively relate to the environment, how to use tools in a good way, how to best relate to others. It is about *logos* but also about *techne*: a *techne* in the relation to people and to things, and environmental *techne*. In contrast to what Hannah Arendt (and Aristotle) thought, such a politics happens not in a separate sphere and should not happen in a separate sphere. The separation between a "political" and a "household" sphere, between "political action" and "work" (and "labour"), between freedom and necessity, is

178 *Implications for Environmental Ethics*

itself problematic. Only if we think of politics in a less dualistic way can we begin to solve the environmental-ethical challenges we face.

Furthermore, in this environmental *polis* "community" and "identity" are not separate, fixed things which one can either reject (Enlightenment revolution) or embrace and hold on to (romantic conservatism). Instead of reifying them, community and identity emerge from the skilled activity and the learning involved in communal practice and personal-social growth. There is a community of learning. The social is neither made nor externally given; it grows within practice, which is at the same time political, technological, and social. There is tradition, where tradition is not understood as a "canon" but in the original meaning of "tradition" as a *handing over* and *giving*. But then something needs to be done with it. Skills are learned, embodied, and used. They are not "things" out there; they only live in the activities and habits of human beings. Similarly, truth, knowledge and wisdom is not pre-given but is revealed, brought-forth, and created by doing things together and by learning from others. There is no "truth" separate from a particular form of life and its practices. Even if we are the kind of beings who can and must question communal and cultural ways of doing (we can 'take distance' in *this* sense), it is only from *within* our community, culture, and so on, that we can use philosophical and other tools to explore different ways of doing. We cannot "take distance" to such an extent that we take a 'view from nowhere'. There can be dialogue (dia-*logos*) and dia-*techne*, and we can learn skills that enable us to connect different cultures and traditions. We can also practice philosophy. But this kind of taking distance and this kind of cross-political engagement remains "environmentally" situated.

Furthermore, this politics is not 'authentic' if this means that here is a fixed, original and authentic tradition. Habits and skills should not be interpreted in a romantic way, as related to some "essence" or "nature". Authenticity means "authoritative", but here authority derives from the quality of the work, not the 'genius' or brute power of the master. The "master" is authoritative, but his authority derives from his skills—that is, from his experience with handling things and people—and is not to be regarded as an expression of his nature or personal genius. In this sense only do we need "authentic" politician-citizens. If they are very skilled, we have good reasons to trust other politician-citizens, but we do not trust them because they are "authentic" in the sense of being "themselves", being "natural", "original" etc. Instead, the most skilled ones are the ones who have *lost* themselves in skilled activity and helped to bring forth something that became so much bigger than themselves.

Finally, the universalism-particularism dilemma articulated as an Enlightenment-Romanticism dilemma can also be resolved by drawing on the "ethics of skill" approach. It is based on a false opposition between reason and feeling, and presupposes either that only disinterested, universalist science and philosophy produces truth, whereas tradition is the breath of

Implications for Environmental Ethics (2)   179

ignorance, or that rationalism and science should be rejected in favour of feeling and love of one's nation and self (and can there be something that is more particular, especially in the romantic imagination?). Moreover, it assumes that "global" and "local" are necessarily opposed.

Instead, a non-modern approach suggests that in skilled engagement with nature, both detached reason and feeling detached from the environment are replaced by thinking and feeling that grow out of one's engagement with the environment. With regard to skilled activity, and especially skilled activity at the "master" level, descriptions that rely on dualisms such as mind-body or mental-material do no longer make sense. In addition, such engaged activity can neither be adequately described in the terms of science—it lacks the objectivist, detached quality of how science is *supposed* to be—nor is it simply the following of fixed traditional rules. Moreover, the identity that emerges is "local", in the sense that it has its locus and origin in the activities, habits, tools, and skills of people situated in specific places, but at the same time the identity is also "global" since those activities, habits, tools, and skills are shared by, and connect, many people around the globe. Even if many skills are not identical, they are similar. Moreover, learning skills is easier today due to the role of electronic information and communication technologies, which do not only spread information but also skills. Perhaps the global-local tension is anyway based on a false contrast: In holistic thinking local change means global change. In such thinking, there is no longer talk of "levels". There is only one ethically relevant "level" for us humans, that of the lived experience and the skilled activity itself, and what we call all other "levels" are related to it and are nourished by it. A politics of environmental skill, therefore, must also be local and global at the same time. If, due to new technologies, our environment has become local and global, online and offline, natural and artificial, etc., then this means that *we* have become local and global, online and offline, and so on. Any environmental ethics and politics that does not sufficiently reflect on the nature, history, and condition of its object—the environment—risks rendering itself irrelevant. Asking the question of this book—*how* to become more "environmental"—has led to asking the question: What is it for us humans to be environmental here and now, in today's globalizing world, in a world shaped by old politics and new information technologies?

Since an analysis and interpretation of contemporary technology and its relation to humans and the environment must be part of any answer to this question, let me say more about technology and environmental skill now—in particular, about the relation between *information technology* and an environmental ethics as an ethics of skill. I have already said something about this in previous work (Coeckelbergh 2011), but here I will discuss Marx and Illich in order to say more about a concept that might be used to highlight or re-frame some key discussions in the previous chapters: alienation.

180 *Implications for Environmental Ethics*

NOTES

1. Note that a similar approach can (and is being) taken to the mind. "My mind" or even "my brain" is seen as something that needs to be controlled, that can be repaired, adjusted, enhanced, and so on. For example, the empirical psychology cited in Chapter 3 could be used in order to better control the mind, to make the mind more "healthy" or more "green".
2. See also Foucault's term.
3. Note that science itself has many aspects, some of which are not objectivist and modern at all. See, for instance, the work of Latour and other STS scholars.
4. In principle, since we must recognize with Hume that talent and circumstance also play a role in the development of virtue and skill—or better: virtue as skill.

11 The Art of Environmental Practice as an Ethics of Skill

Revisiting the Problem of Technology and Its Relation to Alienation

INTRODUCTION

From the previous chapters we can conclude that the main problem of moral-environmental motivation emerges from an alienated relation to the environment and that we have to imagine and especially *try out* ways to more intensely engage with our environment. But what does this conclusion imply for our relation to technology—that is, for our contemporary practices that are highly mediated by technology? Is technology part of the solution to environmental problems, or is it part of the problem? Does a more skill-oriented approach to ethics—an "ethics of skill"—imply that we should reject technology, especially high tech? For example, are the internet and internet-based applications alienating technologies? And what exactly is the meaning of "alienation" here? How does it differ from other uses of the word—for example, by Heidegger or Marx?

In this chapter I first further fine-tune my position by responding to discussions in philosophy of technology. I show how an ethics of skill can navigate between human-centred and artefact-centred theories. By critically responding to Dreyfus, Borgmann, and Illich in a way that avoids a romantic interpretation of their work, I hope to help open up a new direction in the philosophy of technology, while at the same time contributing to the further development of "environmental ethics" broadly construed. I will argue that the advice to live in a way that involves more skilled engagement with one's environment need not imply a romantic rejection of technology, as in work of earlier philosophers of technology and environmental ethicists, but rather that the problem of "technology" concerns the way we relate to our environment and we should evaluate *that* relation. In this sense, an ethics of technology is an environmental ethics, and vice versa.

The chapter then continues with a discussion of information technology and alienation. First I respond to Marxist objections to the internet and argue against Dreyfus' view that the internet is *necessarily* alienating and damaging to the public sphere, and suggest that we should analyze this problem at the level of the activity and the skills involved in particular practices mediated by information and communication technologies. I argue

182 *Implications for Environmental Ethics*

that these technologies do not necessarily make our lives less environmentally good; they only do so in so far as they de-skill us in specific ways and (thereby) alienate us from our environment. Moreover, in line with the previous chapters I argue that this "environment" should not be understood in romantic terms: It may well be at the same time natural and artificial, "offline" and "online". What matters is not how "natural" an environment is, but the precise way of how we relate to it when we perceive and make worlds. Then I use Illich's concept of 'convivial' tools and a 'convivial' society to further develop my position. I will argue that instead of rejecting "technology" we need *different* kinds of technologies and hence a different kind of relation to our environment.

11.1. THE PROBLEM OF TECHNOLOGY AND ALIENATION

Are we "alienated" from "nature"? The term "alienation" can have many meanings, depending on what is identified as the origin of "alienation" (e.g. technology) and on what we are said to be alienated *from* (e.g. from "nature").

In "old style" thinking about technology, modern technology is often seen as the source of alienation. For instance, Heidegger's thinking about modern technology (Heidegger 1977) is often interpreted as meaning that modern technology has alienated us from "authentic" thinking and living, and Ellul has argued that the rationality and efficiency of modern technology creates an artificial system that eliminates the 'natural' (Ellul 1954). These (interpretations) of Heidegger and Ellul are clearly suffused with Romanticism, which also strives for authenticity and naturalness. I have already referred to Heidegger's discussion of the windmill and his admiration for the Greeks that made him long for a lost ancient world.

But Critical Theory also often takes on quasi-romantic features. Here alienation can mean alienation from your human essence and from human nature. It can also mean alienation from the products of your labour, as in Marx. This is his most well-known conception of alienation, but Marx has a much more refined analysis. In the *Economic and Philosophic Manuscripts of 1844* (Marx 1844) he distinguishes between several types of alienation under capitalist technological conditions.

First, the worker is alienated from the product of his labour. In this way labour 'produces not only commodities; it produces itself and the worker as a commodity' (Marx 1844, p. 71). Second, this also implies that labour is 'external' to the worker in the sense that 'it does not belong to his 'essential being': the worker cannot 'affirm' himself and this makes him unhappy (p. 74). The worker is not only alienated from the product of his labour, but also from the act of production. Third, the worker is alienated from his nature as a 'species-being' (p. 75). He should work upon the objective world and thus objectify himself, 'duplicate' himself, and contemplate 'himself in

The Art of Environmental Practice as an Ethics of Skill 183

a world that he has created' (p. 77). But alienated labour 'tears from him his species-life, his real species objectivity' (p. 77) since labour becomes a means to maintain his 'physical existence' (p. 77). Man becomes estranged. Fourth, this also implies an 'estrangement of man from man' (p. 78). The worker is alienated from others. Later, Marcuse has extended and modified Marx's analysis in his critique of consumer society: Consumers recognize themselves in their commodities.

Both Critical Theory and (romantic interpretations of) Heideggerian thinking assume, in contrast to modern technological practices, that there is a "natural", non-alienating way of working and that there are non-alienating technologies, which respect human authenticity (Heidegger) and human nature (Marx). They assume that both modern technology and the human have an "essence", and that both "essences" are irreconcilable. Thus, the concept of alienation is used to set up a dichotomy between humans and technology.

Some contemporary philosophers of technology reject this essentialist and dualistic framework. They have drawn attention to non-intended consequences of artefacts, without using the notion of alienation. For example, Verbeek rejected what he calls the 'alienation thesis' (Verbeek 2005), Ihde has interpreted Heidegger in a 'post-phenomenological' way that does not assume essentialism (Ihde 1990), and several contemporary philosophers of technology have argued that humans and technology are intrinsically bound up with one another (Haraway 1991; Latour 1993, 2005; Verbeek 2005, 2008). But even if we accept these new perspectives on technology, do they necessarily imply that we can do without the notion of alienation altogether?

The notion of alienation may be still useful if it is given a new, non-modern and non-romantic meaning. I have argued in this book that we can relate in various ways to our environment, and one of these can be called "alienating": There is a kind of "environmental alienation" that has to do with modernity, with our modern ways of thinking and doing, and which has resulted in estrangement *from our environment*. But what is the relation between this kind of "environmental alienation" and *technology*?

As I have argued, there is some truth in Heidegger's claim that modern technology reveals humans and "nature" as a 'standing reserve'. And Marx was right to say that modern technology and production alienates the product from the worker and from other workers; this critique seems to tune in with the call for skilled engagement discussed and endorsed in the previous chapters. In these senses, modern technology is a source of environmental alienation: It creates a distance between humans and their (human and non-human) environment. However, while we can learn a lot from these critiques of modernity, if we really want to move towards a thinking that is less modern we must reject Heidegger's and Marx's craving for authenticity and naturalness—say, the *romantic* side of their thinking. Moreover, Marx's view that man must 'duplicate' himself, and contemplate 'himself

184   *Implications for Environmental Ethics*

in a world that he has created' is still very modern: It is a "good" kind of objectification, according to Marx, but an objectification nonetheless. It is the objectification of modern Narcissus, who, after 'duplicating' himself by means of modern technology, is surprised to find himself alienated from his environment. He is looking in the mirror of his creations in order to see himself, rather than opening up to his environment. This non-relationality, this total lack of engagement with one's environment, is what renders environmental motivation and environmental practice impossible.

Thus, technology itself is not the problem, but a specific way of thinking and a specific way of doing. Rather than evaluating technologies or artefacts as such, we must evaluate the way people relate to their environment—a relation that is mediated by specific technologies, a specific culture, etc. Furthermore, the better response to modern alienation is not a romantic rejection of technology or a mystical escape from technology, but skilled engagement with our environment. Here technology can play a role, and perhaps *necessarily* plays a role if it is true, as Plessner said that we are artificial by nature (Plessner 1928). But it has to be the right kind of technology and the right kind of use of technology—with "the right kind" being defined as the kind that helps us, rather than hinders us, to improve our relation to the environment. (Note that "the right kind of use" is not necessarily the use intended by the designers of the technology.)

This approach to technology takes distance from Heidegger, but also, to a significantly lesser extent, from Dreyfus and Borgmann. Let me start with the latter; I will say more about Dreyfus in the next section. As I noted before, Borgmann recommended 'focal practices' as a response to the de-skilling by modern technology (Borgmann 1984). But this advice can easily be interpreted in a romantic way: Some activities that were common in the past may be said to be more "natural" than others. Devices are "artificial"; the old tools were "natural". But some contemporary technologies might even require *more* skill rather than less or at least different skills (re-skilling; see also the next section) and one should avoid attaching value to certain technologies *a priori* (say that they are focal or not). Rather, the same artefacts and perhaps even the same activities and *practices* can be made (or become) more focal or less focal. Practices are morally instable in this sense: They can increase environmental alienation if shaped in one way, but shaped in a different way they might also reduce such alienation.

Perhaps there are certain types of "alienation" and "non-alienation" that cannot be avoided; we might call these "existential" since they seem to belong to the human condition. First, there is a "basic", "objective", "existential" sense in which we are never alienated from our environment as *beings-in-the-world* (Heidegger 1927): we are environmental by "nature" (if we must use this "nature" term at all—a better phrase is that we are *environmental beings*) in the sense that as long as we live, we are "in" a world. We cannot completely detach ourselves from it or be completely detached from it, unless we commit suicide or are killed. Second, there is

The Art of Environmental Practice as an Ethics of Skill 185

another "existential" sense in which we are always alienated in the sense that if we think as *self-conscious*, reflective, and deliberative beings, we take up an "external" position, and in contrast to what Romantics assume, we are never "naturally" and "directly" related to anything. Heidegger talks about *ek-stasis* (Heidegger 1927) and Plessner about eccentric positionality (Plessner 1928). Third, a related "existential" sense in which we are always "alienated", is that in so far as *technology* always mediates our experiences and our actions in one way or another, we cannot have a "direct" relation to our environment as techno-human beings.

However, these are not the meanings of "alienation" that interest us here. They are not immediately relevant for normative ethical analysis since we cannot change our basic existential condition. But we *can* change our relation to our environment, at least in so far as this relation is shaped by us. This relation can be more or less "alienated".

In order to develop this point and to how an "environmental ethics of skill" might work with regard to particular technological practices, I will discuss the relation between environmental ethics, skills, and information technologies. I choose to focus on electronic information and communication technologies since they are so dominant today. I will use Marx, Dreyfus, and Borgmann again, but I will also further develop my position concerning the relation between alienation and technology by using Illich. I will argue that an ethics of skill does not reject technology but requires *different* kinds of technology. Discussing Illich's concept of 'convivial tools' (in the last section) will then help me to explore what kind of different technology and hence what kind of different relation to our environment we need.

11.2. IMPLICATIONS FOR ETHICS OF (INFORMATION) TECHNOLOGY (1): USING MARX, DREYFUS, AND BORGMANN

Are contemporary information and communication technologies (ICTs) alienating, and in what sense are they alienating? Given their pervasive influence in and on our society, it is worth focusing on them in order to further articulate the implications of my "environmental skill" argument.

From a Marxian point of view, one may say that electronic devices turn us into commodities. Not only are the workers who produce these devices alienated (from their products, from other workers, etc.), the consumers are also alienated in the Marcusean sense that they become the extensions of their products. Furthermore, as contemporary Marxism has also argued, consumers of internet services (e.g. social media) are used as data factories and hence alienated from the product of their "labour": The data they produce by using the services are sold off to third parties.[1] Marxism thus seems to provide an attractive and coherent framework for ethical analysis of new

186 *Implications for Environmental Ethics*

information technologies. However, I believe it must be at least modified, if not rejected, for the following reasons.

First, to apply the Marxian commodification/alienation thesis to contemporary information technologies without further qualification may be insensitive to the precise features of contemporary ICTs. Contemporary electronic technologies are not the same as "modern technology" in the industrial age. For example, does use of social media and (other) ICTs really amount to 'indifference' (Marx 1846, p. 66) or to the loss of 'self-activity' (p. 87), given that identity workers care about content, although they may seem indifferent to the data they produce and to others? If users can realize and express their identity in their products, is this not what Marx meant by the kind of "good" (my term) objectification he described? And does using internet-based technologies really require very little *skill*? (See also my response to Dreyfus below.)

Second, while these remarks may be a reason to modify the Marxian alienation thesis or at least to be more careful in applying it, there is deeper, more serious problem with it: it is deeply modern and hence contributes rather than solves the problem of environmental alienation. This is not only so because it is based on essentialist, romantic, and dualist assumptions (see the previous section), but also because it is an analysis in terms of *political economy*, which equates politics with matters of the household. While I argue, against Arendt, that a strict separation between the two spheres is highly problematic, it is dangerous to equate both, especially if in modern times economy, that is, "household", activities are interpreted in terms of "management". Such a thinking does not need capitalism to alienate us: Modern-economical thinking itself, which renders everything part of the household and its management, has already shaped the conditions of possibility for environmental alienation "before" the kinds of alienation described by Marx play out. Marxism does question a specific mode of production, but it does not question modernity and modern-economical thinking itself. Instead, it seems to encourage rather than halt the exploitation of resources and the transformation of "nature" for the sake of the emancipation and self-realization of humans. And although some writings suggest that skilled engagement is good, most work in this tradition seems to foster either (1) a romantic view of technological practices, of a pre-industrial past when there was no capitalism and industrialism, or (2) collective ownership of means of production within a non-capitalist but still modern, industrial mode of production and mode of life, which is at least as alienating as the capitalist mode it tries to replace. These visions are themselves sources of alienation and fail to do justice to the kind of information and communication technologies we have today, which created a new world which is partly capitalist, for sure, but which also appears to have other features which need further analysis.[2]

In response to the problematic *modern* character of Marxian analysis, one may turn to Heideggerian thinking. For example, one may apply

The Art of Environmental Practice as an Ethics of Skill   187

Borgmann's analysis of the 'device paradigm' (Borgmann 1984) to contemporary information technologies and argue that electronic devices are indeed *devices* that hide their workings, prevent skilled engagement with them, and prevent social engagement (the i-devices of this generation ICT). Indeed, it seems that such devices are made for children: to operate them is made easy, and you can play with it on your own. In so far as this is the case, we can conclude from my discussion of Sennett, Pirsig, and others that these devices are indeed environmentally alienating: By de-skilling us, they estrange us from our "natural", material, and social environment.

One may also draw on Dreyfus' critique of the internet (Dreyfus 2001) to argue that the internet disembodies us and prevents engagement, risk-taking, and commitment. Dreyfus' view is close to Borgmann's, and both echo Heidegger's thinking about the "essence" of technology: 'If the essence of technology is to make everything easily accessible and optimizable, then the internet is the perfect technological device' (p. 1–2). In addition, Dreyfus also makes an anti-Platonic argument: He argues that we should not try to get rid of our bodies. He assumes that 'when we enter cyberspace', we 'leave behind our 'vulnerable, embodied selves' (p. 6).

But are electronic artefacts necessarily Borgmannian *devices*? Do they exclude focal practices? And does the internet necessarily exclude commitment, as Dreyfus has suggested? Do we really leave behind our bodies? Borgmann and Dreyfus help us to develop a non-modern, skill-oriented normative approach to evaluating new ICTs and, more generally, to an adequate ethics of technology and environmental ethics. Nevertheless, these objections against contemporary ICTs (1) present a too one-sided picture of these technologies and (2) have a normative view that can all too easily be interpreted in a modern and a romantic way—thus paving the way for more, rather than less, alienation. Let me explain this.

First, how "easy" are contemporary ICTs? Operating particular devices might be easy, but this does not mean that it is easy to integrate them into your life in a good way. This *does* require practical learning and skill, albeit *new* skills (see also below). For example, we may use mobile electronic devices in a way that enslaves us to them and alienates us from the environment, or we may develop skills to use them in such a way that we engage *more*, not less, with others and with the natural, social, material, and artificial (indeed often natural/artificial) environment. And as I already suggested in previous work (Coeckelbergh 2013), when we enter "cyberspace", we do not leave our bodies at home. We remain embodied and we remain beings-in-the-world (as I argued, the basic existential relation we have to the world is not alienating), even if in our experience we become alienated from our body and from our environment (because of specific, technologically mediated relations). This was also the case with using GPS devices: We always remain embodied and connected to the environment in a basic, existential sense, but by using these devices in a "cursory" way we create distance and alienate ourselves from the environment. Thus, it seems that some

188 *Implications for Environmental Ethics*

internet and other electronic technology are in danger of producing such a distance and alienation. But surely there might be other, or other uses of, internet-based technologies that help us to re-connect to our environment?

Second, the more fundamental problem with this kind of objection is that it presupposes a modern, dualistic, and romantic view: an ontological split between the "natural" "off-line" environment versus the "artificial" "on-line" environment. It is only if we presuppose this dualism that we can argue à la Dreyfus that the internet, understood as a non-real, "virtual" and separate world, is dangerous, and that we therefore should retreat to the real, natural world where engagement is still possible. But from a non-modern perspective there is only *one environment*, including when we use these ICTs. When we are "on-line" we are also at the same time "off-line"; the distinction itself is generally not relevant for evaluating how alienated we are from our environment. What needs to be evaluated is the extent to which a particular practice is alienating, regardless of the "ontological status" of the environment.[3] This "hybrid" view of the environment is not a particularly exotic view today. New generations take it for granted that there is only one environment, since they grew up in this *one*, hybrid, blended "on-line"/"off-line" environment. People create and grow up in worlds that depend on this environment and this reality.

In spite of this experience, there are still so many attempts to see the contemporary world in a dualistic way, using categories such as objective/subjective, system/lifeworld, and (of course) natural/artificial. This is especially so when "cyberspace" is seen as a space that is entirely different from other spaces and that constitutes what we may call a *new nature*. This modern and often romantic approach is taken when "cyberspace" is understood as a separate environment that is either (1) objectified—for example, when a scientific or meta-scientific approach understands cyberspace in terms of a collection of information or (better) an information ecology—or (2) subjectified in a romantic "cyber-Rousseau" or "cyber-Jean-Jacques" attempt to retreat into cyberspace understood as a space outside society: an escape into the "virtual" world of reverie, *flaneur*ship (the browser as *flâneur*), and fantasy. Hence there are two kinds of "romantic" responses to new ICTs: one is to escape to the "natural" sphere as opposed to the "artificial" sphere of "cyberspace", and another is to escape to "cyberspace" as a space of freedom, liberated from social constraints, from the artificiality of society. But both the objectivist-scientific view of cyberspace and the subjectivist-romantic view of cyberspace are problematic because they presuppose modern dualism: They presuppose that there is such a separate sphere or domain in the first place.

In order to get beyond these and other dualisms with regard to the relations between humans, technologies, and environment, we had better try to develop a non-modern view of those relations, which avoids the romantic side of Borgmann and Dreyfus as well as what I called "new nature"

The Art of Environmental Practice as an Ethics of Skill 189

approaches. Let me return to my discussion of the epistemology of skill and its application to contemporary information-technological practices.

As Borgmann and Dreyfus have argued, we should avoid an exclusive focus on skill-less, "easy" use. This seems to hinder the development of skillful engagement with the environment. But—and this revises the message Sennett, Pirsig, and others gave us—the alternative is not necessarily that we should all learn how to repair an electronic device (analogy for the "mechanical" age: know how to repair a motorbike). Rather, what is needed is skilled engagement with our *environment*, which may or may not include engagement with a particular technological artefact, which includes the social and "natural" environment, and which today includes those parts or dimensions of the environment created by the internet—which also have a social aspect. Indeed a child or a consumer has *user knowledge* (including know-how concerning use of the interface offered by the device—this requires learning new skills), but (s)he may lack know-how when it comes to coping with the (rest of the) *environment*. She can use an iPad, for instance, but she might not know how to integrate it in a good way of relating to her environment (which is on-line and off-line at the same time). She might miss the skill to re-shape the specific practice she is involved in in order to make it better. This requires additional skill and expertise, probably the skill and expertise that really matters, to our children and to us. It involves a broader kind of skill than only knowing how to "use" the device: the skill to *live* with it in a way that produces human-environmental flourishing. This is what an environmental ethics as an ethics of skill and an ethics of technology aims for.

This kind of skill is not unconnected to the skill to use ICTs, given that our contemporary environment is a hybrid one and includes internet and material devices. But it is broader than knowing how to "use" the device in the strict sense of knowing how to operate; it is the know-how needed for the good life. Thus, having "technical knowledge" and "technical know-how" is not enough. One may recommend the development of practical manual skill, as Pirsig does in his book, as opposed to "mere theoretical knowledge"—the Platonic kind of knowledge that contributes to our environmental alienation. It is true that this kind of know-how and skill seems to have intrinsic ethical and social benefits. It also seems better if one knows how to tinker with a device, rather than merely how to use it. Yet this does mean that such technical knowledge (theoretical knowledge and know-how) is sufficient for environmental alienation to disappear and for environmental good to emerge. If one knows how to cope with a particular technological artefact, even if one has achieved *expertise* in that particular area, this says very little about one's other and one's broader, "meta-skills" to cope in and with the world, to relate properly to one's environment—with or without the particular technology, mediated by the particular technology or not. It says little about how this particular skill (e.g. the skill to repair a motorbike, or the skill to operate an iPad)

190   *Implications for Environmental Ethics*

is related to other skills—to the "ecologies" of skills, so to speak, that matter environmentally. It says little about how we can lead better environmental lives *through* using electronic and other means. This is why becoming a *nerd*—in whatever area of technical competence—may provide interesting opportunities for developing "local" kinds of know-how, for skilled engagement with particular methods, artefacts, and software, but is not sufficient for environmental good. The art of life and the art of environmental practice require the development of "environmental skill", an ethical-environmental expertise necessary and sufficient for (the good) life. The development of skills in the bike workshop and in the computer lab may positively influence the development of this "environmental skill", provided they enable the development of skilled engagement and know-how and provide opportunities to create social and communal relations, but should not be equated with it. These activities may even prevent the development of "environmental skill" if they result in retreat from the wider social-material-technological-natural environment. Practices of technical skill development reveal what kind of knowledge relation we need to develop for relating to the environment in better ways, as I have shown in my reading of Sennett, Dreyfus, Borgmann, and others, but it is not *the same* as the ethics of environmental skill.

Note that such an environmental ethics does not exclude the use of ethical rules and principles. Perhaps we need some instruction as beginners. But if we want to be moral-environmental *experts*, we need to learn the skills necessary to live in, and cope with, the new techno-social, natural-artificial environment that has grown in recent years, and all skills necessary to modify it in a way that produces more virtue and flourishing. We cannot and should not hide from this challenge by trying to escape to "nature" or to the "virtual" world, or to a particular, "local" epistemic area where we gain theoretical knowledge or know-how. To deny that what we do in such "worlds" and "areas" is part of coping with our always changing and evolving environment is itself a condition that makes possible contemporary environmental alienation.

If we now need new technology at all, it will be technology that helps us to attend to, and be responsive to, the new environment's features—indeed to be and live more "environmental" today. "Environment" includes contemporary ICTs and the hybrid worlds they help to create, and our response to this environment is also often mediated by technologies, including electronic tools. Thus, discussions about technology should not be disconnected from the discussion about environmental virtue and skill, and vice versa. If we want people to become environmentally better persons (persons that are more environmentally virtuous) and, therefore, persons that have the right kind of environmental skills, one thing that is required is the development of the right kind of tools. In order to become better we need to engage with the environment in a better way, that is, we need to develop better skills and technologies. In the next section I will further support this point by using Illich's concept of 'convivial tools'.

11.3. IMPLICATIONS FOR ETHICS OF (INFORMATION) TECHNOLOGY (2): USING ILLICH'S CONCEPT OF 'CONVIVIAL TOOLS'

In *Tools for Conviviality* (1973) Ivan Illich criticizes the technocratic and bureaucratic aspects of modern society, which he claims have destroyed people's capacity to work together, to care, to do things themselves, and to realize themselves. He especially targets professionalization and specialization. For example, he describes how the professionalization of health care has resulted in the exclusion of nonprofessionals such as relatives and friends from health care. Health care has become a service, which has made it 'almost impossible for people to *care*' (Illich 1973, p. 3) and which has resulted in the rising power of management and technocracy. He also criticizes the modern obsession with efficiency and "saving time". In traffic, he argues, the creation of faster vehicles such as cars has not saved any time but instead resulted in more time being used by society for the sake of traffic; those vehicles thus 'created more distances than they helped to bridge' (p. 7–8). Indeed, it is well-known that better transportation has made possible the phenomenon of mass commuting, that is, faster means of transport have increased the physical distance between the place where one lives and the place where one works, and this has re-shaped the physical and social geography of the modern world, and of course the lives of people.

For the purpose of this book, it is especially instructive to read what Illich has to say about knowledge in the civilized world. He argues that a high degree of specialization implies that knowledge is no longer shared and becomes a matter of expertise. This means that the individual loses control over knowledge and technology. Only the expert knows how things work and has the appropriate skills; others become mere operators, users, clients, and consumers. Their experience becomes pre-designed and they can no longer learn from their own experience.

> The inhabitant of the city is in touch with thousands of systems, but only peripherally with each. He knows how to operate the TV or the telephone, but their workings are hidden from him. Learning by primary experience is restricted to self-adjustment in the midst of packaged commodities. He feels less and less secure in doing his own thing. Cooking, courtesy, and sex become subject matters in which instruction is required. (. . .) People come to feel that they need "education." Learning thus becomes a commodity.
>
> (Illich 1973, p. 59)

What is lost, according to Illich, is man's 'power to endow the world with his personal meaning'. Man is deprived of 'his deep need to learn what he wants and not what others have planned that he should learn' (p. 60). Like healing and transportation, learning is professionalized and thus given to experts; it is alienated from people's own capacity to heal, to move themselves, and to

192   *Implications for Environmental Ethics*

learn from direct experience, that is, experience not pre-shaped by experts. The result is not only what we may call de-skilling at a personal level but also a crisis at the level of society, according to Illich caused by 'management', which is supposed to cure but instead makes things worse (p. 9).

But if more management does not help, what does? Illich's alternative to 'technocratic disaster' is his vision of what he calls a 'convivial' society and 'convivial' tools. He proposes a new relationship between persons, tools, and collectivity. He argues that we need new tools that enable us to master these tools (rather than being out of proportion to us and enslaving us), to invest the world with our meaning, to pursue our own goals, and to realize ourselves. Although this view still retains traces of Western dualism and Romanticism (see below), it is worth further discussing the implications of Illich's concept for thinking about technology and environment.

If Illich criticizes the tools of his time as being non-convivial, does this mean that we have to return to pre-modern technology? Not necessarily. On the one hand, Illich writes that tools may be simplified 'to enable the layman to shape his immediate environment to his taste' and proposes that laymen can also diagnose and treat many diseases (p. 34). This reminds of the romantic solution: We need more "natural" ways of living. Illich also says that we need more labor-intensive tools and remarks that people value handicraft and personal care as luxuries (p. 44). On the other hand, there might be the possibility to develop tools that 'enable the layman to shape his immediate environment' in a better way, not by giving up contemporary ICTs and revert to older ones, but instead by developing new, *better* ICTs or by modifying existing ones. Illich seems to suggest that modern ICTs *could* be convivial. He did not know the internet yet, of course, but he says about the telephone that 'it is impossible for bureaucrats to define what people say to each other on the phone' (p. 22) and proposes that 'limited resources can be used to provide millions of viewers with the color image of one performer or to provide many people with free access to the records of their choice' (p. 34). Illich wants the tools to be 'modern' *and* 'convivial' at the same time. He is certainly not anti-science:

> Natural and social science can be used for the creation of tools, utilities, and rules available to everyone, permitting individuals and transient associations to constantly recreate their mutual relationships and their environment with unenvisaged freedom and self-expression.
>
> (Illich 1973, p. 34)

Can the internet and internet-based technologies be regarded as such a tool? Can electronic devices be 'convivial'? Illich does not tell us, but we can at least articulate when these tools are *not* convivial: If they are not transparent and come pre-packed as a commodity, if we do not have free access to them, if we cannot significantly modify or repair them without being "experts," and if they are used by managers and bureaucrats to exercise power over us. To the extent that we are "passively acted upon" by electronic devices, that

The Art of Environmental Practice as an Ethics of Skill   193

for their functioning we are entirely dependent on external "expert" parties such as technicians in multinational corporations, and that we become mere consumers that are controlled by means of the devices, they are not convivial. If only experts can fix them and we can only *adapt* to them, they are not convivial. If they promise us speed, but actually take more time (think about traffic but also about e-mail, which makes communication faster but now occupies time we previously used for other activities), they are not convivial. If they pre-design our experience and if we cannot 'endow the world with our personal meaning' because of them, then they are not convivial. If, on the other hand, they contribute to self-realization and enable 'individuals and communities to choose their own styles of life through effective, small-scale renewal' (p. 73), they *are* convivial.

Is this possible today? Although technologies and their uses are never one-dimensional—surely the internet has a 'convivial' aspect in much the same way as the media Illich describes—it is clear that we are (still?) far removed from the kind of convivial tools I suggest in the description above. Some people use ICT in 'convivial' ways, perhaps, for example when they hack software and hardware (thus doing other things with them than intended) and, for example, use 3D printers not as machines that produce pre-designed things (a "consumption," "instant" way of using them) but as tools for making new tools, that is, for really changing the way we do things. Although the electronic tools they play with and modify are made in such a way that this requires a lot of pre-acquired formal and explicit expertise, there is a possibility of skilled learning and craftsmanship practices here and clearly there are "workshop" settings where people work together and learn from one another. Yet the "knowing-that" aspect of the practice seems still dominant because of the nature of contemporary ICTs: For instance, software has a "know-how" aspect, for sure (think also of what it means to learn other, "natural" languages), but also a considerable "know-that" aspect.

In addition, ICT is today still often (if not mainly) used for bureaucratic and management purposes. Illich fears a world of social engineering, in which others define for us what we ought to do. Think about the current proposals (and they are already being translated into policy) of 'nudging' as mentioned earlier in this book. Choice architects seem to be the new social engineers. Illich's warning is very relevant here:

> Overprogramming can transform the world into a treatment ward in which people are constantly taught, socialized, normalized, tested, and reformed.
>
> (Illich 1973, p. 76)

And:

> People would be confined from birth to death in a world-wide schoolhouse, treated in a world-wide hospital, surrounded by television

194   *Implications for Environmental Ethics*

screens, and the man-made environment would be distinguishable in name only from a world-wide prison.

(Illich 1973, p. 101)

Do internet and other communication technologies create this world-wide prison? Does the current management and bureaucracy contribute to it? The answer is probably not "yes" or "no" but somewhere in between. But again Illich provides a clear (negative) criterion for convivial tools and a convivial society.

What does this mean for environmental ethics? Connecting the main argument of this book with Illich's analysis and with the question regarding new ICTs, we may conclude: The problem with contemporary ICTs is not that they are "artificial" or create "artificial" worlds. The problem is that these technologies do too little to enable and promote skillful engagement with the environment (they rather promote engagement with the device and with the products of the company) and that they are often used to promote more bureaucracy and management rather than less. Indeed, Illich's notion of 'conviviality' seems to be very compatible with my "environmental skill" criterion for evaluating contemporary technologies. The environmental skills and environmental technologies argued for in the previous sections and chapters should be 'convivial' in Illich's sense, and the meaning of 'conviviality' can be helpfully defined in a more "environmental" way. Illich himself suggests this connection. He writes:

The only solution to the environmental crisis is the shared insight of people that they would be happier if they could *work* together and *care* for each other.

(Illich 1973, p. 50)

Thus, Illich does not separate the "environmental" question, the "social" question, and the question of "technology". The convivial tools and the convivial society he envisions are also solutions to the environmental crisis. He warns that the preservation of the environment can become hijacked by management and bureaucracy: 'the preservation of the physical milieu can become the rationale for a bureaucratic Leviathan' (p. 50). Again, with Illich we can conclude that we need not more management to solve the environmental crisis (which is at the same time a social crisis); instead, we need convivial tools and convivial work, understood as tools and work that help us to shape a better relation to our social, material, and natural/artificial environment. Bureaucratic and managerial control over people and control over the environment turn out to be rooted in one and the same way of life (a modern, non-convivial way of life), and to counteract this requires the reform of practices based on learning from direct experience and skilled and communal work, which leads to forms of shared knowledge not delegated to experts, and thus forms of social organization that are far less oppressive

The Art of Environmental Practice as an Ethics of Skill 195

than the "treatment ward" and the "schoolhouse", where the distribution is of knowledge is entirely asymmetrical.

In his pro-environment argument, however, Illich still heavily relies on the modern-romantic distinction between the "natural" and the "artificial", and the "human" and the "technological". He fears that

> man will find himself totally enclosed within his artificial creation, with no exit. Enveloped in a physical, social, and psychological milieu of his own making, he will be a prisoner in the shell of technology, unable to find again the ancient milieu to which he was adapted for hundreds of thousands of years. The ecological balance cannot be re-established unless we recognize again that only persons have ends and that only persons can work towards them.
>
> (Illich 1973, p. 51)

His argument against a technoworld without exit is interesting. Illich writes: 'Man would live in a plastic bubble that would protect his survival and make it increasingly worthless' (p. 101). This would then require 'the psychogenetic tooling of man himself as a condition for further growth' (p. 101)—say, human enhancement. Illich also shares the modern fear that 'machines enslave men' (p. 10).

However, I disagree with his interpretations of technology here. The modern-romantic natural/artificial distinction is problematic: We have always been artificial and natural at the same time. In contrast to Illich, I think that human beings have always built shells by transforming their physical milieu. With Sloterdijk I agree that we create bubbles in order to attempt to achieve immunity, and recently I have argued that we have always used technology in an attempt to reduce our vulnerability, but that this has always also transformed the human and that it has created new vulnerabilities (Coeckelbergh 2013). The environmental-ethical question, therefore, is not how to get rid of technology and the "artificial", but how to use technology in a way that is 'convivial' in Illich's sense, although this will always involve a particular way of protecting us from risks and will necessarily incur new risks. We will always make ourselves dependent on the tools we use, even if they are 'convivial'. We will always build new shells. And they will always be as much "artificial" as "natural", social and technological, human and technological. As I argued in the previous section, we need to think beyond dualisms such as artificial/natural, human/technological, and ends/means.

However, Illich's vision of convivial tools and a convivial society—and its implications for environmental ethics—can be articulated without relying on these dualisms. His own view that we should have the power to 'endow the world with our personal meaning' is non-dualistic if we read this phrase not as presupposing a split between a world-object that is meaningless and a human-subject that gives meaning, or between a

196 *Implications for Environmental Ethics*

"natural" world that is then interpreted and transformed into something "artificial", but as presupposing an active relation towards the environment, which "receives" and "gives" meaning at the same time. If we are skillfully engaged with our environment in a 'convivial' way, we do not create a separate "artificial" world as opposed to a "natural" one, and the personal meaning Illich writes about is not something we impose on the world. Rather, in skilled activity we humans and our actions are already "environmental" and therefore at the same time artificial and natural, and personal meaning emerges from this interaction and engagement with our environment. Meaning is not something that we "give" or "deliver" to an external world; rather, it emerges within and from the environmental-existential relation.

Illich is right to stress that this meaning and this experience should not be pre-designed by experts and that we should not be enslaved to our tools. But, as he himself suggests, avoiding this 'treatment ward' does not mean that we should reject technology, but rather that we create and use different tools and create different and better, more convivial shells and spaces. The bureaucratic and managerial nightmare (in which we are already living to some extent) is not made possible by "technology", but by *the wrong kind of technology* and the wrong kind of use. If we want to re-think and re-shape our world and our practices and habits (in particular, not only what we do but especially *how* we do things), part of what we need to do is re-thinking and re-shaping the tools we use.

Acting in a "pro-environmental" way, then, does not mean that one rejects the "artificial" in favour of the "natural", but that one reshapes one's relation to the environment in a way that creates more environmental good, personal meaning, and community at the same time. Illich's analysis suggests that under conditions of modern 'management' and 'bureaucracy' this is very difficult indeed, since *both the environment and the human being* are manipulated in a way that (1) precludes direct experience and skilled engagement with one's environment and (2) precludes caring for others, working together, sharing knowledge—in other words precludes *living together* (con-viviality).

Note that, if interpreted in a *narrow* sense, skilled engagement and conviviality may not constitute a *sufficient* condition for human-environmental flourishing. Skilled engagement might also be used in practices that produce violence, and bad people may be very 'convivial' amongst themselves but do bad things to others. But I have rejected such a narrow, technical interpretation of environmental skill and environmental *techne*. When it comes to environmental questions, technical skill is certainly a *necessary* condition and it certainly *motivates*. It also provides one important criterion to evaluate new technologies—whatever other criteria might be used. But "environmental skill" is broader; we need more kinds of know-how to attain the habits, know-how, and wisdom of the good environmental life and the environmental good life.

The Art of Environmental Practice as an Ethics of Skill   197

Current information and communication technologies, it turns out, are ambiguous with respect to how 'convivial' and "environmental" they are, how much they can contribute to the good environmental life and the environmental good life. On the one hand, electronic ICTs seem to contribute to the prison, the schoolhouse and the treatment ward: the managed and controlled environment in which we are manipulated by experts and 'surrounded by television screens' (p. 101). Electronic devices, for instance, seem to pre-program our experience, turn us into consumers (and laborers—we produce data for companies and governments), and as non-transparent devices they make us dependent on experts. Consider, for example, how the experience of video games is pre-designed and pre-programmed, and how difficult it is for a lay person to repair an electronic device. Electronic ICTs are also used in various management and professional contexts, such as health care and education. They are used in order to "save time" but in fact they also take up time that cannot be used for other activities (e.g. the computer in a doctor's consult). And we adapt. We are educated. We are disciplined. We are given goods to consume and services are delivered to us. Using these tools, we "have" education and we "have" sex (another example from Illich). In these ways, contemporary technologies—especially ICTs—can shield us from our physical and social environment. It seems that they can even alienate us from the material environment, when they enable us to be imprisoned in a world of words and images.

On the other hand, electronic ICTs such as smart devices, the internet, and social media also give us freedom and possibilities for self-realization. As "social" tools, they enable people 'to constantly recreate their mutual relationships and their environment with unenvisaged freedom and self-expression' (p. 34). They can also assist our self-care and self-learning, as opposed to care and learning that is provided as a "service". They can be used to share knowledge and to give people the opportunity to learn skills—including environmental skills. They can, in principle, distribute power rather than monopolize it. They can also, in principle, help us to live in a more ecological way and to engage with our environment. They can help people "to do their own thing" and thereby help people to live in a more ecologically friendly way. For example, they can help to monitor energy use and to self-manage one's own energy production, they can give us information about our ecological footprint and about how to cook and eat in a different way. Thus, they certainly have a 'convivial' aspect, or at least they might help to create conditions under which conviviality can grow.

Yet the ambiguity remains. There is always the danger that at the same time these ICTs alienate us from our physical and social environment, reduce time and possibilities for direct experience of our environment and of working and living with others, and turn us into the hands of those who want to manage and control us, our environment, and our relation to our environment "for our own good"—indeed, sometimes in the name of "ethics".

198 *Implications for Environmental Ethics*

But with Illich we may want to remain optimistic: We can dispense with the managers since we *have* the native capacity to do our own thing, that is, to transform our environment in a more spontaneous, meaningful and sustainable way. To recover and develop this capacity, we do not need to reject technology, live in more "natural" ways, or avoid "artificial" environments; the challenge is rather to develop new tools and new forms of living together that provide the conditions for more environmental engagement and conviviality. This means: developing new skills and building new shells, growing into new forms of dwelling and thus new forms of human being and human existence.

In their introduction to a volume on climate change, Thompson and Bendik-Keymer rightly argue that in response to new global ecological conditions (in particular, climate change) we will need to adapt "humanity itself": We will need to adjust our moral character and our social institutions, and we will need to adjust practices of restorations and indeed the virtuous themselves. They argue that 'the challenge of adapting to global climate change is fundamentally an ethical challenge of adjusting our conception of humanity, that is, of *understanding human flourishing in new ways*' (Thomson & Bendik-Keymer 2012, pp. 7–8). I agree with the authors, but I would like to add that we also have to adapt ourselves to changing social-*technological* conditions—which we do not fully control—and that we will not only have to change our understanding of human flourishing and our institutions but also *the human* itself. Both technology and the human will change anyway and *are* changing anyway because of the new technological-environmental changes, and if this is true, then we better try to change them in ways that promote human and non-human flourishing.

However, this should not be interpreted as a plea for a "Brave New World." On the contrary, after interpreting Illich we now also have a better idea about if and how science and technology can help us become more environmentally virtuous. Empirical psychology and other "human" sciences can assist us in our efforts to become environmentally virtuous, but with Illich we must be cautious that they are not used by others and by ourselves for the purpose of psychological and social engineering, turning our minds and bodies into "standing reserves" for data mining and manipulation. For example, the psychology of flow can help us to achieve a better relation to our environment, but it can also be used by employers to manage and control us—and indeed by individuals to exercise self-management, self-control, and self-manipulation. As I remarked earlier in this book there is a thin line between these two approaches. Even "non-scientific" Eastern practices such as specific forms of meditation are ambiguous in this respect: They can help us to better relate to our environment, but they can also be used by "human resource managers" to make us more productive employees. And electronic devices may attend us to specific features of the environment and of our body (features we might not have been fully aware of before), but they can also become tools that turn the human

The Art of Environmental Practice as an Ethics of Skill 199

person into a "smart body", a "quantified self", a collection of data. (Again, this quantification can be done by others, but there is also the practice of self-quantification—for instance, by using apps that measure bodily parameters.) These electronic devices can let the environment appear as a flat grid that is a 'standing reserve' for my purposes (e.g. a path from A to B) or indeed for the purposes of those who 'manage' us and for human purposes (only). They can help us to heal ourselves and achieve a better relation to our environment, but they can also mediate and materialize the duty of self-management, self-monitoring, and self-regulation, producing feelings of guilt and fear. They can be used to "re-design" and "re-engineer" the human, or they can help us to adapt to changing global and local conditions and support our efforts to do this in a way that produces more flourishing. They can give us more self-knowledge in the sense of making possible and enhancing direct experiences from which we can learn, or they can give us "self-knowledge" by revealing our "data" and patterns in these data. Virtue is about becoming better persons, not about becoming better (self-)managers. It is about human excellence, not about numbers and data. It is about quality, not about quantity. Nevertheless, re-thinking human excellence (*arete*) or virtue will also and always involve re-thinking science and technology and our relation to science and technology, including our relation to numbers and data, software and hardware, electronic devices and the internet. Re-shaping what human excellence means requires also re-shaping our relation to technology. A new (environmental) ethics requires new tools, including new 'convivial' ICTs.

NOTES

1. See for example the work of Christian Fuchs on the political economy of the internet and other new media. I have also discussed this in a recent conference paper, in which I used Marx and Heidegger to talk about 'data milking'.
2. Again, there are interesting responses to new technologies in contemporary Marxism. See, for example, Fuchs and Dyer-Witheford; however, they remain within modern thinking.
3. This view can be characterized as a 'mono-environmentalism', so to speak, but not a 'mono-worldism': There is one environment, but there are different worlds—that is, different ways of seeing and doing, depending on human subjectivity and human agency.

12 Conclusion
The Possibility of a New Environmental Ethics

12.1. SUMMARY OF THE BOOK

The argument of this book can be summarized as follows. My starting point was the observation that there is a gap between knowledge and action when it comes to responding to what may be called the environmental challenge: We know what is ethically required from us; we know that we have to change our lives, but most of us do not make significant changes. In the first two chapters I provided some moral-psychological explanations for this gap, drawn from philosophy but also from empirical psychology. Although this was and is a worthwhile exercise in itself, I have then drawn attention to what I see as a deeper problem which makes environmental change difficult, and which transcends individual moral-psychological issues: the problem of modernity. I have shown that our current thinking about the environment is still heir to what I see as the two faces of modernity: on the one hand, the Enlightenment, with its focus on rationality, control of nature, objective science, and political liberation and emancipation, and, on the other hand, Romanticism, with its emphasis on feeling, naturalness, authenticity, and nostalgia—translated into conservation or restoration. While the first face of modernity has already received much attention in environmental philosophy, I have highlighted the much less-often discussed *romantic* heritage of contemporary environmentalism. I have shown how much we are still the children of Rousseau and Thoreau, caught up in the dialectic of Romanticism and Enlightenment. Then I have (re)constructed some attempts to go beyond modern thinking and I have argued that there is one promising route which deserves more attention: Skilled practical engagement with the environment may overcome the detached, alienated modern attitude which prevents us from acting in a more environmentally friendly way. The problem with the gap between knowledge and action was that, as moderns, we understood "knowledge" as knowing-that to the exclusion of knowing-how. What is needed in environmentalism, I argued, is more of the latter kind of knowledge: We need the ethical-environmental knowledge that emerges from skilled engagement with the environment, from environmental *habitus*, from our involvement as environmental beings in natural-social practices, in embodied and materially and culturally mediated activities. If we have *that* kind of knowledge, I concluded, we can bridge the gap between knowledge and action; in skilled activity, we are already moved and "internally" motivated. What we need is not so much more moral principles and theories, or more information and more facts, but "environmental skill" and "environmental habitus". In the remainder of the book I then explored what this plea for more "environmental skill" implies for our thinking about (environmental) ethics (in particular, environmental virtue ethics), for our thinking about technology, for our thinking about environmental politics, and of course for our practices. In my discussions of walking, health care, eating, providing energy, etc. I have made suggestions for a more "environmental" understanding of these issues and I have shown how difficult it is to take distance from modern language and modern practices and habits, which still captivate us. I conclude that we need to develop new environmental skills and know-how, new environmental habits, and therefore also new technologies that render our lives more environmental and more 'convivial', but that there are limits to how much and how fast we can change given our modern 'form of life'. In this last chapter I will further reflect on the contribution of this book to environmental ethics and on those *limits*: I will outline some of the conditions of possibility for moral change.

12.2. A NEW ENVIRONMENTAL ETHICS?

The previous chapters can be read as a contribution to a new environmental ethics, which shifts from a modern approach focusing on "nature" (external and internal) and recommending self-control, a strong will, independent thinking, liberation, purity, knowledge (know-that), rationality, feeling, naturalness, and authenticity, to a non-modern, more relational approach that starts with recognizing our 'being-in-the-world' and which recommends skilled engagement with the environment and better environmental know-how as a way to deal with the problem of moral-environmental motivation and, indeed, with the environmental problems, to the extent that these problems are generated by a lack of this motivation. This approach also turns out to be in tune with studies in environmental psychology that emphasize the importance of experience and is compatible with an account of environmental ethics in terms of 'environmental virtue', especially if this virtue is understood in a roughly Humean fashion.

However, formulated in this way it seems that I assume that in environmental ethics we need something "new", an "alternative", and that once we have a new or alternative "concept" or "idea", we can then "apply" this concept to our actions and our living, we can "implement" the new ethical-environmental program in policies and personal plans, we can

202   *Conclusion*

"execute" the new code and "follow" the new law. But these assumptions are rooted in the same modern tradition and, ultimately, in the same Platonic/Socratic tradition that created the problem of moral motivation in the first place. It presupposes the moral-epistemological and moral-motivational priority of theoretical knowledge over practice and experience. It presupposes that we can and must shape and re-shape the world based on our concepts and theories, which should be new, original, and authentic. And it presupposes that the philosopher or master-mind, the "genius", can come up with such theories and that they will solve our problems.

But the turn to skilled engagement in this book should neither be interpreted as proposing a romantic "arts & crafts" return to pre-modern technology, nor as a rationalist-modernist tool we can use to "fix" a problem. So far I focused on distinguishing my approach from Romanticism; I think the latter claim still needs some more explanation.

First, thinking can change things, but its power is limited. Modern culture, like any culture, is *not* comparable to a motorbike. A conceptual framework is something that can be changed, for sure, and we can develop philosophical meta-skills to work on such frameworks. This is partly what I have done in this book. Philosophers can act as conceptual mechanics or (Platonic) conceptual designers. They might also assume a "therapeutic" role, as Wittgenstein recommended. Language is a very important aspect of the problem, as I already mentioned and will further show below. But words alone cannot change a culture, let alone words from philosophers. A culture cannot simply be re-written, even if writing is an important cultural technology. When we think, there is already a language given to us; language is undoubtedly difficult to change. And culture is more than a language: Words are related to embodied and technologically mediated habits, to practices, and to institutions. These are also hard to change. Perhaps philosophy cannot do much more than conceptual tattooing, while the cultural body moves on.

Second, guided by ideas and concepts such as "ethics of skill" and "environmental virtue", we might *want* to change our lives, as individuals, in order to "regain control". But this very desire to design our lives and identity is rather romantic, and I have also observed that relying on will-power, control, management, disciplining, etc. is itself a very modern thing to do; hence, we remain caught up in one of the paradoxes of modernity. I already discussed "the archer's challenge" and suggested that changing our relation to the environment cannot be a matter of will, decision, and agency alone, and that we have to learn by experience and patiently move on from there—very much in the spirit of the moral epistemology of skilled activity itself. But there is more to be said about moral change and its implications for environmental motivation and environmental change. In the next pages I will draw on what I said about moral change in my work on moral status (Coeckelbergh 2012) to discuss this problem and to draw conclusions from what has been done in this book.

12.3. WHY IT IS SO HARD TO BECOME GREENER IN A NON-MODERN WAY

In my introduction I asked why, in spite of increasing knowledge about environmental problems, most of us are not motivated enough to change the way we act and live. In the previous chapters I have tried to answer this question. At first sight, it seemed that the problem was lack of self-control and independent thought: We are too weak-willed and do not think independently enough to take distance from the conventions and ideologies that shape our lives; this is why we do not manage to really make a change. The solution for this problem appeared to be a kind of "environmental Enlightenment", which uses reason and science (including empirical psychology) to re-gain control over our lives and the environment, and which includes an environmental politics focused on liberation or conservation. However, both the Enlightenment and the romantic reaction to it, both of which have been so tremendously influential in creating the contemporary face of modern environmentalism, are forms of modern thinking, and this turns out to be part of the problem rather than the solution, at least in so far as modern thinking itself promotes a detached attitude and alienates us from our environment (not from "nature" or from the "nature" of our "true", "authentic" self, as the Romantics thought—I have argued that these ideas themselves are alienating).

Therefore, the question of motivation should be followed by this question: Can we move beyond a *modern* environmental ethics, and if so, how? In the previous chapters I have discussed some attempts to do so and I have proposed the concept of "environmental skill" as a way to get closer to a non-modern approach. I have also reflected on the implications of this concept for virtue ethics, for politics, for our way of living, and for coping with technology. However, in so far as "environmental skill" remains a "concept" or a "theory", it seems to face the same problem I mentioned in the beginning of the book: We might "know" what to do, but there remains a gap between knowledge and action. As long as it remains a knowing-that, rather than a knowing-how, environmental knowledge remains impotent. It seems that even if we are no longer chained to our book cases of reports and our hard disks full of "environmental" data, we are still imprisoned by philosophy as theory: In desperation we call for a new approach, but we forget that we are lamed by the very "knowledge" we think we have. Is the approach to environmental ethics that emerges in this book still too much a "knowing-that" rather than a "knowing-how"?

If it is, then perhaps we need to make a kind of moral-practical "leap" and just start doing things that make us engage more closely and more intensely with the environment, such as working in "nature" or collaborating with designers to make more "green" technology that encourages and facilitates a more direct relation to the environment. But thinking in terms of a "leap", as, for example, Kierkegaard did in his (proto)existentialist

204   *Conclusion*

thinking, is a hyper-voluntarist way of thinking. This thinking denies the moral force of modern ways of thinking and thus prevents us from making the change—indeed, it is impossible for it to recognize this, since voluntarism is itself a typical modern way of thinking.

The opposite of voluntarism would be fatalism. Here we may consider Heidegger's suggestion in his later work that the modern way of thinking (which he misleadingly called 'modern technology') is a kind of fate. If this is true we have to await better times and be patient (see also the notion of *Gelassenheit* mentioned in a previous chapter). Indeed, Heidegger talks about destiny and 'destining' (Heidegger 1977, p. 24). But while it is good to recognize that humans do not have full control over the conditions under which they have to exist and live, and that patience is an important meta-virtue, it would be also wrong to say that we are the passive recipients of "fate", that we are entirely constrained by outer conditions which form our thinking. This would assume an externalist view of the environment (including ways of thinking) and indeed of the human being, according to which we are entirely separated from our environment. Instead, as I said (inspired by Ingold and Berleant), humans and their environment mutually constitute one another. One advantage of the concept of skilled engagement is that it takes seriously Heidegger's own claim (in his earlier work) that we are-in-the-world, which implies that we can only know and experience "modernity" as *environmental* beings, as beings which are actively related—in perception and activity—to the environment. Modernity does not have an independent existence; it does not exist independent of our perception-in-relation and our action-in-relation. In this sense, we are *part* of modernity; it is not an external "fate" that hovers above our heads, as a sword of Damocles. Rather, if it can be compared to a sword at all, it is a sword that we handle and are *used* to handling. Modernity is in the form of our actions, our words, our bodies, our comportment, our technologies, our thinking, and our experience. We *modernize*, so to speak. We modernize in our daily lives, in our habits, in our practices. The truth in the argument against voluntarism is that we cannot change those forms by an act of will. But the forms change and grow in various ways, and what we do, say, think, and experience is part of that process of change and growth. This means that what we do matters, even if as individuals we are only a small part of the whole. To believe the opposite is not only de-motivating, as empirical psychology shows; it is simply a mistake.

It is worth noting that even Heidegger rejects the "fatalistic" interpretation of his claim that enframing 'belongs within the destining of revealing': he says that by using the term *fate* he does not mean 'the inevitableness of an unalterable course' and argues that 'sojourning within the open space of destining (. . .) in no way confines us to a stultified compulsion to push on blindly with technology' (Heidegger 1977, p. 25). Instead, he suggests that there might be a 'saving power', but if there is, it would be very modern indeed to try to want to 'lay hold' of it (p. 29). Rather, he suggests that *art* may 'foster the growth of the saving power' if art is called to 'poetic revealing', that we must continue questioning (I interpret: we must continue philosophy), and that 'the closer we come to the danger (. . .) the more questioning we become' (p. 35). But is questioning enough to "save" us? As I argued in this book, the art of being environmental requires more than (changing the) words.

In order to continue *my* questioning, let me ask a more precise question than the question how we might be "saved" from "the danger": What are the conditions of possibility of moving from modern environmentalism to a non-modern environmentalism? What keeps us from more practical environmental engagement and more environmental skill, know-how? And what would be conditions that make such a change possible?

Consider the following conditions of possibility of moral change, which I have distinguished and analyzed more comprehensively in my work on moral status (Coeckelbergh 2012), but which are applicable and highly relevant to the problem of moral environmental change as well, and which can helpfully be connected to the main argument in this book.

Language. As I already suggested with my reference to Wittgenstein in Chapter 10, an important barrier to environmental change is the language we use to talk about the environment. For example, if we talk about the environment in terms of "nature" or "ecosystems", we carry the luggage of modern thinking with us. Using Heidegger's metaphor we may also say that we live in the house of modern language. Some environmentalists are aware of this. As White has correctly observed, using scientific language does not help us to resist ways of thinking and doing that are detrimental to the environment but rather turns us into collaborators who "negotiate" with nature, finding a balance between the needs of the economy and the needs of the natural world (White 2007, p. 15). But rationalism and science alone are not to blame—and not even "science" as such but its modern, alienating dimension, which may be different from scientific *practice* (the same holds for the Enlightenment). As I have emphasized in this book, modernity also has a non-rationalistic and non-scientific dimension: Romanticism. The romantic language of "nature" turned out to be yet another barrier to finding a better relationship to nature. At present we seem to be caught up in modern thinking, that is, in modern language. The language of "skill" and other concepts might help us to move to different ways of thinking, but it is difficult to move away from the moral-environmental language we are used to. We are as much the backpack of modernity as modernity is our backpack. Surely, it is not only unavoidable but also good that there is already a language, that it is given to us. Otherwise we couldn't say anything. But if language is the house of being, as Heidegger said in his later work, and if we recognize that the specific language we have is problematic, can we move out of it? Or do we have to rebuild it bit by bit? But non-modern thinking would mean: re-building the house of language without merely executing a plan, without a blueprint, without a design. Here human-centred, that

206   *Conclusion*

is technology-centred metaphors have limited value since we tend to use modern language to talk about architecture; perhaps we had better turn to life-oriented ones. Changing the architecture of our moral language would need to be a process of growth and evolution, to which we contribute but which we cannot fully control or predict. We cannot know its ultimate form, since the future form does not only depend on us and since there is no "ultimate" form (and no "original" form). Developing environmental skill "while talking" or "while writing", and indeed *by* talking and writing, then means: using words as *part* of learning how to respond adequately to the environment, trying to achieve a more engaged relation, good "flow", and more (environmental) virtue. We can only hope that, partly influenced by our efforts, language changes in a direction that helps us to think differently about the environment and especially to *act* and *practice* differently in relation to the environment. Thus we can contribute to this change.

Society. If we want a different relation to our environment, we are confronted with the problem that we already live in a society in which "they" (Heidegger: *das Man*) do things in a particular way and think about the environment in a particular way. The modern-romantic response of existentialists and of contemporary individualists is then to assert the independence and authenticity of the individual, but this response denies that we cannot live without a social environment, and that if we want to change society this cannot be done from *design*. Rather, society is like the house of language: a living, growing, and in the best case flourishing house, in which we are only temporary guests, who contribute to what goes on in the house but do not own or master it. Acquiring more environmental skill means then: to engage in a collective learning process, which supports us as persons and as a community in our efforts to become more environmentally virtuous (the social can thus play a positive role; it is not necessarily the source of alienation and there is no "state of nature"), but without guarantee that we can move to a perfect, "pure" form, and without fixed individual or collective identity. Again, we can contribute, with words and with deeds, but then we can only *hope* that the form of our societies evolves into something that supports better environmental relations.

Bodies and technologies. Our thinking is dependent on physical/bodily and material conditions. This is true in an abstract, linguistic sense (we use "bodily" metaphors when we think—see, for example, the work of Lakoff and Johnson), but also in a very concrete, practical sense: If we want to move beyond modern thinking, we have to *do things in a different way*, develop different *habits* and *skills*. But if this is true, then if we want change then we must take into account and question the precise form of the material and technological mediation of our relation(s) to the environment. The objects and technologies we use today shape our relation to the environment and our thinking about that environment. If we want to achieve a less detached, less alienated relation to the environment, then we need different technologies and different body-technological relations.

But although we can design objects and produce products, we cannot fully control the precise human-technology relations that follow, and we should be aware that design and control of artefacts, of ourselves, and of the environment can assume a modern, managerial, and bureaucratic mode, which turns humans and their environments into objects of manipulation, in things that "stand reserve." Moreover, we are—literally—so *used* to our technologies that we cannot change our thinking and doing related to these technologies by *wanting* to. Skills are connected to habits, to ways of doing that may be difficult to acquire but also difficult to get rid of. Thus, the concept of skill attends us to the specific embodied and technological ways we relate to the environment, which always imply specific ways of moral thinking and doing, and which make environmental change difficult.

Religion and spirituality. In the first chapters of this book I observed that although many of us would call themselves and their society "secular"[1], we might still be (post-)Christian in our moral-psychological coping with environmental problems (think about the psychology of guilt and the problem of conversion). Later I also mentioned Callicott's discussion of the 'Judeo-Christian religious belief system' which sets 'man apart from the rest of creation' (Callicott 1989, p. 137) and Szerszinsky's thesis that the world was never disenchanted (Szerszinsky 2005a, 2005b). This suggests that there are deep cultural-religious patterns from which we cannot simply take distance by means of an act of will. If we would want to change our culture—for example, from a modern to a less modern one—then we must take this into account. Any culture is always also a *religious* culture: It comes with a luggage of concepts, metaphors, habits, and practices that are not always easy to change partly *because* they are entangled with religious meaning and practice (now or in the past). Changing cultural-religious patterns is possible but it takes a long time. For instance, it took Christians more than a millennium—if not more—to convert "pagans", and it could only do so by incorporating forms of "paganism" into its practices, imagery, language, etc. (in what is now called Catholicism). Similarly, Enlightenment reason has not *convinced* all Christians, and even if it has convinced a lot of them, changing beliefs should not be confused with changing ways of thinking and doing (for example moral-psychological patterns). Thus, even if one would want to "convert" moderns to non-moderns, or "convince" moderns that it is better to live in more non-modern way (which is perhaps a rather Socratic and modern thing to want), this is not easy. Moreover, even if change is possible, "conversion" may not be the best way to describe the change and growth of a (religious) culture. People and things cannot just be "turned around"; transformation is slow. For environmental ethics, acknowledging this relative inertia of culture implies accepting that our attitudes and our practices with regard to "environmental" issues cannot easily be changed in so far as they have roots in historically grown cultural forms (forms of thinking and doing), including historically grown religious

208   *Conclusion*

forms thinking and doing. There is what Wittgenstein calls a 'form of life,' and changing this form is hard.

(Historical) spaces. The way we think about the environment and the way we relate to it is very dependent on the spaces in which we live and the way we order and use these spaces. For example, romantic thinking has grown in response to modern urban spaces. An important aspect of Romanticism is the desire to move out of the city into "nature", into the "wild", or the move out of the house (sometimes literally, as when Rousseau leaves the table to go to his boat), to the "outdoor", into spaces where no human trace can be found (at least this is what Romantics wish). It is also well known that, ironically, many contemporary "environmentalists" and "greens" live in urban environments, out of which they want to escape into "nature"; but they tend to return to the city. The importance of space for our thinking means that to change our environmental thinking and doing, we need to live in different spaces (not necessarily "natural" ones). But to know *which* kind of spaces is difficult, since our thinking is constrained by the spaces in which we live, spaces that have emerged in the course of history. Both their form and their meaning are historically shaped. This has again consequences for change. Here too we have to accept a process of skilled learning and growth, which works with what is "given". This attitude is very different from the one of modern architecture, which wants to force form onto the world, wants to make an *imprint*, wants to order the world (see, for example, the early Wittgenstein and the house he designed).

To conclude, since our relation to the environment is interwoven with specific (for example: modern) linguistic, social-cultural, bodily-technological, religious-spiritual and spatial conditions that make possible our thinking and doing, but also limit it, becoming "environmentally" better people and living in "environmentally" better ways is, literally, in our hands, but also at the same time *not* in our hands—out of hand, so to speak. We can only superficially explore this paradox in thinking; in order to really *know* what this non-duality means we have to practice. To *cope* with this condition is a meta-skill we need if we want a better environment and better people.

It seems that if we want moral-environmental change, then we have to be a kind of moral meta-craftsman in relation to the environment, to others, and to ourselves. Rather than (a) trying to rationally explain and manage "nature" and "society", or trying to design or follow moral-environmental principles and laws, or trying to apply insights from empirical science to better manage ourselves and others (modern-rationalist thinking and doing), and rather than (b) trying to escape from society and from the "artificial" into "nature," or trying to achieve an "authentic" self and a "natural", "authentic" life (modern-romantic thinking and doing), we better (c) skillfully engage with our environment—human and non-human—and try out *together* and in *practice* how we can live in a more "environmental" way given the language, society, culture, and spaces we inherited. Developing environmental skill and conviviality is a process of trial and error, of

Conclusion 209

experiment; there is no final design, no blueprint, no original state of nature that can save us.

This also means that as philosophers, we should neither be arrogant conceptual designers who want to control the world nor self-absorbed, nostalgic dreamers. We should make sure that our questioning does not become ghostly reason or impotent and self-absorbed romantic sentiment but remains connected to our practices—indeed, emerges from our active engagement with our environment. It is in that here and now, in that art-full human-environmental communion of *techne, poiesis*, and *physis* that the problems of environmental ethics have their roots, and it is in that living metamorphosis alone that answers can grow. These answers need not necessarily reveal themselves in the form of *logos*. They might "happen to us" in other ways; for example, they might light up in the flow of our skilled activity in a particular situation and practice—even if we cannot, and should not try to, control or force this happening and should practice some *Gelassenheit* (letting-go). Environmental ethics is an art, and influencing and accompanying the coming into being of a new ethics is also an art: the art of loving, committing, waiting, caring, hoping, and—in the best case—giving and attending birth. Perhaps philosophers should indeed be a kind of midwife, but then not only by using dialogue but *also* by acting in this, largely *non-Socratic*, less logos-oriented way. (Incidentally, this less annoying style of philosophy may also increase their chance of *not* being condemned and executed by their fellow citizens.)

12.4. CONCLUSION

I conclude from this reflection on change in environmental ethics that the previous chapters should not be read as an argument for a "new", "alternative" environmental ethics, which replaces the modern, rationalist and/ or romantic version. Although at first sight it may seem to well-meaning environmental philosophers that what environmental ethics needs today is a powerful vision, good political will, and immediate action—perhaps based on "ethics of skill" as a new "concept" and "vision"—this is not how moral-environmental change can or will happen.

First, it has been argued that moral-environmental change is neither only a matter of will nor of switching ideology. Both anti-consumerism centred on self-control and liberationist, anti-conservative ideologies (liberalist and Marxist) are forms of *modern* environmentalism. It has been shown how contemporary environmentalism has roots in Enlightenment rationalism and its attempts to control "nature", but also in romantic longing for naturalness and authenticity, both of which contribute to more rather than less alienation, and therefore hinder rather than promote moral-environmental change.

Second, even if modernity is part of the problem, it is wise to realize that we cannot just "leave" modernity. If our thinking and doing needs to

210　*Conclusion*

change (for example, in the direction of more and better skilled engagement with our environment) then this means that a whole culture and tradition needs to change. Having considered several conditions of possibility for moral-environmental change, we must acknowledge that modern and romantic thinking are entangled with the way we talk about the environment (e.g. in terms of "nature"), with the way we have organized society, with the way we move our body, with the technologies we use, with the forms of religion and spirituality our tradition offers, and with the historically shaped spaces in which we think and act. These conditions thus resist our efforts to think and act in a non-modern and non-romantic way and hence hinder our efforts to change modern environmentalism and modern environmental ethics into something else.

Thus, rather than new conceptual design, a new moral vision, or a fresh ideal, environmental ethics needs philosophers who are willing and able to "accompany". "Accompanying" moral-environmental change requires the skills of conversation and criticism, but also the skill of moral-environmental midwifery. We need philosophers who do not so much try to re-*design* environmental ethics (a design which then awaits implementation), but rather assist in the birth of better environmental practices by enhancing moral-environmental know-how and meta-know-how, thus contributing to the growth of "environmental skill".

NOTE

1. Secularism can be interpreted as part of cultural-religious history; it is only meaningful *in response* to religion and is part of a particular cultural development. It is not 'prior' to religion.

Bibliography

Ajzen, Icek. (1991). The theory of planned behavior. *Organizational Behavior and Human Decision Processes, 50*(2), 179–211.

Allan, Julia L. (2008). The intention-behaviour gap–it's all under control (executive control). *The European Health Psychologist, 10*(3), 62–64.

Annas, Julia. (1995). Virtue as a skill. *International Journal of Philosophical Studies, 3*(2), 227–243.

Annas, Julia. (2011). *Intelligent Virtue*. Oxford: Oxford University Press.

Arendt, Hannah. (1958). *The Human Condition*. Chicago: University of Chicago Press.

Arendt, Hannah. (1963). *Eichmann in Jerusalem: A Report on the Banality of Evil*. New York: Viking Press.

Aristotle. (1984). *Nicomachean Ethics*. In Barnes, Jonathan (Ed.), *The Complete Works of Aristotle* (Vol. 2). Princeton, NJ: Princeton University Press.

Armitage, Christopher J. & Conner, Mark. (2000). Social cognition models and health behaviour: A structured review. *Psychology and Health, 15*(2), 173–189.

Ash, Solomon E. (1952). *Social Psychology*. Englewood Cliffs: Prentice-Hall.

Ash, Solomon E. (1956). Studies of independence and conformity: A minority of one against a unanimous majority. *Psychological Monographs, 70*(9), 1–70.

Augustine. (1961). *Confessions* (trans. R.S. Pine-Coffin). London: Penguin Classics.

Babbitt, Irving. (1919). *Rousseau and Romanticism*. Boston and New York: Houghton Mifflin Company.

Bandura, Albert. (1986). *Social Foundations of Thought and Action: A Social Cognitive Theory*. Englewood Cliffs, NJ: Prentice-Hall.

Bandura, Albert & McClelland, David C. (1977). *Social Learning Theory*. Englewood Cliffs, NJ: Prentice-Hall.

Bandura, Albert, Ross, Dorothea, & Ross, Sheila A. (1961). Transmission of aggression through imitation of aggressive models. *The Journal of Abnormal and Social Psychology, 63*(3), 575–582.

Baumeister, Roy F., Gailliot, Matthew, DeWall, C. Nathan, & Oaten, Megan. (2006). Self-regulation and personality: How interventions increase regulatory success, and how depletion moderates the effects of traits on behavior. *Journal of Personality, 74*(6), 1773–1802.

Bengson, J. & Moffett, M. A. (Eds.). (2012). *Knowing How: Essays on Knowledge, Mind, and Action*. New York: Oxford University Press.

Bentham, Jeremy. (1789). *An Introduction to the Principles of Morals and Legislation*. Oxford: Clarendon Press, 1907.

Benton, Ted. (1993). *Natural Relations: Ecology, Animal Rights and Social Justice*. London: Verso.

Berleant, Arnold. (2005). *Aesthetics and Environment: Variations on a Theme*. Aldershot/Burlington: Ashgate.

212 Bibliography

Berlin, Isaiah. (1958). *Two Concepts of Liberty*. Reprinted in *The Proper Study of Mankind: An Anthology of Essays*. London: Chatto & Windus, 1997.

Berlin, Isaiah. (1999). *The Roots of Romanticism* (Ed. H. Hardy). Princeton, NJ: Princeton University Press, 2001.

Bolter, Jay D. & Grusin, Richard. (2000). *Remediation—Understanding New Media*. Massachusetts: MIT Press.

Bond, Rod and Smith, Peter B. (1996). Culture and conformity: A meta-analysis of studies using Asch's Line Judgment Task. *Psychological Bulletin, 119*(1), 111–137.

Bookchin, Murray. (1980). *Toward an Ecological Society*. Montreal: Black Rose Books.

Borgmann, Albert. (1984). *Technology and the Character of Contemporary Life: A Philosophical Inquiry*. Chicago/London: The University of Chicago Press.

Bourdieu, Pierre. (1990). *The Logic of Practice*. Cambridge: Polity Press.

Brennan, Andrew & Lo, Yeuk-Sze. (2008). Environmental ethics. In *Stanford Encyclopedia of Philosophy*. Retrieved from http://plato.stanford.edu/entries/ethics-environmental/#DeeEco

Cafaro, Philip. (2004). *Thoreau's Living Ethics: Walden and the Pursuit of Virtue*. Athens and London: University of Georgia Press.

Cafaro, Philip. (2005). Gluttony, arrogance, greed, and apathy: An exploration of environmental vice. In Sandler, Ronald & Cafaro, Philip (Eds.), *Environmental Virtue Ethics* (pp. 135–158). Lanham, MD: Rowman & Littlefield.

Callicott, J. Baird. (1989). *In Defense of the Land Ethics: Essays in Environmental Philosophy*. Albany: SUNY Press.

Carman, Taylor. (1994). On being social: A reply to Olafson. *Inquiry, 37*(2), 203–223.

Chawla, Louise. (1999). Life paths into effective environmental action. *The Journal of Environmental Education, 31*(1), 15–26.

Coeckelbergh, Mark. (1999). Rousseau's idea(s) of freedom. *UEA Papers in Philosophy, 9*, 28–62.

Coeckelbergh, Mark. (2007). *Imagination and Principles*. Basingstoke/New York: Palgrave Macmillan.

Coeckelbergh, Mark. (2010). The spirit in the network: Models for spirituality in a technological culture. *Zygon: Journal of Religion & Science, 45*(4), 957–978.

Coeckelbergh, Mark. (2011). Environmental virtue: Motivation, skill, and (in)formation technology. *Journal of Environmental Philosophy, 8*(2), 141–170.

Coeckelbergh, Mark. (2012). *Growing Moral Relations*. Basingstoke/New York: Palgrave Macmillan.

Coeckelbergh, Mark. (2013). *Human Being @ Risk: Enhancement, Technology, and the Evaluation of Vulnerability Transformations*. Dordrecht/Heidelberg: Springer.

Coeckelbergh, Mark. (2014). Moral craftsmanship. In Moran, Seana, Cropley, David, & Kaufman, James (Eds.), *The Ethics of Creativity* (pp. 46–61). Basingstoke/New York: Palgrave Macmillan.

Conner, Mark & Armitage, Christopher J. (1998). Extending the theory of planned behavior: A review and avenues for further research. *Journal of Applied Social Psychology, 28*(15), 1429–1464.

Cooke, George Willis. (1881). *Ralph Waldo Emerson: His Life, Writings, and Philosophy*. Honolulu, Hawaii: University Press of the Pacific, 2003.

Cooper, John M. (1997). Introduction to Protagoras. In Plato, *Protagoras*. In Cooper, John M. & Hutchinson, D. S. (Eds.), *Plato: Complete Works* (pp. 746–747).

Crawford, M. B. (2009). *Shop Class as Soulcraft: An Inquiry into the Value of Work*. New York: The Penguin Press.

Bibliography 213

Crocker, Lester G. (1968). *Rousseau's Social Contract*. Cleveland: The Press of Case Western Reserve University.

Csikszentmihalyi, Mihaly. (1990). *Flow: The Psychology of Optimal Experience*. New York: HarperCollins.

Dewey, John. (1922). *Human Nature and Conduct: An Introduction to Social Psychology*. London: Allen and Unwin.

Diekmann, Andreas & Preisendörfer, Peter. (2003). Green and greenback: The behavioural effects of environmental attitudes in low-cost and high-cost situations. *Rationality and Society, 15*(4), 441–472.

Dobson, Andrew. (2000). *Green Political Thought* (3rd Edition). London: Routledge.

Donlan, Josh. (2005). Re-wilding North America. *Nature, 436*, 913–914.

Doris, John M. (1998). Persons, situations, and virtue ethics. *Nous, 32*, 504–530.

Dreyfus, Hubert L. (2001). *On the Internet* (Revised 2nd Edition). London and New York: Routledge.

Dreyfus, Hubert L. & Dreyfus, Stuart E. (1991). Towards a Phenomenology of Ethical Expertise. *Human Studies, 14*(4), 229–250.

Dreyfus, Hubert & Kelly, Sean Dorrance. (2011). *All Things Shining. Reading the Western Classics to Find Meaning in a Secular Age*. New York: Free Press.

Eckersley, Richard. (1992). *Environmentalism and Political Theory*. London: UCI Press.

Ellul, Jacques. (1954). *La technique ou l'enjeu du siècle*. Paris: Armand Colin. (Translated Wilkinson, J., *The Technological Society*. New York: Knopf, 1964.)

Emerson, Ralph Waldo. (1836). Nature. In Emerson, Ralph Waldo (Ed.), *Nature, Addresses and Lectures* (pp. 13–17). Honolulu, Hawaii: University Press of the Pacific, 2001.

Enzle, Michael E. & Ross, June M. (1978). Increasing and decreasing intrinsic interest with contingent rewards: A test of cognitive evaluation theory. *Journal of Experimental Social Psychology, 14*(6), 588–597.

Feenberg, Andrew (1995). *Alternative Modernity: The Technical Turn in Philosophy and Social Theory*. Berkeley/Los Angeles: University of California Press.

Festinger, Leon & Carlsmith, James M. (1959). Cognitive consequences of forced compliance. *Journal of Abnormal and Social Psychology, 58*, 203–210.

Frankfurt, Harry. (1971). Freedom of the will and the concept of a person. *The Journal of Philosophy, 68*(1), 5–20.

Foot, Philippa. (2002). *Hume on Moral Judgement*. Oxford: Oxford University Press.

Foreman, Dave. (2004). *Rewilding North America: A Vision for Conservation in the 21st Century*. Washington, DC: Island Press.

Garner, Robert. (1996). *Environmental Politics*. Hemel Hempstead: Prentice Hall/Harvester Wheatsheaf.

Germov, John, Williams, Lauren, & Freij, Maria. (2011). Portrayal of the Slow Food movement in the Australian print media: Conviviality, localism and romanticism. *Journal of Sociology, 47*(1), 89–106.

Goodin, Robert E. (1992). *Green Political Theory*. Cambridge: Polity.

Haraway, Donna. (1991). Cyborg Manifesto: Science, technology, and socialist-feminism in the late twentieth century. In Haraway, Donna (Ed.), *Simians, Cyborgs and Women: The Reinvention of Nature* (pp. 149–181). New York: Routledge.

Harman, Gilbert. (1999). Moral philosophy meets social psychology: Virtue ethics and the fundamental attribution error. *Proceedings of the Aristotelian Society, 99*, 315–331.

Haslam, S. Alexander & Reicher, Stephen D. (2008). Questioning the Banality of Evil. *The Psychologist, 21*(1), 16–19.

214 Bibliography

Heidegger, Martin. (1927). *Being and Time: A Translation of Sein und Zeit* (Trans. Joan Stambaugh). Albany, NY: State University of New York Press, 1996.

Heidegger, Martin. (1954). The Question Concerning Technology. In Lovitt, William (Trans.), *The Question Concerning Technology and Other Essays* (pp. 3–35). New York: Harper & Row, 1977.

Heidegger, Martin. (1971). Building Dwelling Thinking. In Hofstadter, Albert (Trans.), *Poetry, Language, Thought* (pp. 145–161). New York: Harper Colophon Books.

Heidegger, Martin. (2000). *Elucidations of Hölderlin's Poetry* (Trans. Keith Hoeller). New York: Humanity Books, 1981.

Horkheimer, Max & Theodor, W. Adorno. (1947). *Dialektik der Aufklärung*. Amsterdam: Querido. (Translated *Dialectic of Enlightenment*, New York: Seabury, 1972.)

Hulliung, Mark. (1994). *The Autocritique of Enlightenment: Rousseau and the Philosophies*. Cambridge, MA: Harvard University Press.

Hume, David. (1739/40). *A Treatise of Human Nature: A Critical Edition* (Eds. David Fate Norton & Mary J. Norton). Oxford: Clarendon Press, 2007.

Hung, Iris W. & Labroo, Aparna A. (2011). From firm muscles to firm willpower: Understanding the role of embodied cognition in self-regulation. *Journal of Consumer Research, 37*(6), 1046–1064.

Hungerford, Harold R. & Volk, Trudi L. (1990). Changing learning behavior through environmental education. *Journal of Environmental Education, 21*(3), 8–22.

Hursthouse, Rosalind. (2007). Environmental Virtue Ethics. In Walker, Rebecca & Ivanhoe, Philip J. (Eds.), *Working Virtue: Virtue Ethics and Contemporary Moral Problems* (pp. 155–172). Oxford: Oxford University Press.

Ihde, Don. (1990). *Technology and the Life World: From Garden to Earth*. Bloomington, IN: Indiana University Press.

Illich, Ivan. (1973). *Tools for Conviviality*. Berkeley: Heyday Books.

Ingold, Tim. (2000). *The Perception of the Environment: Essays on Livelihood, Dwelling and Skill*. London/New York: Routledge.

Ingold, Tim. (2004). Culture on the ground: The world perceived through the feet. *Journal of Material Culture, 9*(3), 315–340.

Ingold, Tim. (2010). Footprints through the weather-world: Walking, breathing, knowing. *Journal of the Royal Anthropological Institute, 16*(Supplement s1), S121–S139.

Ingold, Tim & Vergunst, J. Lee. (2008). *Ways of Walking: Ethnography and Practice on Foot*. Aldershot: Ashgate.

Jamieson, Dale. (2008). *Ethics and the Environment: An Introduction*. Cambridge: Cambridge University Press.

Jenkins, Richard. (2000). Disenchantment, enchantment and re-enchantment: Max Weber at the millennium. *Max Weber Studies, 1*, 11–32.

Jonker, Laura, Efferink-Gemser, Marije T., & Visscher, Chris. (2009). Talented athletes and academic achievements: A comparison over 14 years. *High Ability Studies, 20*(1), 55–64.

Kamtekar, Rachana. (2013). Ancient virtue ethics: An overview with an emphasis on practical wisdom. In Russell, Daniel C. (Ed.), *The Cambridge Companion to Virtue Ethics* (pp. 29–48). Cambridge: Cambridge University Press.

Kaplan, Stephen. (2000). Human nature and environmentally responsible behavior. *Journal of Social Issues, 56*(3), 491–508.

Kitsantas, Anastasia. (2000). The role of self-regulation strategies and self-efficacy perceptions in successful weight loss maintenance. *Psychology and Health, 15*(6), 811–820.

Bibliography   215

Kollmuss, Anja & Agyeman, Julian. (2002). Mind the gap: Why do people act environmentally and what are the barriers to pro-environmental behaviour? *Environmental Education Research, 8*(3), 239–260.

Kuhl, J. (1987). Action control: The maintenance of motivational states. In Halisch, Frank & Kuhl, Julius (Eds.), *Motivation, Intention, and Volition* (pp. 279–291). Berlin: Springer.

Latour, Bruno. (1993). *We Have Never Been Modern* (Trans. C. Porter). Cambridge, MA: Harvard University Press.

Latour, Bruno. (2004). *Politics of Nature* (Trans. C. Porter). Cambridge, MA: Harvard University Press.

Latour, Bruno. (2005). *Reassembling the Social: An Introduction to Actor-Network-Theory*. Oxford: Oxford University Press.

Lee, Jo & Ingold, Tim. (2006). Fieldwork on foot: Perceiving, routing, socializing. In Coleman, Simon & Collins, Peter Jeffrey (Eds.), *Locating the Field: Space, Place, and Context in Anthropology* (pp. 67–86). Oxford/New York: Berg.

Leopold, Aldo. (1949). *A Sand County Almanac*. Oxford/New York: Oxford University Press, 1989.

Maiteny, Paul T. (2002). Mind in the gap: Summary of research exploring 'inner' influences on pro-sustainability learning and behaviour. *Environmental Education Research, 8*(3), 299–306.

Marx, Karl. (1844). Economic and philosophic manuscripts of 1844. In Marx, Karl & Engels, Friedrich, *Economic and Philosophic Manuscripts of 1844 and the Communist* Manifesto. Amherst, NY: Prometheus, 1988.

Marx, Karl. (1867). *Capital: A Critique of Political Economy* (Vol. 1). London: Penguin, 1976/1990.

Marx, Karl & Engels, Friedrich. (1846). The German Ideology. In Marx, Karl & Engels, Friedrich, *Karl Marx and Friedrick Engels Collected Works* (Vol. 5). New York: International Publishers/Moscow: Progress Publishers, 1976.

McKibben, Bill. (1989). *The End of Nature*. London: Bloomsbury, 2003.

Merleau-Ponty, Maurice. (1945). *Phénoménologie de la perception*. Paris: Gallimard.

Merritt, Maria. (2000). Virtue ethics and situationalist personality psychology. *Ethical Theory & Moral Practice, 3*, 365–383.

Milgram, Stanley. (1963). Behavioral study of obedience. *Journal of Abnormal and Social Psychology, 67*(4), 371–378.

Mintz, Sidney W. & Du Bois, Christine. (2002). The anthropology of food and eating. *Annual Review of Anthropology, 31*, 99–119.

Mischel, Walter, Shoda, Yuichi, & Rodriguez, Monica L. (1989). Delay of gratification in children. *Science (New Series), 244*(4907), 933–938.

Næss, Arne. (1973). The shallow and the deep, long-range ecology movement. *Inquiry, 16*, 95–100.

Nietzsche, Friedrich. (1882/1887). *The Gay Science* (Ed. Walter Kaufmann). New York: Vintage, 1974.

Nussbaum, Martha C. (1994). *The Therapy of Desire: Theory and Practice in Hellenistic Ethics*. Princeton, NJ: Princeton University Press.

Oaten, Megan & Cheng, Ken. (2006a). Improved self-control: The benefits of a regular program of academic study. *Basic and Applied Social Psychology, 28*(1), 1–16.

Oaten, Megan & Cheng, Ken. (2006b). Longitudinal gains in self-regulation from regular physical exercise. *British Journal of Health Psychology, 11*(4), 717–733.

Olafson, Frederick A. (1994). Heidegger à la Wittgenstein or 'Coping' with Professor Dreyfus. *Inquiry, 37*(1), 45–64.

Olafson, Frederick A. (1998). *Heidegger and the Ground of Ethics: A Study of* Mitsein. Cambridge: Cambridge University Press.

216 Bibliography

Palmberg, Irmeli E. & Kuru, Jari. (2000). Outdoor activities as a basis for environmental responsibility. *The Journal of Environmental Education, 31*(4), 32–36.

Pepper, David. (1986). *The Roots of Modern Environmentalism*. Beckenham, Kent: Croom Helm.

Petty, Richard E. & Cacioppo, John T. (1986). The elaboration likelihood model of persuasion. *Advances in Experimental Social Psychology, 19*(1), 123–205.

Pilbeam, Bruce. (2003). Natural allies? Mapping the relationship between conservatism and environmentalism. *Political Studies, 51*, 490–508.

Pirsig, Robert M. (1974). *Zen and the Art of Motorcycle Maintenance*. New York: HarperTorch.

Plato. (1997a). *Alcibiades*. In Cooper, John M. & Hutchinson, D. S. (Eds.), *Plato:Complete Works* (pp. 557–595). Indianapolis/Cambridge: Hackett Publishing Company.

Plato. (1997b). *Protagoras*. In Cooper, John M. & Hutchinson, D. S. (Eds.), *Plato: Complete Works* (pp. 746–790). Indianapolis/Cambridge: Hackett Publishing Company, 1997.

Plessner, H. (1928). *Die Stufen des Organischen und der Mensch* (Gesammelte Schriften Vol. IV). Frankfurt/M: Suhrkamp, 1981.

Popper, Karl R. (1934). *Logik der Forschung*. Tübingen: Mohr. (Translated *The Logic of Scientific Discovery*. New York: Basic Books, 1959.)

Pottter, Andrew. (2010). *The Authenticity Hoax: How We Get Lost Finding Ourselves*. New York: Harper Collins.

Preuss, Sigrun. (1991). *Umweltkatastrophe Mensch. Ueber unsere Grenzen und Moeglichkeiten, oekologisch bewusst zu handeln*. Heidelberg: Roland Asanger Verlag.

Quick, Brian L. & Stephenson, Michael T. (2008). Examining the role of trait reactance and sensation seeking on perceived threat, state reactance, and reactance restoration. *Human Communication Research, 34*(3), 448–476.

Regan, Tom. (1983). *The Case for Animal Rights*. Berkeley, CA: University of California Press.

Ringold, Debra Jones. (2002). Boomerang effects in response to public health interventions: Some unintended consequences in the alcoholic beverage market. *Journal of Consumer Policy, 25*(1), 27–63.

Rousseau, Jean-Jacques. (1762a). *Emile or On Education* (Trans. A. Bloom). London: Penguin Classics, 1991.

Rousseau, Jean-Jacques. (1762b). *On the Social Contract* (Trans. G. D. H. Cole). Mineola, NY: Dover Publications, 2003.

Rousseau, Jean-Jacques. (1782a). *Confessions* (Trans. A. Scholar). Oxford: Oxford University Press.

Rousseau, Jean-Jacques. (1782b). *The Reveries of the Solitary Walker* (Trans. Charles E. Butterworth). Indianapolis, IN: Hackett, 1992.

Ruiter, Robert A. C., Abraham, Charles, & Kok, Gerjo. (2001). Scary warnings and rational precautions: A review of psychology of fear appeals. *Psychology and Health, 16*(6), 613–630.

Russell, Paul. (2013). Hume's Anatomy of Virtue. In Russell, Daniel C. (Ed.), *The Cambridge Companion to Virtue Ethics* (pp. 92–123). Cambridge: Cambridge University Press.

Ryle, Gilbert. (1945). Knowing how and knowing that. *Proceedings of the Aristotelian Society, 46*, 1–16.

Sandler, Ronald L. (2005). Introduction: Environmental virtue ethics. In Sandler, Ronald & Cafaro, Philip (Eds.), *Environmental Virtue Ethics* (pp. 1–14). Lanham, MD: Rowman & Littlefield.

Bibliography 217

Sandler, Ronald L. (2007). *Character and Environment: A Virtue-Oriented Approach to Environmental Ethics.* New York: Columbia University Press.

Sandler, Ronald L. & Cafaro, Philip. (Eds.). (2005). *Environmental Virtue Ethics.* Lanham, MD: Rwman & Littlefield.

Scheper-Hughes, Nancy & Lock, Margaret M. (1987). The mindful body: A prelogomenon to future work in medical anthropology. *Medical Anthropology Quarterly (New Series), 1*(1), 6–41.

Schulz, Dieter. (1997). *Amerikanischer Transzendentalismus.* Darmstadt: Wissenschaftliche Buchgesellschaft.

Sennett, R. (2008). *The Craftsman.* New Haven & London: Yale University Press.

Sheeran, Paschal. (2002). Intention—behavior relations: A conceptual and empirical review. *European Review of Social Psychology, 12*(1), 1–36.

Singer, Peter. (1975). *Animal Liberation.* New York: HarperCollins, 2002.

Smith, John E. (1954). Rousseau, Romanticism and the Philosophy of Existence. *Yale French Studies, 13*, 52–61.

Soper, Kate. (2004). Hedonist Revisionism. In Albritton, Robert, Bell, Shannon, Bell, John R., & Westra, Richard (Eds.), *New Socialisms: Futures Beyond Globalization* (pp. 125–138). London/New York: Routledge.

Stalnaker, Aaron. (2010). Virtue as mastery in early Confucianism. *Journal of Religious Ethics, 38*(3), 404–428.

Stern, Paul C. (2000). New environmental theories: Toward a coherent theory of environmentally significant behavior. *Journal of Social Issues, 56*(3), 407–424.

Szerszynski, Bronislaw. 2005a. *Nature, Technology and the Sacred.* Oxford: Blackwell.

Szerszynski, Bronislaw. 2005b. Rethinking the secular: Science, technology, and religion today. *Zygon: Journal of Religion and Science, 40*, 813–822.

Thaler, Richard & Sunstein, Cass. (2008). *Nudge: Improving Decisions about Health, Wealth, and Happiness.* New Haven, CT: Yale University Press.

Thompson, Allen & Bendik-Keymer, Jeremy. (2012). Introduction: Adapting Humanity. In Thompson, Allen & Bendik-Keymer, Jeremy (Eds.), *Ethical Adaptation to Climate Change: Human Virtues of the Future?* (pp. 1–26). Cambridge, MA: MIT Press.

Thoreau, Henry David. (1854). *Walden.* Princeton, NJ: Princeton University Press, 2004.

Thoreau, Henry David. (1862). *Walking.* New York: Cricket House Books, 2010.

Tranströmer, Tomas. 2006. 'Morning Birds.' In Tranströmer, Tomas, *The Great Enigma: New Collected Poems* (transl. Robin Fulton), New York: New Directions Books.

Urry, John. (2006). Travelling times. *European Journal of Communication, 21*(3), 357–372.

Varela, Francisco J. (1999). *Ethical Know-How: Action, Wisdom, and Cognition.* Stanford, CA: Stanford University Press.

Varela, Francisco J., Thompson, Evan, & Rosch, Eleanor. (1991). *The Embodied Mind: Cognitive Science and Human Experience.* Cambridge, MA: MIT Press, 1993.

Vaske, Jerry J. & Kobring, Katherine C. (2001). Place attachment and environmentally responsible behaviour. *The Journal of Environmental Education, 32*(4), 16–21.

Verbeek, Peter-Paul. (2005). *What Things Do.* University Park, PA: Pennsylvania State University Press.

Verbeek, Peter-Paul. (2008). Cyborg intentionality: Rethinking the phenomenology of human-technology relations. *Phenomenology and the Cognitive Sciences, 7*(3), 387–395.

218 Bibliography

Weber, Max. (1919). Science as a Vocation. In Gerth, H. H. & Mills, C. Wright (Eds. and trans.), *From Max Weber: Essays in Sociology* (pp. 129–156). New York: Oxford University Press, 1946.

Wensveen, Louke van. 2000. *Dirty Virtues*. Amherst, NY: Humanity Books.

White, Curtis. (2007). The idols of environmentalism. *Harper's Magazine*, August 2007, 13–18.

Wikipedia. (2014). 'Ecosystem services.' Available at http://en.wikipedia.org/wiki/Ecosystem-services.

Wilkins, Burleigh Taylor. (1959). The nature of Rousseau. *The Journal of Politics*, 21(4), 663–684.

Willim, Robert. (2007a). *Walking Through the Screen: Digital Media on the Go*. Paper presented at the Department of Anthropology, University College London. October 29, 2007. Available at www.pleazure.org/robert/rw_gps.pdf

Willim, Robert. (2007b). *Walking the Cognisphere: Navigation and Digital Media on the Go*. Conference Proceedings of INTER: A European Cultural Studies Conference in Sweden, organized by ACSIS, Norrköping, June 11–13, 2007. Available at www.ep.liu.se/ecp/025/067/ecp072067.pdf

Winkelman, Michael. (2009). *Culture and Health: Applying Medical Anthropology*. San Francisco, CA: Jossey-Bass/Wiley.

Wittgenstein, Ludwig. (1953). *Philosophical Investigations* (Revised 4th Edition, Eds. P. M. S. Hacker & Joachim Schulte). Malden, MA/Oxford: Wiley-Blackwell, 2009.

Zajonc, Robert B. (1968). Attitudinal effects of mere exposure. *Journal of Personality and Social Psychology,* 9(2, Pt. 2), 1–27.

Zimbardo, P. (1982). Pathology of imprisonment. In Krebs, D. (Ed.), *Readings in Social Psychology: Contemporary Perspectives* (pp. 249–251). New York: Harper & Row.

Index

acting-in-the-world 4
Action Control, theory of 30
addiction 18–22, 25–6, 35; *see also*
    unwilling addict
akrasia 17, 27
Alcibiades (Plato/Socrates) 115–16
alienation 3–9, 80, 87, 92–103,
    111–14, 132–3, 138, 143,
    161–3, 170, 179, 181–90,
    206, 209; environmental (*see*
    environmental); existential 7,
    92; food alienation 163–4; from
    "nature" 182; labour 182–3;
    Marx on 100, 181–3, 186; self-
    alienation 7, 94, 96, 132
animal liberation *see* animals
Animal Liberation (Singer) 59
Animal Liberation Front 59
animals 1, 3, 9, 16, 18–19, 32, 44–8,
    51, 57–63, 69–70, 73, 80, 85–7,
    111–12, 120, 126, 144, 149,
    152, 156–7, 163–70; death of
    156; de-contextualization of
    156; de-skinning of 156; ethics
    46, 164–6; killing of 126, 156;
    liberation 45, 58–62, 69; as pets
    or friends 165; relations 164–8;
    rights 59
anthropocentrism 57–8
apatheia 18
apathy 37, 95, 113, 117
appearance 14–16, 45, 71, 77–8, 107,
    165
Arendt, H. 25–7, 99, 104, 154, 170,
    177, 186
Aristotle 4–5, 8, 17–18, 26–7, 30, 99,
    121–33, 177
art 2, 10, 14, 88, 90, 98, 105–12, 121,
    148; 172; 181, 202, 205, 209; as
    fostering the saving power 205;

environmental ethics as 209;
    of being environmental 108–9,
    205; of environmental living
    2; of environmental practice
    181–99; of life 112, 190; of
    measurement 14
artificial 5, 10, 67–91, 127, 132,
    138–44, 153–9, 162, 169, 174,
    179, 182–98, 208
askesis 18
A Treatise of Human Nature (Hume)
    127, 131
attitude 5–8, 27, 31–9, 47, 62, 68,
    76, 79–80, 88, 93–5, 109, 113,
    123, 138, 141–4, 154, 200, 203,
    207–8
Augustine 2, 22–6, 67, 100
authenticity 2–4, 7, 26, 63–71, 75–8,
    83, 86, 91, 105, 108, 113, 116,
    138, 144–5, 154–5, 162–4, 167,
    169, 172–8, 182–3, 200–9
autonomy 5, 26, 83, 91, 102
avatar 147, 151–2, 155

Bacon, F. 9, 24, 45, 51, 175
banality of environmental evil 6,
    26–56, 125–6
Being and Time (Heidegger) 26, 86
behaviour 6, 20–1, 28–39; intention-
    behaviour gap 29–30; pro-
    environmental 28, 33, 36–9;
    theory of Planned Behaviour
    30–3
being-in-the-world 85–6, 201
beings-in-relation 5
Benjamin, W. 141, 155
Bentham, J. 59
Berleant, A. 7, 87–91, 141, 158, 204
Berlin, I. 19–21, 59, 63, 173
biocentrism 60

220 Index

biospheric egalitarianism 55, 60, 93
birth 10, 209–10
body 35, 50, 69, 88–90, 99, 105,
110–12, 117, 122, 132, 138–62,
179, 187, 198, 202, 206, 210
Borgmann, A. 4, 8, 68, 73, 104–5, 140,
167–8, 181–90
Bourdieu, P. 139, 155
bureaucracy 54, 80, 194–6

Cafaro, P. 3, 5, 8, 113–14
calculation 14–17, 63, 115, 151
Callicott, J.B. 47–8, 93, 95, 130, 207
change: moral-environmental 3, 10,
176, 208–10; see also moral,
environmental
Christian 5, 13, 22–5, 29, 57–8, 67,
73–9, 93, 103, 169, 207; post-
Christian 23–5; pre-Christian 24
climate change 3, 9–10, 17, 30, 36, 44,
50, 56, 58, 157, 169–71, 198
Club of Rome 10, 17
Coeckelbergh, M. 64, 72, 118, 165,
179, 187, 195, 202, 205
cognitive dissonance 31, 36
conditions of possibility 2, 6, 8, 10,
176, 186, 201, 205, 210; of
environmental change 2, 6, 176,
205, 210
Confessions (Augustine) 22–3, 67
Confessions (Rousseau) 65–6, 69, 79
conformity 26–9, 86
consequentialism 114
conservation 44–6, 55–7, 200, 203
conservationism 46, 56–9
conservatism: metaphysical 57–8, 60;
political 55–6
contemplation 8, 15, 55, 57, 77, 84, 94,
98, 122, 141–2, 149, 153, 174
context of discovery v. context of
justification 48–9
control 2, 5–8, 15–28, 30, 34, 45,
51–4, 58, 61, 63, 66, 72–5,
80–90, 94–6, 108, 115–17, 132,
144, 154–61, 169, 172, 177,
180, 191–4, 198–209; self-
control 2, 5–6, 15, 17–28, 34,
66, 72–5, 95–6, 115–17, 132,
169, 198, 201–3, 209; see also
self-control
conversion, problem of 22–3, 207
convivial 10, 164, 170, 182, 185,
190–9; ICTs 192–4, 199; society
182, 192, 194–5; tools 10, 182,
185, 190–5

craftsmanship 3, 14, 101–2, 107–9,
115–18, 132, 168, 193, 208;
moral 115, 118, 208
Crawford, M.B. 3, 8, 102–7
Critical Theory 51–4, 83, 182–3
culture 6, 10, 21, 23–9, 34, 38–9,
51–5, 61, 64, 68, 80, 89, 94–5,
101, 118, 130–3, 138–9, 160–8,
175–8, 184, 202, 207–10
cursor 147–51, 187

death 151, 154, 156, 193
death of the environment, the 151
democracy 9, 173–7
deontology 114, 172
Descartes, R. 51, 100, 115, 158,
160–1, 165
desire 5, 18–22, 45, 57, 65, 68, 72–8,
94, 112, 138, 175, 202, 208;
first-order v. second order
18–19
de-skilling 102–5, 148–50, 167, 182,
184, 187, 192
de-skinning 156
detachment 2–7, 18, 21, 51–2, 66, 76,
80, 96–7, 100, 114, 116, 121–3,
141–3, 150, 153, 159, 174, 179,
184, 200, 203, 206
device 15, 73, 91, 102–8, 145–55,
184–9, 192–9
Dewey, J. 3, 9, 92, 97–8, 103, 118,
125, 130, 174
disciplining 18, 30, 34, 76, 120, 174,
197, 202
disenchantment 7, 64, 76, 80, 83, 87,
207
disengagement 2, 5, 8, 100, 104–5,
113, 138, 141–3, 148–9, 156,
165
disinterestness 3–4, 88, 90, 95, 108,
112, 141, 144, 150, 178
distance 21, 37–8, 54, 92, 95–6, 123,
132, 137, 144, 158, 162–70,
178, 183, 187, 188, 191, 201,
203, 207; moral distance 165
Dreyfus, H. 3, 4, 8–9, 87, 97–108,
116–18, 124, 148–9, 176, 181,
184–90
dualism 4, 7, 9, 22–3, 48–9, 52, 61,
69, 76, 80–9, 94–6, 99, 113,
115–16, 132–3, 139–40, 153,
155,158, 175, 178–9, 183–95;
non-dualism 4, 9, 22–3, 48, 76,
80, 83, 89, 94–5, 113, 132–3,
139, 155, 158, 175, 178, 195

duty 26, 59, 120, 124, 169, 199
dwelling 143, 198

eating 9, 24, 35, 57, 111–12, 162–6,
    201
ecology 15, 44, 46, 53, 60, 80, 92–5,
    154, 175, 188
*Economic and Philosophic Manuscripts
    of 1844* (Marx) 182
ecosystem 1, 44–5, 53, 123, 154,
    169–72, 175, 205; management
    154; services 44, 53, 123, 172
ecotourism 65, 76
Elaboration Likelihood Method 31
embodiment 2, 35, 96, 98, 100,
    110–13, 132, 139–51, 178, 187,
    201–2, 207
Emile (Rousseau) 65, 72–5, 110–12
Emerson, R.W. 54, 78, 112
emotion 2, 18, 36–8, 47–8, 63–4, 71,
    73, 77, 78, 114, 119–28, 144
empathy 47–8, 144
enchantment 64, 80, 87;
    disenchantment 64, 80, 87; re-
    enchantment 64
energy 3, 9, 45, 84–5, 120, 157,
    166–70, 197, 201; management
    167–8
engagement 2, 5–9, 29, 32, 39, 48, 79,
    89, 91, 96–107, 110, 114–19,
    123, 128–9, 137–43, 148,
    152–7, 162, 167, 170–90,
    194–210; disengagement (*see*
    disengagement); environmental
    (*see* environmental); ethics of
    89; skilled engagement 2, 9, 29,
    32, 48, 96–107, 110, 114–19,
    128–9, 137, 142–3, 148, 157,
    161–2, 171–90, 194–210 (*see
    also* skill *and* environmental
    skill); world 98, 105, 140
Enlightenment 2, 6–7, 26–7, 41–63,
    68, 71–6, 79–80, 83, 93, 96–7,
    101, 110, 113–16, 132, 143,
    158, 174–8, 200–9; rationalism
    6, 46–7, 76, 113, 209
environment: active relation to 2, 79,
    159, 166, 196; built 87, 89, 143;
    death of the 151; denial of 159;
    mastery of 45, 58; natural 38,
    47, 52, 56, 59, 66, 89, 109, 113,
    138–47, 154, 160–3, 173, 189,
    190; perception of 3, 52, 77;
    relation to 10, 21, 25, 45, 52,
    79, 95, 116, 138, 141–4, 154–8,

163, 168, 171, 177, 181, 184;
    196, 202–8; skillful engagement
    with 129, 162, 172, 181, 184,
    189, 194; social 26, 89–91, 123,
    128–9, 161, 170, 187, 197, 206
environmental: action 1, 29–33, 39, 45,
    54–5, 60–1, 79, 95, 125, 174;
    alienation 3–4, 9, 80, 99, 183,
    132, 162, 184–90; assessment
    16; behavior 28, 30, 33–9;
    beings 5, 9, 85, 95, 151, 159,
    162, 184, 204; change 1–3, 6,
    10, 23, 38, 55–8, 62, 96, 175–6,
    198, 200–10; crisis 1, 4–5,
    194; education 16, 29, 37–8,
    73, 75, 102–3, 111, 121, 130,
    152, 164, 191, 197; emotion 38,
    63, 119; engagement 119, 155,
    198, 205 (*see also* engagement);
    ethics 1–10, 13–17, 21–8, 30,
    34, 47–9, 60–4, 73, 76, 89, 92,
    96–100, 104, 107, 114–25,
    131–3, 135–56, 166, 168,
    172–3, 176, 179, 181, 185–90,
    194–5, 199, 200–10; evil 6,
    22–5, 51; Fall 24–5; good 2, 6,
    13–28, 50, 97–100, 107–13,
    123–4, 130, 133, 153, 173,
    189–90, 196–7; guilt 24, 26,
    37, 120–4, 199, 207; knowledge
    3, 13–29, 35–9, 96–118, 124,
    200, 203; language 10, 23–4,
    32, 53–4, 54, 61–2, 89, 103,
    113, 158–9, 164–5, 168, 170,
    201–8; management 2, 5, 9,
    32, 34, 43–4, 80, 90, 120, 123,
    132, 140, 154, 169–77, 186,
    191–202; motivation 2, 6–7,
    11–39, 43, 48–9, 54–5, 60–4,
    69, 97, 100, 104, 107, 128, 154,
    181–4, 201–2; non-modern
    environmental ethics 10, 76, 96;
    nudging 20–1; philosophy 4, 7,
    92, 200; politics 9, 43, 55–60,
    171–80, 201, 203; psychology 6,
    13–39, 63, 201; science 16–17,
    44, 124, sin 13, 22–3; skill 2,
    8–10, 29, 39, 49, 89, 96–142,
    157–79, 185, 190–7, 201–10;
    thinking 5, 10, 43, 54, 58,
    96–118, 155, 158, 171, 175,
    208; virtue 3, 5, 8–9, 14–15, 28,
    33, 39, 113–14, 118–33, 137,
    149, 154, 174, 177, 190, 201–2,
    206; virtue ethics 3, 5, 8, 28, 33,

222   Index

39, 114, 119–28, 201; zombies
6, 57
environmentalism 5–9, 41–94, 167,
171, 174–5, 199–210; modern
9, 41–94, 171, 174–5, 203–10;
technological 45
episteme 4
ethics: consequentialist 32, 114, 120,
123–4; deontological 32, 45,
59, 60, 114, 120, 123–4,
164, 172; environmental (*see*
environmental); of engagement
89 (*see also* engagement); of
skill 5, 8, 10, 98–118, 132–46,
155–7, 172–199, 202, 209 (*see
also* skill); social 89, 132; virtue
(*see* environmental virtue ethics
and virtue); walking 142
evil 6, 22–28, 51, 92, 109;
environmental (*see*
environmental)
existentialism 80
experience 6, 87–91, 98–133, 138–56,
160, 162, 166, 176–9, 185–204;
direct experience 6, 33–9,
110–12, 123, 192–9
expertise 9, 14–16, 55, 98–100, 115,
124, 130–2, 175–7, 191–7

failure 5, 17, 19–21, 65, 117
Fall 24–5, 78, 159
fatalism 7, 204
fear 33, 120–5, 199
feeling 2, 4, 24, 32–7, 47–8, 63–80,
85, 88, 97, 101–2, 107–10, 113,
121, 139, 144, 178–9, 199–201;
for the environment 2, 63
Feenberg, A. 51–2
flâneur 141–4, 153, 155, 188
flourishment 3, 116, 123, 125
flow 103, 206
focal practices 104–6, 140, 184, 187
food 3, 9, 17, 34, 65, 68, 73, 80, 124,
144, 156–8, 162, 172; food
alienation 163–4
footprint 169–70, 197
form of life 10, 117, 139, 158, 178,
201, 208; modern 139, 201
Form of the good 16
Forms, theory of 15
Frankfurt, H. 18–20, 25, 29

Gelassenheit 7, 94–5, 117, 204, 209
Gestalt 148

global 9, 30, 33, 44, 47, 56, 62, 71,
120, 175, 179, 198–9; global *v.*
local 9, 56, 179, 199
globalization 56, 175
good 6, 8–9, 13–28, 43, 46–50, 57,
64–5, 68–70, 78–9, 96–100,
103, 105, 107–10, 113–33,
141–5, 153, 155, 161–4, 171–7,
182–90, 196–7; doing 17–18,
100, 109; environmental 6,
13–22, 27–8, 46–7, 50, 57, 64,
97–100, 107–10, 113–14, 118,
121, 123–33, 141–5, 153, 173,
177, 182, 189–90, 196 (*see also*
environmental); knowledge of
the (*see* knowledge); seeing the
15; turning away from 6, 22;
vision of the 15
good life, the 9, 49, 70, 97, 99, 110,
113–14, 124, 161, 172, 189–90,
196–7
GPS 101, 145–55, 187
gratitude 124
greens 44–5, 53, 56–7, 62, 75, 208
Growing Moral Relations
(Coeckelbergh) 165
growth 9–10, 109, 117, 171–8,
204–10; of environmental skill
10, 174, 208, 210; societal
growth 9, 171, 174, 206
guilt 24, 26, 37, 120–4, 199, 207;
environmental guilt 37
guns 144

Habermas, J. 4, 51–4, 83, 172
habit 2, 5, 8, 27, 30, 36–9, 97–8,
109, 117–28, 139, 153, 155,
168–9, 173–9, 196, 200–7;
environmental 37, 97, 124,
200–2
habitus 124, 139, 153, 200–1;
environmental 200–1
health 3, 9, 20, 30, 34–5, 39, 60, 92,
122, 124, 133, 154, 157–62,
165, 168, 180, 191, 197, 201
health care 9, 158, 160–1, 191, 197,
201
hedonism 133
Heidegger, M. 3–9, 23, 26, 48, 51–4,
61, 76, 79–87, 92, 95, 101, 105,
109, 116–18, 121, 130, 143–4,
155, 165–70, 181–7, 199,
204–6
hubris 24

human nature 4, 182–3
Hume, D. 8, 46–8, 63, 92, 95, 101, 119, 122–3, 126–32, 172, 180, 201
hunter-gatherers 144–5
hunting 70, 112, 143–5, 163

Icarus, myth of 24
ICT (Information and Communication Technology) 167, 185–99
Illich, I. 4, 10, 161, 170, 179, 181–2, 185, 190–8
incontinence 17, 26–7, 30
Ingold, T. 7, 52–3, 76, 87, 139, 140–50, 155–8, 204
intention 6, 22, 26, 29–30, 60, 126, 152; intention-behaviour gap 29–30
Intergovernmental Panel on Climate Change 10, 17
internet 9, 105–6, 181, 185–99

joy 33, 35, 113, 123–6, 133; the joys of environmental virtue 123–4

Kant, I. 27, 59–60, 71, 74, 88, 100, 150
know-how 2–3, 10, 79, 97–126, 132, 176–7, 189–90, 193, 196, 200–5, 210
knowledge 2–8, 11–39, 44–7, 54–6, 64, 66, 69, 75, 79, 87, 96–118, 120–8, 132–3, 150, 176–8, 189–203; environmental (see environmental); moral (see moral); scientific 15 (see also science); of the good 17, 97, 99; theoretical 3, 5–6, 14–17, 47, 97, 120, 189–90, 202

language 10, 23–5, 32, 53–4, 61–2, 89, 103, 113, 158–9, 164–5, 168, 170, 193, 201–2, 205–6; environmental (see environmental); modern 61–2, 158–9, 168, 201, 205–6; moral-environmental 165, 205; of 'ought' 32; romantic 164
Latour, B. 49–52, 146, 180, 183
Leopold, A. 5, 47, 80, 92–3
liberalism 55–60; free market 57; liberalism v. conservatism 60; neo-liberalism 55, 57

liberation 7, 43, 45, 55, 58–62, 69, 103, 138, 174, 200–3, 209; liberationism 7, 43, 55, 59–60, 69, 209; see also animal liberation
libertarian paternalism 20; see also nudging
liberty 19–21, 44, 59–60, 74; negative 20, 59; positive liberty 19, 173; positive v. negative 19–20, 59
lifestyle 1, 38, 75, 122, 161, 171
logos 5, 8, 18, 23, 53, 95, 98, 103, 154, 177–8, 209
luck 48, 119, 129–30, 172

machine 24, 61, 64, 67, 73, 105, 108, 150, 157–8, 165, 193, 195
Man, das 26, 83, 86, 206
management 2, 5, 9, 34, 43–4, 80, 90, 120, 123, 132, 140, 154–77, 186, 191–9, 202; ecosystem 154; energy 168; planet 9, 120, 169; self-management 34, 123, 132, 159, 162, 168, 198–9; wildlife 154
Manicheism 22
map 145–56
marshmallow study 34–5
Marx, K. 7, 51, 55–8, 100–4, 179–86, 199, 209
mastery: and apprentices 176–8; as obedience to the law which we prescribe to ourselves 74; of nature 21, 45, 58–9, 85; of new land 70; of skills 115–16, 131, 178–9, 139; of technology 84, 98, 192; self-mastery 21–26, 102, 115; the household 99, 116
materiality 4, 8, 10, 49, 51, 61, 76, 79, 95, 97–9, 101–4, 115–16, 153–4, 161, 165, 174, 179, 187, 189–90, 194, 197, 199, 201, 206; intimacy, dialogue, and engagement with the material 101, 103
meaning 4, 7, 18, 24, 32–8, 53, 55, 64, 68, 76, 85–111, 139–42, 148–53, 156, 160–5, 191–8, 207–10
measurement 14–16, 44, 169, 199; the art of 14
metaphysics: as words 111; craving for 96; dualist 22–3, 140; ecological thinking as 92; heavy

224　*Index*

25; metaphysical conservatism 55–60; metaphysical egalitarianism 60; metaphysics of Quality 107; notion of intrinsic value as 93

midwifery 10, 209–10

Milgram experiment 26

modern 2–10, 14–18, 23–9, 34, 41–97, 101, 105–19, 129, 132–45, 150–210; environmentalism (*see* environmentalism); form of life 10, 139, 201; non-modern 2–11, 49, 76, 80–7, 92–6, 133, 114–16, 139, 144–5, 155, 157, 160–4, 167–71, 175–6, 179, 183, 187–8, 201–7, 210; post-modern 4; pre-modern 4, 55, 64, 168, 192, 202; thinking 6–7, 17, 23, 29, 34, 43, 48, 52, 85–7, 94, 105, 129, 137, 142, 145, 157–60, 165, 170, 175, 200–10

modernity 2, 6–8, 24–5, 28, 39, 43, 46–62, 65, 70–1, 76, 79–85, 92–5, 101, 114–15, 132, 138, 152–60, 168, 183, 186, 200–5, 209; alternative 52; as verb 204; Janus Face of 6, 41, 47, 72, 75–6, 110, 112, 200; objectivist 46 (*see also* objectivism)

moral: alienation 7; change 3, 10, 124, 176, 201–10; craftsmanship 115, 118; development 32, 115, 124; distance 163–5; education 121; epistemology 2, 97–8, 202; expertise 14, 55, 98, 115; imagination 47, 118; justification 2, 48; know-how 115; knowledge 2, 14–28, 56, 97–8, 104, 115, 126, 128; language 165, 206; moral-environmental 3, 10, 48–9, 54, 57, 60–4, 116, 124, 176, 181, 190, 201, 205, 208–10; motivation 2, 13, 16, 19, 43–8, 54, 56, 60, 63, 93, 101, 118, 181, 201–2; philosophy 17; psychology 2, 6, 13–29, 48, 63, 93–7, 117, 125, 133, 171, 200, 207; sentiment and emotions 3, 8, 47, 118–130; skill 122, 129–30; status 10, 45, 49, 58–60, 165, 205; wisdom 118

morality 6, 13, 18, 23, 127

Mother Earth 7, 92, 169

motivation 1–9, 11, 13–38, 43–69, 79, 92–3, 97, 100–7, 113, 118–21, 125, 128, 131, 144, 154, 181, 184, 201–3; a-motivation 33; environmental (*see* environmental); intrinsic *v.* extrinsic 32; moral (*see* moral)

mysticism 7–8, 48, 51, 83, 94–6, 112, 117, 184

Næs, A. 60, 92–3

narcissism 76, 84

Narcissus 77, 84–5, 184

nationalism 9, 85, 102, 171–5

natural 2–10, 37–8, 44–7, 51–91, 99, 104, 108–19, 127–63, 169, 173–210; environment 38, 47, 52, 56, 59, 66, 89, 109, 113, 138, 143, 147, 154, 160–3, 173, 189–90

Nature (Emerson) 78

nature: alienation from 63, 158, 182, 203; as computer game 155; as phenomenon 78; as standing reserve 7, 53, 84–5, 167, 183; as thing external to us 9, 45, 51–4, 85, 89, 92, 108, 163, 170; back to 65–7, 70; being in nature 141; beliefs about 46; beyond 81–98; care about 1, 37; colonization of 52; control of 85, 94, 108, 200, 209; construction of 45, 50–1, 61, 77; destruction of 4; domination of 52; end of 67; engagement with 179; environmental nature of the human (environmental by nature) 2, 7, 89, 170, 184; escape to 69, 106, 138, 172, 190, 208; essence 108, 178; experiencing 37; feeling for (and love of) 2, 7, 54, 63–71, 77, 93, 116, 142–3; human 4, 182–4; human-nature dualism 4, 87; idealized 106; imagining 47; immersion in 66; intrinsic value of 61; knowledge 55; language of 4, 7, 51–4, 91, 138–42, 155, 164, 184, 205, 210; leaving alone 59–61, 89–90, 167; liberation of 7, 59–9; living in harmony with 18, 24, 78; management of 27, 43–5, 172, 175, 208; manipulation of 7,

21, 43–5, 52, 80; mastery of 21; metabolism of 99; nature-in-itself 87; new nature 94, 83, 94–6, 188; of environmental good 16; of ICTs 193; of the nation 173; original 80, 209; overcoming 73–4; politics of 54, 172–3; preservation of 1; protecting 43–5, 54, 57; pure 50, 60, 67; reconnect to 159; re-enchanting 7, 64; relation to 24, 38, 43, 55, 109, 205; restoration of 54, 59, 173; return to 65–71, 93, 158; re-wilding 67; Romantic feeling for 63–5; Romantic thinking about 3, 63–92, 164; second 95, 147; state of 76, 111, 169, 206, 209; study of 44–5, 72, 142, 149, 154; transformation of 45, 59, 94, 154, 186; walking in 3, 7–8, 66, 68, 78, 113, 137–53; wild 45, 57, 67, 90, 208 (*see also* wild); working in 8, 79, 113, 153–4, 176, 203

navigation 101, 145–52, 157, 181; by using GPS 101, 145–55, 187; *see also* wayfinding

neo-liberalism 55, 57

Nicomachean Ethics (Aristotle) 5, 17, 26–7, 30, 121–3

Nietzsche, F. 23, 64, 101

non-modern *see* modern

nudging 20–1, 28, 75, 193; *see also* environmental

Nussbaum, M. 18

objectification 7, 88–9, 95, 182–6

objectivism 3, 46–55, 63–4, 97, 107–17, 119, 130, 142, 157–62, 176, 179–80, 188, 200; in science 3, 51, 111–2, 142, 157–60, 176, 180, 188, 200

objectivity 108, 147, 188

oikos 99, 143, 154

online and offline 172, 179, 182, 188–9

original sin 24–5

outdoor 38, 63, 138, 145, 152–3, 167, 208

overjustification effect 31

paganism 169, 207

passenger 150, 155, 174

passions 17–19, 27, 63, 66, 72–3, 127

paternalism 20; libertarian 20

patience 8, 114, 117, 204

Paul 23

Phaedrus (Plato/Socrates) 18–19, 115

phenomenology 3, 118, 137, 144–55, 159, 165, 183

Philosophical Investigations (Wittgenstein) 158

phronesis 122

physis 109, 209

Pirsig, R.M. 3, 86, 107–16, 187–9

planet 9, 33, 38, 46, 67, 120–2, 154, 169–70; as spaceship 67; management 9, 120, 154, 169–70

Planned Behaviour, theory of 30, 33

Plato 2, 14–19, 25, 28, 55, 97, 99–100, 108, 115–16, 122, 126, 133, 174–5, 187–9, 202

poiesis 109, 209

polis 14, 16, 99, 177–8

political economy 172, 174, 185–6, 199

politics 1–2, 6–9, 13–16, 23, 27–8, 43–4, 54–61, 68, 76, 99, 194, 118, 122, 125, 157, 160–1, 164, 171–8, 186, 200–3, 209; environmental (*see* environmental); green 13; of nature 50, 54, 172–3; of skill 9, 172–9; participatory 174–7

Popper, K. 28, 48

polytheism 101

pragmatism 3, 32, 106, 111, 114, 121, 125

Prometheus, myth of 24

Protagoras 14–19, 114

psychology (*see* environmental); moral-psychological (*see* moral)

purification 49–51, 64, 66, 71

puritanism 133

quality 102–9, 177–9, 199: metaphysics of 107

ratio 18, 46

rational 14–20, 44, 47–54, 59, 63–5, 86, 91, 115, 122, 174, 208

rationalism 2, 6, 36, 44–54, 61–4, 74–6, 80–4, 91–6, 113–4, 132, 172–5, 179, 202–9; Enlightenment 6, 46–54, 63, 74–6, 113–4, 132, 174–5, 200, 209 (*see also* Enlightenment)

226 *Index*

rationality 4, 14, 18–19, 51–4, 63, 80, 83, 114, 150, 175, 182, 200–1
real, the 90–1, 151; animal 144; self 173; thing 68; world 72, 188
reason 2, 7–8, 18, 26–7, 43–55, 61–4, 71–5, 96–7, 101, 104, 107–14, 120, 123–4, 126–8, 150, 174, 177–9, 203, 207; Enlightenment 7, 43–4, 51–2, 96–7, 101, 207; the ghost of 108, 114, 209
re-enchantment 7, 64, 100
relational 60–1, 76, 85, 87, 91–8, 103, 109, 115, 140–2, 151–9, 162–3, 184, 201
religion 23, 25, 50, 64, 74, 93, 101, 163, 169, 207–10
Regan, T. 59, 164
Republic (Plato) 15
re-skilling 150, 184
reveries 65–79, 93, 112, 144
Reveries of the Solitary Walker 65–9, 93
rewilding 4, 45, 57, 59
romantic 2–10, 18, 24, 26, 41–117, 133–210: non-romantic 2, 8, 48, 81, 96, 106–7, 155, 157, 175, 183, 210; reverie 71, 80, 93, 109, 113, 116, 172 (*see also* reveries); thinking 2, 7, 86, 106, 114, 144, 158, 163, 168–70, 208–10
Romanticism 2–8, 41, 43, 51, 54, 62–85, 93–6, 102–210
Rousseau, J.-J. 2–3, 7–8, 64–93, 104, 110–12, 126, 128, 133, 138, 144, 173, 188, 200, 208

science 1–8, 16–17, 24, 35, 43–54, 63–5, 71, 75, 80–4, 92–8, 110–16, 120–4, 129–32, 142, 145, 154, 157–62, 169–70, 175–80, 192, 198–208
science and technology studies (STS) 49
second nature 95
self: divided self 18
self-control 2, 5–6, 15–28, 34, 66, 72–5, 95–6, 115–17, 132, 169, 198, 201–3, 209
self-discipline 18, 30, 34, 120
self-management 34, 123, 132, 159, 162, 168, 198–9
self-monitoring 34, 199
self-regulation 6, 28, 34, 199
Sennett, R. 3, 8, 102–6, 110, 114, 116–17, 176, 187–90

sentiment 3, 8, 24, 46–8, 65, 95, 112–19, 126–8, 209: moral 3, 8, 46–7, 118–19, 126, 128
shells 195–8
Silent Spring (Carson) 5, 10
sin 13, 22–5, 37, 169; original 24–5; *see also* environmental
Singer, P. 44–6, 59–60, 164
skill 2–9, 29, 32–9, 48–9, 79, 89, 92, 96–133, 137–55, 157–205; animal relations 164–6; climate change and 169; community of 174; de-skilling 102–5, 148–50, 167, 182, 184, 192; energy skills 166–7; environmental (*see* environmental skill); ethics of 5, 8, 10, 98, 102, 110, 114, 118, 132–46, 155, 172, 175, 178–182, 185, 189, 202, 209; food and eating skills 162–4; health skills 157–61; meta-skills 159, 189, 202, 208; political (politics of) 9, 171–7; re-skilling 150, 172, 184; self-regulation 34; skilled activity 96–110, 114, 117, 128, 132, 140, 174, 178–9, 196, 201–2, 209; skilled engagement 2–3, 8–9, 29, 32, 48, 96–119, 128–9, 137, 142–3, 148, 157, 161–2, 172–9, 181–90, 194, 196, 200–10 (*see also* engagement); skillful play 106–7; to live with technology 189; virtue and 119–130, 152, 180, 190; walking 149, 155
Slow Food 164
soccer mom example 125–6
Social Cognitive Theory 29, 36
Social Learning Theory 33
Socrates 6, 8, 14–18, 54, 66, 96–9, 115–16
spaces 88, 103, 174, 187–8, 196, 208–10; cyberspace 187–8; historical spaces 208–10; social space 103
spirituality 10, 207, 210
standing reserve 7, 52–4, 61, 80, 84–8, 154–5, 164–7, 171–2, 183, 198–9
Stoicism 2, 5, 18, 47, 66–7, 72–6, 80, 95–6, 110–13, 116; anti-Stoic 5; non-Stoic 2, 96
sustainability 1, 10, 44–5, 58, 121, 168, 171, 198

sympathy 47, 130
Szerszinsky, B. 7, 76, 87, 207

techne 4–5, 9, 104, 141, 177–8, 196,
    209; dia-*techne* 178
technocracy 9, 126, 175, 191–2
technology 2–10, 24–5, 44–54,
    61, 64, 67–8, 76, 79–109,
    115–20, 135, 140–210, GPS
    101, 145–55, 187; information
    105–6, 179–81, 185–91 (*see
    also* ICT); philosophy of 4–5,
    135, 181; skill to live with 189;
    'The Question Concerning
    Technology' (Heidegger) 67, 84,
    167; wayfinding (*see* wayfinding)
The Human Condition (Arendt) 99
theoria 4, 15
Thoreau, H.D. 2–8, 54, 64–79,
    110–13, 123, 137–8, 144, 200
Tools for Conviviality (Illich) 191–9
tourism 65, 68, 76, 155; ecotourism 65,
    76, 155
transcendental 3, 140–1, 155
Transcendentalism 78, 112
transformation 45, 54, 59, 61, 94–5,
    109, 153–5, 159, 163, 166, 186,
    193–8, 207
transport 19, 139, 150, 168, 191
tree farms 140

Umwelt-Vergessenheit 9, 170
unwilling addict 19–21, 25
utilitarianism 45, 59–60, 123, 164, 172

Value-Belief-Norm theory 38
virtual 90–1, 147, 151, 188, 190; body
    147; environment 90, 147, 151;
    nature 147; reality 90; self 151;
    world 90–1, 188, 190
virtue 3, 93, 105, 108, 113–33, 137,
    149–180, 190, 199, 201–6; and
    skill (*see* skill); approach 114,
    125; environmental virtue ethics
    (*see* environmental); ethics 113,
    119, 121, 124–8, 164–6, 172,
    203; Humean interpretation
    of 128–32, 201; objective list
    of virtues 119, 130; patience
    as meta-virtue 204; stability

of 131–2; the virtue of skilled
    activity 110–23, 137, 180;
    walking 149
vision 10, 15–6, 44–6, 55, 94, 100–1,
    105, 115, 121, 150–1, 174, 186,
    192, 194–5, 209–10
voyeur 143

Walden (Thoreau) 69–73, 111–13
Walking (Thoreau) 68, 71, 112, 137–8
walking 7–9, 65–6, 69, 78, 113,
    137–57, 201; and wayfinding
    technologies (*see* GPS *and*
    wayfinding); as technique of the
    soul 66; ethics 141–2; ethics of
    137, 146; in nature 7–8, 66,
    137–44, 149; phenomenology
    of 137–45; screen walking 147;
    skills 145–53
wanton 19–20, 25–6, 57; *see also*
    unwilling addict
wayfinding 9, 145–55; modes 145;
    technologies 145 (*see also* GPS)
weak will 6, 17, 203; *see also* akrasia
webcam 143–4
Wensveen, L. 3, 5, 114
White, C. 53–4, 113, 205
wild 4–7, 45, 57, 67–72, 80, 90, 140,
    154–5, 208; nature 57, 59, 67;
    rewilding 45, 57, 59 (*see also*
    rewilding); wilderness 7, 67, 69,
    87, 138
will 6, 15–23, 30, 35, 43, 75, 102, 117,
    129–30, 173, 176, 201–4, 207,
    209; divided 18–19, 22; evil
    22; general 173; like a muscle
    30, 35; political 209; unwilling
    addict 19–20, 25; weak 6, 17,
    203 (*see also* akrasia)
wisdom 27, 98–9, 118, 122, 178,
    196; practical 98, 122 (*see also*
    phronesis)
Wittgenstein, L. 62, 158, 202, 205, 208
working in nature 8, 79, 153–5, 176
workshop 103, 190, 193
wuwei 8, 95

Zen 107, 112, 117
*Zen and the Art of Motorcycle
    Maintenance* (Pirsig) 107